PATTERNS OF EXCELLENCE

PATTERNS OF EXCELLENCE

THE NEW PRINCIPLES OF CORPORATE SUCCESS

Danny Samson and David Challis

PEARSON EDUCATION LIMITED

Head Office:
Edinburgh Gate
Harlow CM20 2JE
Tel: +44 (0)1279 623623
Fax: +44 (0)1279 431059

London Office:
128 Long Acre, London WC2E 9AN
Tel: +44 (0)171 447 2000
Fax: +44 (0)171 240 5771
Website: www.business-minds.com

First published in Great Britain 1999

© Pearson Education Limited 1999

The right of Danny Samson and David Challis to be identified as authors
of this work has been asserted by them in accordance with the
Copyright, Designs, and Patents Act 1988.

ISBN 0 273 63876 9

British Library Cataloguing in Publication Data
A CIP catalogue record for this book can be obtained from the British Library.

All rights reserved; no part of this publication may be reproduced, stored
in a retrieval system, or transmitted in any form or by any means, electronic,
mechanical, photocopying, recording, or otherwise without either the prior
written permission of the Publishers or a licence permitting restricted copying
in the United Kingdom issued by the Copyright Licensing Agency Ltd,
90 Tottenham Court Road, London W1P 0LP. This book may not be lent,
resold, hired out or otherwise disposed of by way of trade in any form
of binding or cover other than that in which it is published, without the
prior consent of the Publishers.

10 9 8 7 6 5 4 3 2

Typeset by Northern Phototypesetting Co. Ltd, Bolton.
Printed and bound in Great Britain by Biddles Ltd, Guildford & King's Lynn.

The Publishers' policy is to use paper manufactured from sustainable forests.

ABOUT THE AUTHORS

Danny Samson (left) has been a professor of management at the University of Melbourne, Australia for the past decade, with prior appointments at the Universities of Illinois and New South Wales. His career began as a chemical engineer with ICI, followed by a PhD in management. He has written five books and over 50 scholarly articles on management. He is a company director and regularly consults to businesses in a variety of industries in Asia, Europe, Australia, New Zealand and the USA on strategy, operations improvement, organizational change, business excellence and improvement and the achievement of the business principles outlined in this book. He is an outstanding executive educator and conducts regular executive education programs for companies wishing to transform themselves using these principles. His clients over the past decade have included a global financial services organization and major corporations in the oil, plastics, building, automotive, textiles and consumer goods industries. He has worked on numerous high-level government inquiries in the field of technology management, manufacturing management, leadership, industry competitiveness, and market policy and restructuring. E-mail d.samson@ecomfac.unimelb.edu.au

David Challis (right) has spent the last 20 years consulting to organizations in Europe, USA, Australia and Asia in the area of stategic organizational change. He has worked at all organizational levels: board through middle management through shop floor and has an outstanding track record as an effective change agent. He has extensive consulting experience in assisting executives in many different businesses, to assess business health and organizational effectiveness and then transform their operations utilizing a broad range of processes and models, including those described in this book. David has also facilitated the introduction of many different consulting interventions including strategic repositioning, work and process redesign, capability assessment, leadership and team development, continuous improvement, change planning and culture change. He has also been a member of numerous taskforces in areas concerned with industry competiveness, technological innovation, manufacturing excellence and workplace reform. David holds bachelor's and master's degrees in Engineering and a PhD in management. E-mail: challisd@wscg.com.au

CONTENTS

Preface	xi
Acknowledgements	xv

Part 1 • PATTERNS OF EXCELLENCE — 1

1 Patterns of excellence – beyond organizational 'mid-life' crisis — 3
Introduction — 3
How and what you manage — 6
The present state of play – organized chaos — 9
How good could it (or should it) be? — 10

2 Towards world-class management and leadership — 19
Company 'New' – what would it look like and what wouldn't it look like? — 19

Part 2 • MANAGEMENT BY PRINCIPLES — 27

3 Management by principles — 29
Introduction — 29
How management by principles works — 31

4 Principle 1: Alignment — 35
Introduction — 35
Evaluation of alignment — 41
Benefits of alignment — 43
Improving a company's alignment — 43
Summary — 46

5 Principle 2: Distributed leadership — 47
Introduction — 47

	Evaluation of distributed leadership	51
	Benefits of distributed leadership	55
	Improving distributed leadership	55
	Summary	57
6	**Principle 3: Integration**	**58**
	Introduction	58
	Evaluation of integration	63
	Benefits of integration	64
	Improving integration	64
	Summary	67
7	**Principle 4: Being out front**	**68**
	Introduction	68
	Evaluation of out front	74
	Benefits of out front	75
	Improving out-front status	76
	Summary	78
8	**Principle 5: Being up front**	**79**
	Introduction	79
	Evaluation of up front	85
	Benefits of the up-front principle	85
	Improving up-front status	86
	Summary	87
9	**Principle 6: Resourcing the medium term**	**88**
	Introduction	88
	Evaluation of resourcing the medium term	96
	Benefits of resourcing the medium term	96
	Improving on resourcing the medium term	99
	Summary	99
10	**Principle 7: Being time focussed**	**101**
	Introduction	101
	Evaluation of time focus	107
	Benefits of the time-focus principle	108
	Improving time focus	109
	Summary	111

11 Principle 8: Embracing change — 112
- Introduction — 112
- Evaluation of the embracing-change principle — 117
- Benefits of embracing change — 118
- Improving on the embracing-change principle — 120
- Summary — 122

12 Principle 9: Learning focus — 123
- Introduction — 123
- Evaluation of the learning principle — 129
- Benefits of learning — 130
- Improving on the learning-focus principle — 131
- Summary — 132

13 Principle 10: Being disciplined — 133
- Introduction — 133
- Evaluation of the principle of discipline — 144
- Benefits of discipline — 144
- Improving and sustaining discipline — 145
- Summary — 145

14 Principle 11: Measurement and reporting — 147
- Introduction — 147
- Evaluation of measuring and reporting — 155
- Benefits of measurement and reporting — 158
- Improving the organization's measurement and reporting — 158
- Summary — 159

15 Principle 12: Customer value — 161
- Introduction — 161
- Evaluation of the customer-value principle — 169
- Benefits of customer-value creation and focus — 170
- Improving and sustaining customer value — 171
- Summary — 172

16 Principle 13: Capabilities — 175
- Introduction — 175
- Evaluation of capabilities — 177
- Benefits of the capabilities principle — 179
- Improving capabilities — 180
- Summary — 181

17 Principle 14: Micro to macro — 182
Introduction — 182
Evaluation of micro to macro — 187
Benefits of micro to macro — 188
Improving micro to macro — 188
Summary — 190

Part 3 • IMPLEMENTATION — 191

18 Implementation steps — 193
Introduction — 193
Step 1: Building awareness and executive buy-in — 197
Step 2: Strategic focussing – business/organizational direction — 197
Step 3: Performance assessment – business/organizational — 212
Step 4: Diagnosis and development of the change case (gap analysis) — 214
Step 5: Project planning — 214
Step 6: Implementation and review — 214
Summary — 214

19 Key Success Factors – the system of management — 216
Introduction — 216
KSF 1: Understanding the changing nature of business strategy: from plan to process — 219
KSF 2: Integrated management of business strategy and organizational development systems — 222
KSF 3: Know the magnitude of the gap, know how long there is and know the culture — 224
KSF 4: Know the limits of restructuring and the business growth breakpoint: is the organization at risk of becoming anorexic? — 229
KSF 5: Develop an exceptional sense of reality — 231
KSF 6: The ability to avoid 'fad-surfing' — 234
KSF 7: Keep it relevant and keep it simple — 235
KSF 8: Getting into specifics: managing the detail, not the concept — 236
KSF 9: Leadership of the change process — 238
KSF 10: Stakeholder engagement — 239
Summary — 240

Conclusion and epilogue — 242

Bibliography — 246

Index — 249

PREFACE

Let's face it. For many of us, our organizations are not as well organized as we would like. For most companies, there is lots of room for improvement. We do not see this as any criticism or negative factor, but as a major challenge and opportunity for further and future wealth creation.

If one considers return on investment, there is a large variance between the best and the rest in any industry. Why have so many companies failed to achieve their maximum potential? A major cause is the lack of systematic and holistic vision and connection right across the company. By this, we mean that the business strategy, operational actions, management of performance and rewards for employees are not fully aligned. All companies set strategy, have operations and processes, measure their outputs and reward their people, but for mediocre companies it seems that these four activities are done in a vacuum, or – more to the point – in four separate vacuums.

We see the world's best companies as having achieved a powerful linking up of these four critical factors – strategy, actions, consequences and rewards. When these excellent companies choose a path or change initiative it works and it sticks. Lesser companies are constantly searching for solutions to their problems. In many cases, they have tried many or all of the populist fads and management initiatives proposed by our academic colleagues and a slew of consultants. These companies then become cynical within themselves and over the past decade we have seen them resort repeatedly to the only sure-fire way of increasing their competitiveness, which is cost-cutting. This can be a fine practice, for again, who is going to argue against being lean, but what happens after all the fat is cut away and the only things left to cut are actually the muscle and bones of the organization? Cost cutting can be successfully mandated and achieved in even a mediocre organization, but it is the other value-creating changes that go differently in the excellent and poorly led companies. It is in areas such as time compression, service and quality improvement, new product development, waste elimination and delivery reliability that we see the excellent companies making real progress and the others in the pack being backward.

Through first-hand experience, we know how difficult these initiatives are to implement in these 'ordinary' companies. We believe that the fundamental reason for this is a lack of basic connections between longer-term strategy, shorter-term action plans, performance and rewards. For example, consider one of the major improvement initiatives of the late decade, total quality management. The basic ideas of total quality are very sensible. Who can argue against improved customer focus, stronger leadership and vision, better employee involvement and stronger measurement, control and stability of operational processes? So why has total quality had such a mixed record ranging from startling successes to dismal failure? Why did companies like Xerox and Harley Davidson achieve fabulous turnarounds based on total quality while others failed completely? There must be something else even more fundamental than the elements of total quality which needs to be in place first in order to make it work. Our first objective in this book is to articulate these fundamentals. The same applies to improvement attempts in the areas of re-engineering, benchmarking, process redesign, team building, culture change, employee participation, innovation, customer service, supplier management, production scheduling, segmentation, brand repositioning, ... you name it.

The second major objective of this book is to articulate how these connections between strategy, actions, outcomes and rewards are achieved. We have observed that ordinary companies lack a unifying set of central principles that are the foundations of all aspects of their behavior, but that great companies have these in place. The closest human characteristic we can ascribe to this is that ordinary companies have no apparent 'soul' or 'heart'. Specifically, let's consider the following factors that characterize companies which we call 'ordinary' in terms of whether a company is mature in its position and achievements. 'Ordinary' companies are characterized by a number of traits:

- A lack of alignment between employee behaviors and company values and direction.
- People at all levels not taking full responsibility for actions and the organization not having clear accountability for its performance, particularly its failed projects.
- Work being organized and done in functional hierarchies and not within value-creating processes.
- Being a lagger, not a leader, in setting industry standards and practices.
- Not having the highest standards of integrity and openness.
- Inability to balance short-term and medium-term issues and requirements.
- Not managing time as a critical resource and organizational value.

- Generally being poor at implementation and, as a result, experiencing slippage and poor effectiveness in change initiatives.
- Not having everyone excited by their personal development and learning experiences.
- Being 'undisciplined' in terms of procedures, standards and work processes.
- Failure to provide all employees with timely, effective information about their work performance.
- Not having all employees focused on creating customer value.
- Having no explicit notion of what its key capabilities are, hence not having a plan for developing and exploiting these.
- Poor connection in employees' minds between individual contribution and organizational success.

Imagine trying to implement even a conceptually sound approach, such as total quality, in a company that scores poorly on the criteria above. Would it catch hold, stick and make a difference?

We believe that these are some of the deeper questions that executives should be asking, and these questions clearly raise issues about the fundamental building blocks and connections that are needed in a company on which specific change interventions can be based. Hence our second objective is to convince readers to accept, and act on, basing their organization's future on a set of axiomatic principles, which we have observed are the distinguishing features of the world's best companies. We have deduced these from close study of hundreds of companies all around the world in every conceivable sector and industry.

We have organized the book into three parts:

- **Part 1** amplifies the ideas above and demonstrates that these ideas are little more than applied common sense within a disciplined, structured framework. The hard part is implementation. By the end of Chapter 1, the need for fundamental, enduring systems will be established and their role as behavioural guides established. In the rest of Part 1 a systematic approach and the need for a set of principles are developed and illustrated.
- **Part 2** sets out the 14 principles that we have observed as common to world-class companies. Each of these is developed and illustrated as a guide to action. Part 2 brings together the systematic approach to management that aims to connect strategy, actions, performance and rewards, all guided by a set of underlying principles.
- **Part 3** is focused on *implementation*. Whereas Parts 1 and 2 elaborate on what drives the world's best companies, Part 3 describes how to proceed as

the best do. It also provides a set of key success factors for moving into implementation, and making the transition from an ad hoc approach to management and business improvement, into a systematic and 'principles driven' mode.

Finally, we have written this book for practising managers and executives with the intent of keeping the 'theoretical foundations' to a minimum. We have extensively reviewed the existing knowledge base of the relevant fields of general management and field tested our work empirically. Interested readers can access this material at the website www.excellentpatterns.com

ACKNOWLEDGEMENTS

● ● ● ● ● ● ● ● ● ● ● ● ● ● ● ● ●

We sincerely want to thank the many people who have made it possible for us to write this book.

First come our families – Jeanette, Sarah, James and Rachel Samson, and Mardi, Anna, Stephen and Clare Challis.

Second are the executives, change agents and professors whom we most admire and have learned from over the past decade. In particular we are grateful to Don Argus, David Sixton, Clay Whybark, Oscar Hauptman, Laurie Conole, John Stevens, Ewen McConchie and Wick Skinner for their wisdom and contributions to our knowledge.

Third, we wish to thank the University of Melbourne, a world-class institution that provided the infrastructure and support for this work to be completed.

Finally, we are also grateful to the Financial Times Prentice Hall team who brought this book to fruition, particularly Iain Campbell and Penelope Allport.

Danny Samson and David Challis

Part 1
PATTERNS OF EXCELLENCE

The first part of this book introduces a major point of difference between the world-class companies we have visited and worked with, and those that comprise the rest of the pack. The world's best companies have a systematic way of connecting what they manage and how they manage, relating the key elements of strategy, actions and operations, management of performance and rewards to each other. Further, the key market domains in which managers operate, namely the market for their products and services, the labor market and the capital market are sensibly connected in excellent companies.

We articulate the unfortunate state of 'fad-based management' that many companies are caught in. In comparing this state of management to that of companies that we have observed as following the 'patterns of excellence' of the world's best, a number of strong differences arise. These are not just differences of *degree* but of *kind*.

Part 1 describes and illustrates the patterns we have observed to be followed by truly excellent companies.

- They have a single, integrated improvement strategy.
- They do not fall prey to fads.
- They have a conscious focus on using a set of fundamental principles of management to guide behavior in their organization.
- They actively manage performance.
- They link rewards for all employees to organizational performance.
- They benchmark themselves against other leading companies and set corresponding stretch goals.
- Most importantly, they link together the elements of strategy, actions and operations, performance and rewards in powerful, sensible ways.

1
Patterns of excellence – beyond organizational 'mid-life crisis'

Significantly better leadership and management must be the answer to what ails many of our organizations today, as much as poor management and leadership has been the problem. The proof is nothing less nor more than those truly great companies that are getting superior results.

INTRODUCTION

Are today's organizations having a mid-life crisis? We argue that the answer to this question is generally 'yes'. Many organizations are struggling to gain control of their own destiny and, for them, the transition out of the wilderness and into growth is frequently a painful process. Other organizations exhibit an overwhelming sense of fear and desperation, as their recipe for past success no longer assures continued success. Still others are in a state of panic and reach for the latest management fad as an escape. Most are anxious, some are downright neurotic.

Despite our concerted efforts to turn our organizations around during the last decade or so, many firms report that their performance and relative competitiveness today is little better (and often considerably worse) than before these efforts began. Despite our concerted efforts to become responsive and customer focused, many companies report continued loss of business to competitors and new entrants. Despite our concerted efforts to develop a committed and satisfied workforce, employee opinion surveys often show that employee morale is lower today than at any time in the past. Things must change. Organizations are increasingly becoming sufficiently self-aware to realize that they must make some hard choices and decide what to believe in and what to do.

The number of books exhorting managers to follow a formula, recipe or to adopt a certain approach, seems to be already large and increasing exponentially. Most of these books provide lists of initiatives, e.g. strategic scorecards, re-engineering, self-managed teams or total quality management – often presented as if '*this*' approach will be the savior of the corporate world. However, it is not that simple. We are restructuring, revitalizing, re-engineering and reskilling but these are tactics. What is nearly always missing is a strategic and holistic view and approach of long-term, sustainable and systemic management fundamentals that is implementable and that increases shareholder value.[1]

Our work is based on closely observing the key differences between the best companies in the world and the many which are mediocre, distilling the common and the distinguishing features of the best and then gaining an understanding about what the best are trying to achieve in their future development. This book does not focus on any particular type of initiative. Rather, it incorporates various advances in management knowledge and focuses on the deeper issues that need to be put right first, before such initiatives are introduced. In our worldwide reviews of excellent companies and their management activities, we found no companies that were doing everything in a 'best' manner, but a few which were well along the way and could demonstrate a clear link between elements such as managerial action and customer satisfaction, business growth, environmental management, safety performance, unit cost, employee satisfaction and shareholder value. These companies include Asea Brown Boveri (ABB), British Airways, Boeing, Chase Manhattan Bank, Du Pont, Ericsson, Hoechst, Honda, Kellogg, Kodak, General Electric, Intel, MBNA, Medco, Motorola, National Bank, Norwest Bank, NUMMI, Proctor and Gamble, Shell, Siemens, South West Airlines, State Farm Insurance, Taco Bell, Walmart and Xerox. We believe that it is both possible and very useful to develop a view of what 'best of the best' looks like in order to plan progress towards that state.

Our endgame in this book is the same as that which excellent executives want for their companies. We want to develop a management approach which will be robust and which will provide an enduring but dynamic framework through which managers and others can make decisions, allocate resources and confidently lead their organizations through an increasingly complex and competitive environment. In other words, this book is an attempt to attack 'the big question' head on – how to gain and sustain competitive advantage and therefore create lasting shareholder value and financial returns. However, we will not be considering marketing strategy, financial and technical decisions and practices. Our focus is on unlocking the enormous energies inside companies through better management and leadership.

Two analogies are worth briefly considering. The first is between our companies and the human brain. We have all heard statements along the lines that we only actually use about 10 percent of our potential brainpower in everyday behavior. The reason cited relates to the poor connections between different subsystems or 'departments' of the brain. This sounds like many companies that we all know, both in cause and effect. There is an incredible amount of 'potential energy' waiting to be unlocked in most companies, and we need to reflect on why it is locked up and how to unlock it. It is a source of major frustration both for executives and their workforces. Why, despite our very considerable efforts, haven't we been able to release the other 90 percent of our organization's potential?

A second comparison is between managerial systems and technical control systems. Let's start this analogy with a contentious statement: we believe that if we ran the technical systems in oil refineries and chemical plants with the same degree of (lack of) control and discipline that we achieve in our organizational systems, there would be major explosions in most cities most days of the week! Our companies are often out of control or close to it and in many cases the reason we survive and sometimes prosper is that our competitors are similar.

> *There is an incredible amount of 'potential energy' waiting to be unlocked in most companies*

Technical systems such as oil refineries do not go out of control for the following reasons.

We understand the *fundamental principles* of their operation to a degree that allows us to know how changing a particular control leads to certain consequences. There are certain principles of physics, chemistry, electricity, etc. that we can use to design the systems correctly in the first place and which also guide our ongoing management of these technical systems. Managerial life would be wonderful if we could only articulate and enact an analogous set of organizational principles! Of course this is going to be more complex, because organizations and people are considerably more complex than oil refineries[2] and molecules but we believe it can be done. Hence, despite the complexity, one major objective of this book is to articulate these principles and describe how to use them to guide behavior. The power of these organizational principles will be a function of their simplicity and practicality.

Within an oil refinery there are clearly defined technical *relationships* between technical strategy, operating actions and states, improvements to these actions, consequences of these actions in terms of outputs, and system performance measures. Because of the existence of fundamental principles and our understanding of these interconnections, we can be disciplined and controlled in the design and operation of these systems. This is the second high-level requirement of well run systems (the first being a set of principles), namely knowing and accounting for the connections between strategy, actions, behavior, consequences and system performance measures. Just as the fundamental principles of management are always going to be less precise than Ohm's law (for electricity) and Newton's laws of motion and gravity, we argue that they are nevertheless of considerable value in our quest to gain better control over our corporate destiny and better satisfy our various stakeholders. Hence our second major objective is to provide a framework which allows managers to use the fundamental principles in a systematic way. We will begin with this issue, of moving from a state of 'management by educated guesswork'[3] to a higher state of organization and connection between important elements of a company, namely its strategy, operations, change initiatives, outcomes and performance.

Although we have not yet seen a company that we could give full marks to in terms of the systems and principles, there are quite a few that are making a lot of progress towards real managerial excellence. We have observed the patterns of excellence across many of these, and assembled a picture of the 'best of the best'.

To summarize, consider the joy of working in a company in which we manage through an integrated management system with our actions driven by a practical, actionable set of management principles. In this company, everyone understands the nature of the connections between these principles, business strategies, improvement initiatives, objectives and performance outcomes. We will also argue the importance of strong leadership and effective performance management, i.e., actively managing both performance and under-performance and linking rewards to performance outcomes in achieving these connections. We can control our management system's inputs, processes and outputs and gain a true understanding of the relationship between managerial action and shareholder value. We measure these outputs and use the measures as feedback to drive improvement by 'closing the loop' and aligning an organization's strategy, action initiatives, operational system, human behaviors and outcomes. The world's best companies are well on the way to achieving this!

HOW AND WHAT YOU MANAGE

One thing we have learnt in the last decade about the important factors required to successfully lead and manage an enterprise is that 'how to manage' is as important as 'what to manage'. The 'what' of management involves the structural side of an organization's strategy including issues such as what products to have, what markets to be in, what segments to be positioned in within those markets, what pricing policies and customer value propositions to have, what technologies and systems to use and how to organize and resource the operations strategy to produce and distribute those products (see Figure 1.1).

Our learning about the ingredients for successful organizations over the past decade has shown us that the 'how' question is also a critically important ingredient associated with getting it right for the customer and therefore for the shareholder. The 'how' question involves getting internal and external relationships right in terms of the elements of the service profit chain.[4] Figure 1.1 attempts to provide some clarity about the 'how' and 'what' of getting management and leadership right. It is clear that if an organization excels at only one of these dimensions, it is doomed to failure. We believe that many industrial firms in the 1970s and early 1980s focussed very much on the structural side of getting their business strategy right – they worked hard at the question of

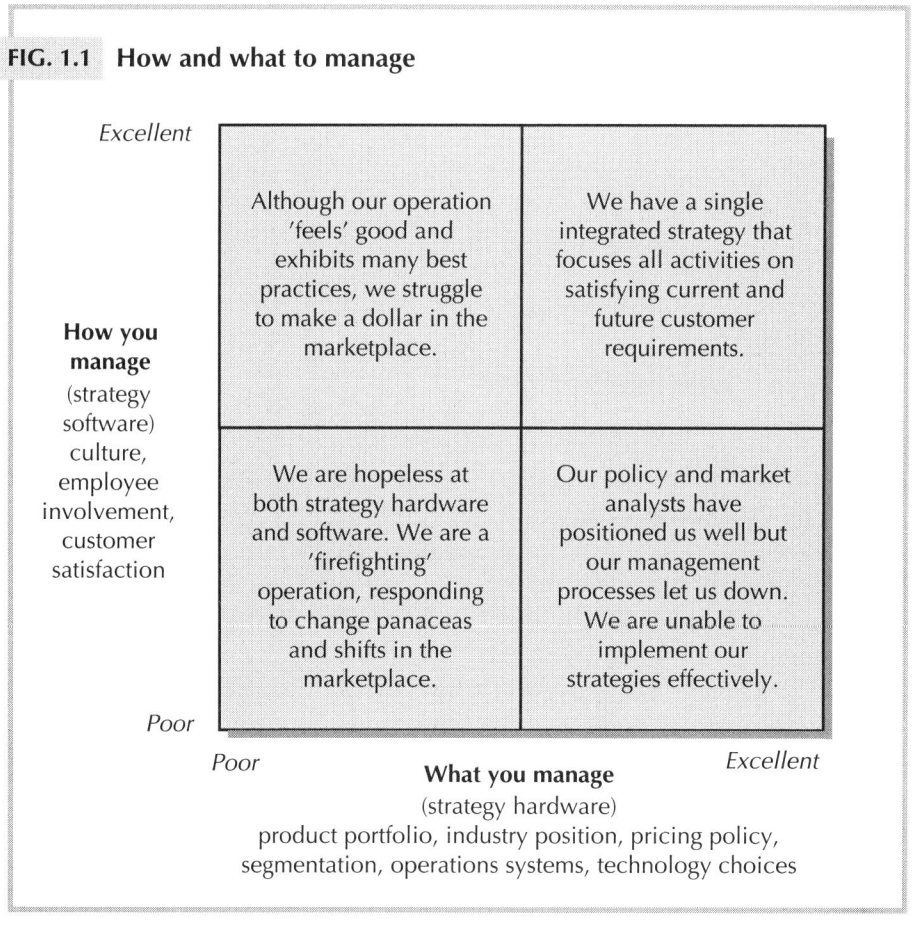

FIG. 1.1 How and what to manage

'what'. For the specific design of their operational systems, this 'what' question includes: make versus buy decisions; organizational structure; workforce and job design; supplier roles and relationships; quality control systems; employment contracts, etc. During the 1980s, many organizations refocussed very much on the question of 'how', with generic concepts and fads like decentralization, restructuring, downsizing, customer focus, relationship management, core competence, the learning organization, shared values, employee empowerment and culture change taking over as the main change paradigms in many organizations.

There is no clear delineation between 'what' and 'how', and the distinction is a little artificial. However, we believe it is a useful framework with which to view managerial action, particularly as many organizations have tried to use 'what' levers to affect changes to 'how' elements. Consider culture change, for example. During the 1980s many firms changed their operational system by redesigning individual and team roles and responsibilities, developing measurement and reporting systems, developing employee business, technical and interpersonal skills, introducing forums and processes to enhance workforce participation and involvement, etc. It was generally believed that these changes would lead to improvements in business performance and changes in employee behavior by creating a work environment that supported new ways of thinking and working. This has not proved to be the case.

The use of teams is a good example. Many firms introduced 'what' team interventions as a vehicle for teamwork and cultural change only to find that the development of a work environment that supports teamwork does not necessarily result in teamwork, as the level of interdependency maybe insufficient, or perhaps existing cultural norms are such that employees are unable or unwilling to change their behavior. Leadership development has been very similar in many respects. Many firms have introduced processes to develop employee leadership capability but have been unable to translate this individual capability into an organizational capability as the intervention has inadequately addressed barriers to changing employee behavior.

One of the major barriers that has stopped many firms from truly becoming successful has been that they have separately worked on improving their 'what' and their 'how', and that their strategies and practices in these regards have not only not been integrated, but in many instances have in fact been competing. This book provides the principles and implementation guidelines for producing a single integrated strategy by which managers in organizations of all sizes and shapes will be able first to think through and formulate, and then to implement a combined process for collectively working the 'how' and the 'what' issues together. This single integrated strategy for improvement requires a management system and a set of guiding principles from which practices and on-the-ground actions can be coherently strung together.

Part of the reason we believe that the 'how' of management is critically important is that the 'what' factors do not explain the huge variance in operational and corporate business performance. Pick an industry – airlines, automobiles, banking, consumer electronics, hotels, machine tools, you name it. In each sector, there are companies that are efficient and highly profitable and others that are going backwards. For example there are banks making significant profits (such as MBNA, Wells Fargo, Citibank, Lloyds, Hong Kong & Shanghai and National Bank) while others go bankrupt! In terms of the 'what' of strategy, the best and worst are not so different. Their products are certainly similar, as are their prices and distribution systems. So, what explains the high variance in their business performance? It must be a function of *how* they manage their assets.[5]

THE PRESENT STATE OF PLAY – ORGANIZED CHAOS

Many organizations, even some that we can say are leaders in terms of their performance, resemble the state of organization depicted in Figure 1.2. They reach for programs and initiatives in an unco-ordinated and unstructured way, often depending on what the latest fad[6] is. They do not have a medium to long-term plan associated with how they are going to improve the way in which they satisfy their employees, customers and shareholders. These organizations do have business plans and strategy documents, but very often they cover one to three years and are little more than statements such as 'How many can we make and sell?' Further, there is often no serious accountability when things do not go according to the plans which were signed off by executives. So everybody knows that the planning process is a painful ritual but not much more, because the loop of planning, action, performance and accountability is not closed.

Figure 1.2 shows the organizational model where many supposed improvement initiatives have been applied, such as total quality management, best practices, re-engineering, culture change, visioning, industrial reform, downsizing, etc., usually with annual or bi-annual cost-cutting exercises interspersed between these programs. Different groups or individuals often manage these programs with no overarching strategy driving them and little, if any, co-ordination between them. However, it even gets worse than that – we have observed in many organizations that the sequencing of the application of these initiatives is often almost ad hoc when one looks at it after the fact, and that new initiatives often undo achievements from past initiatives, further fuelling resistance to change. No wonder many organizations make relatively little progress over a two or three year period. No wonder the success rate of re-engineering or team development attempts is so low. No

PART 1 • PATTERNS OF EXCELLENCE

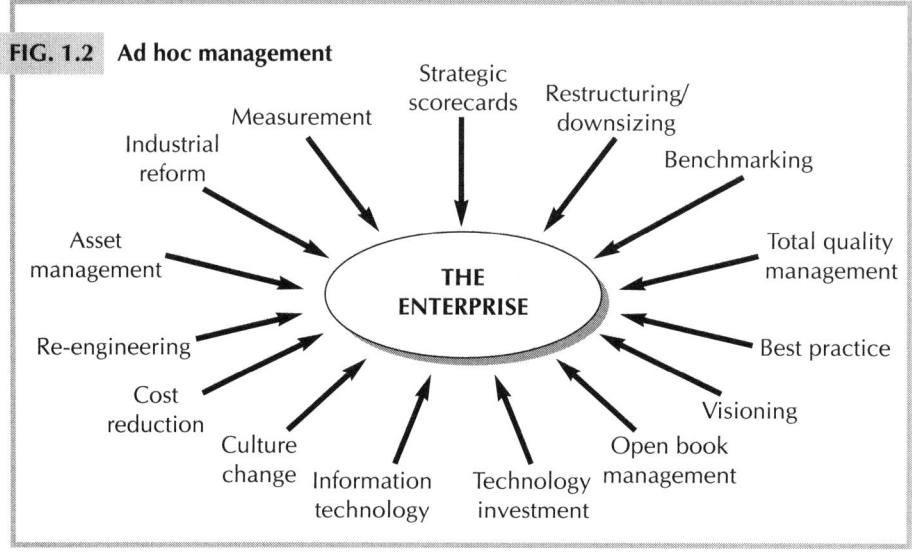

FIG. 1.2 Ad hoc management

wonder there are so many new product and new process technology failures. No wonder they resort to short-term cost-cutting measures such as staff reduction. No wonder employee morale is so poor and the relationships between an organization's leaders and its workforce are often so strained. No wonder we see shareholder value destroyed through companies lacking the policies that drive value creation.

And all this mediocrity of outcome occurs despite the earnest efforts of highly intelligent, hard-working people with the best interests of the organization at heart. These teams of executives and managers are challenged with responding to ever-increasing customer requirements, best international practices and turbulent, dynamic business contexts so they are highly motivated to pursue improvement.[7]

HOW GOOD COULD IT (OR SHOULD IT) BE?

Let us compare and contrast the overall model of management for a firm shown by Figure 1.2 with that of Figure 1.3. In Figure 1.3, the enterprise is shown (labelled as element 2) along with its business plan, which is not really a strategic plan but answers the questions of 'How many we can make and sell?' and 'What resources will we need in order to that over the next couple of years?' What distinguishes Figure 1.3 from many of the firms that are more like the representation in Figure 1.2 is that there is only one improvement initiative (element 1 in Figure 1.3) and it is the integration of the 'what' and 'how' components of strategy. The strategies and practices used to improve

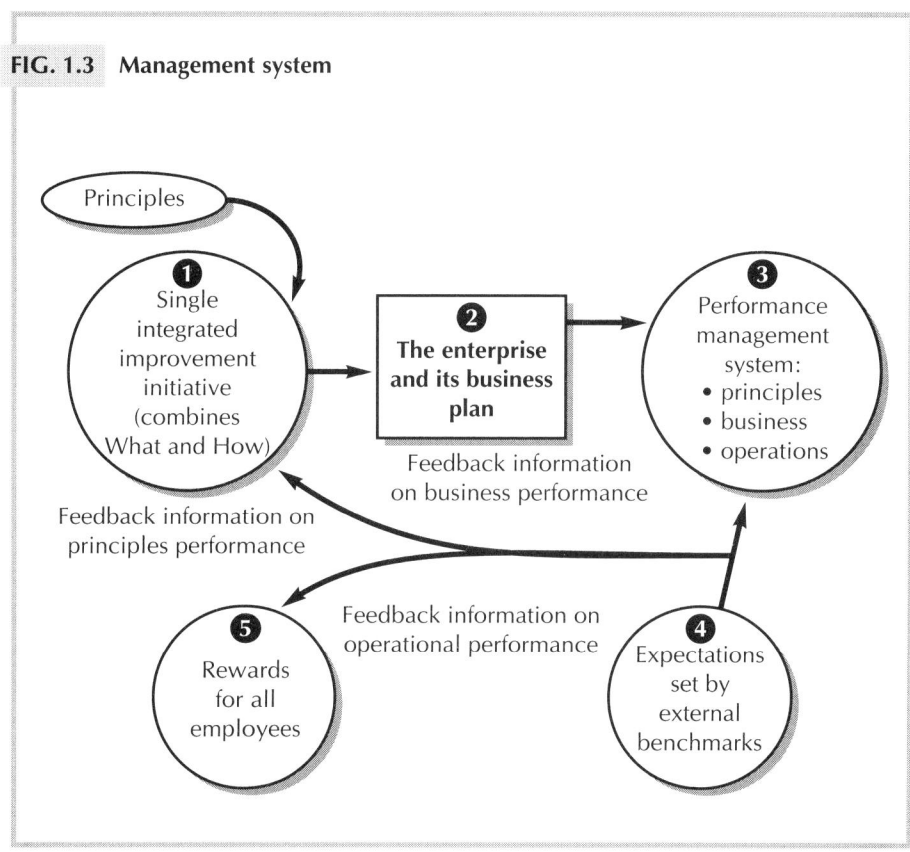

FIG. 1.3 Management system

all facets of the value chain in ways that realize business objectives, are integrated and aligned with the strategies and practices used for organizational improvement. This single strategic improvement initiative may have many parts but it has been thoroughly thought through and comprehensively planned. Its implementation is 'project managed' in a synergistic way. As this single initiative is the result of the collective efforts of many people, it is collectively owned by many people. Further, leading edge firms appear to drive this initiative through a key set of management principles. This set of driving principles serve as a roadmap against which to gauge organizational effectiveness and review organizational improvement activity. Hence, these principles ensure constancy of purpose and therefore the creation of a 'closed loop' system where organizational performance may be continually reassessed against them and deficiencies corrected.

This behavior can be contrasted to that of Figure 1.2 that is based on the 'open loop' system. That is, through some appropriate analysis of the external environment the future state is defined, typically using a five-year time horizon, the current state assessed, gap-closing strategies developed and interventions implemented. The system is 'open' because the nature of the environment determines the nature of the relationships within the system and hence management is largely about the rational processes of diagnosing the environment and developing an organizational form and gap-closing strategy appropriate to it. We believe the failure of many firms to achieve success with 'open loop' systems is due to the scale and pace of changes within the business, industry, competitor and operating environments. Competitiveness is fast becoming a war of movement (Stalk, 1988). For many firms this results in a new future state needing to be developed about every 6–12 months rather than every five years, resulting in a mismatch between the objectives of the planned change activity and the actual change needs of the organization.

If elements 1 and 2 of Figure 1.3 were the only system elements, then our approach would be grossly deficient. Element 3 is a performance management system. For each part of the single integrated improvement initiative applied to the firm, performance expectations are set on a wide-ranging set of dimensions over three levels, the principles themselves (typically 12–24-month review cycle), business performance (typically 6–12-month review cycle), and operational performance (typical 1–3-month review cycle). The best performance management systems that we have seen, even with their apparent shortcomings, are the quality award systems such as the Baldrige system in the USA, the Australian Quality Award framework, and the Balanced Scorecard Approach (Kaplan and Norton, 1995). Unfortunately, many firms use only some aspects of these systems or use them as a performance measure rather than a performance management system. That is, they simply develop sets of measures, targets and trend performance and address deficiencies rather than use these systems to drive strategy, behavior and investment.[8]

These systems are both rigorous and quite comprehensive, as a starting point. In other words, they measure much of 'the right stuff'. The performance measurement system and performance expectations are set by element 4 of our model (Figure 1.3), i.e. external performance comparisons and benchmarks. There is always a set of feedback loops in good companies from the measures of performance back to the firm's operations, the business plan of the firm and back to the single integrated improvement initiative of the organization. These feedback loops allow for change actions, correction of plans and communication to all involved at the right level of aggregation of information, such that everyone in the enterprise can connect their actions and work processes with the effects of these on performance. At ground level, this means understanding how the efforts of individuals and teams affect customer service, quality and productivity. At executive level, this means understanding how product designs and various resource allocations, decisions and investments impact on market share, sales growth, and profitability. At the business plan level, it means balancing resources and productive capacity on a monthly through to yearly basis, with trends in demand across product lines and markets.

Finally, the performance of all employees is actively managed (see element 5 of Figure 1.3). First, consider rewards. Employee rewards are derived from exactly the same set of measures as those that define organizational success more broadly. In excellent organizations that we have observed, everybody has a variable component of their remuneration aligned to organizational performance and its key drivers. Just as shareholders have put their capital at risk where the return is variable depending on organizational performance, employees provide human capital and the alignment of part of the return to this effort with organizational performance, when this alignment is done well, provides both incentives and satisfaction. This approach is little more than good, applied common sense in an organizational context.

Many people have uttered one of the following two sayings: 'Take their minds there and their hearts will follow'; 'Take their hearts there and their minds will follow. Which is true? Which works better? Are both true to some extent? Should we appeal to employees' logic and let them internalize the company's needs, and generate their passion and motivation, or should we make impassioned speeches and emotionally ask them to sign on in order to motivate them to come with us on the journey? We believe that we need to do both but that even doing both of these well is not enough. Here is another maxim that leading organizations also use effectively as a change lever: 'Take their wallets there and both their hearts and minds will follow'. Let's use logical arguments to explain to employees why and how we must change, let's appropriately use emotion too, but let's also use money! In most of the companies we visit or work with that are high performance organizations, there is a close alignment of the financial outcomes of the company's owners and its employees at all levels. Perhaps the simplest and clearest statement we can remember of this came from a middle manager at Medco in New Jersey when asked how the immense sense of energy is sustained right across the company. 'When the company prospers, so do I, and my family knows and supports that. Further, everyone here is part of the same system.'

So what should we say to those who state that money is not a motivator and that it is a sense of job satisfaction and goal achievement that counts in motivating people?

- Job satisfaction and goal achievement are important, so make sure that they are in place as critical elements of the work culture – but they don't make for everything.[9]
- Use every lever available to generate focus, alignment and energy in the workplace, and it is clear that some people respond strongly to financial incentives.

- If structured sensibly, the cost of bonuses or variable components of remuneration are small compared to the net gain for the company.
- Visit Medco, or others such as Microsoft, Saturn, Edison Mission or BF Goodrich. Or visit any other high-performance workplace where people are switched on to alignment of company and staff objectives for the long term, at least partially because of the alignment of company and staff financial outcomes.

We do not want to give the impression that leading organizations actively manage (i.e. reward) achievement only. We have observed that they also actively manage underperformance. They have agreed sets of behavioral standards and ethics with their workforce. Leading firms spend considerable effort in ensuring everyone knows and understands their behavioral limits. In many organizations, the work culture has evolved to such a mature level that these standards are gatekept by peers, possibly other team members. Positive behavior is reinforced, unacceptable behavior is confronted.

To summarize, there is an alternative to the ad hoc and short-term approach represented by Figure 1.2. Many of our best firms are acting at least partially in the mode as represented by Figure 1.3 but very few have all the connections right and fully implemented in a mature manner. The first generation of firms who have moved from the ad hoc mode of improvement initiatives towards the single integrated plan and closed-loops system of Figure 1.3 came to many of these changes through crisis. These companies include Xerox, Kodak, IBM and General Motors. It is something of a sad reflection on the nature of organizations and indeed the individuals who lead and drive those organizations that many of our most forward-thinking and best-organized companies today were those which were deep in crisis some time during the previous decade. But there is hope, because there is a lot of learning being done in this regard!

The hope is that this crisis-driven process is not the only mechanism by which firms systematically pursue improvement strategies as against pursue the wasteful, ad hoc model. A newer breed of companies has emerged which have at least partially implemented the integrated model of management.

The best organizations are managed as an integrated set of closed loops. There are three basic closed loops involved. These revolve around the company's major stakeholders – customers, employees and investors – and really define management's job in a fundamental way.

First, there is a closed loop around the customer (see Figure 1.4). Customer requirements drive product and service designs that drive supply and operations systems that in turn satisfy customer requirements.

Figure 1.4 comes from our study and practice of total quality management, and relates to being competitive in the market as well as being well-controlled and organized in the company's value-adding production and distribution processes.

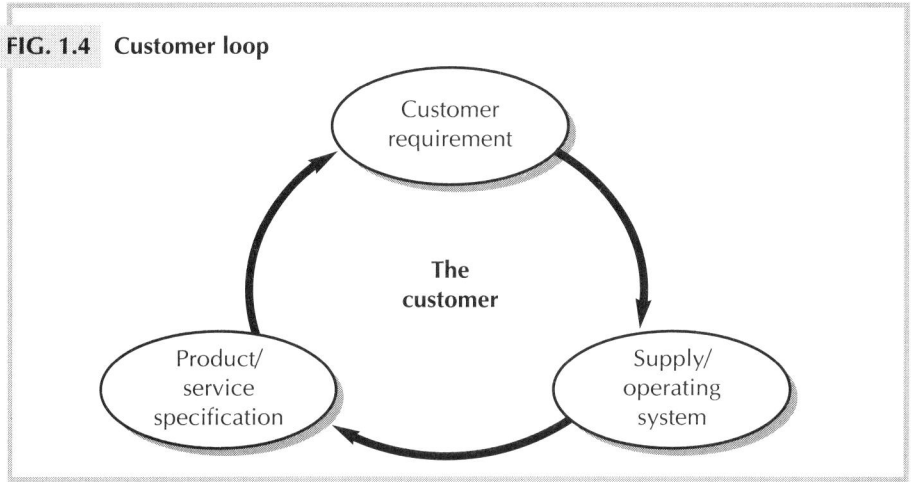

FIG. 1.4 Customer loop

Second, there is a closed loop around employees as shown in Figure 1.5. Goals/objectives are articulated, employees are skilled and given the tools, resources and support to achieve these goals and performance assessed against these goals and other behavioral standards and norms. Incentives are provided to reward the achievement of agreed goals to specified standards and unacceptable behavior is flushed out and actively managed.

Third, there is a closed loop for the owners of the enterprise (see Figure 1.6). Investment targets are explicitly stated, performance is measured against target measures and related to owner rewards, with investors having directors and governance processes as controls.

In this context, management's job is really to bring these various stakeholders together in an enterprise that will bring value to each of these three closed loops and their sub-elements (see Figure 1.7).

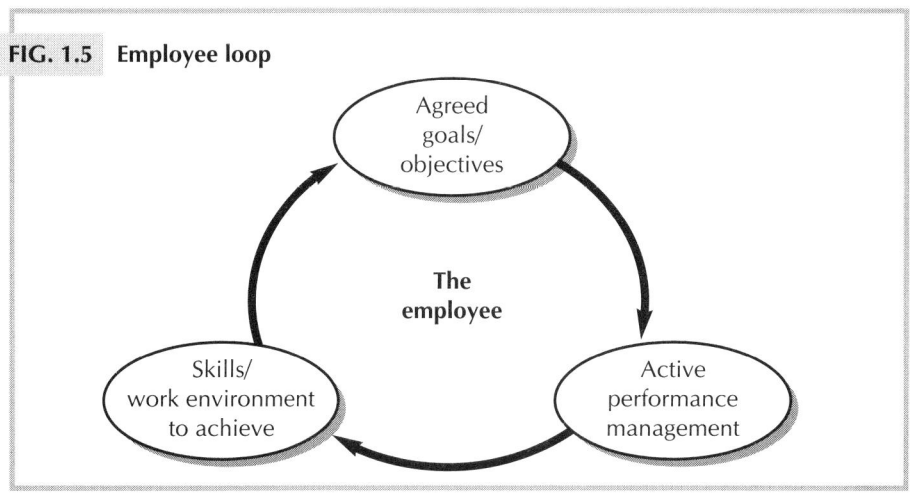

FIG. 1.5 Employee loop

PART 1 • PATTERNS OF EXCELLENCE

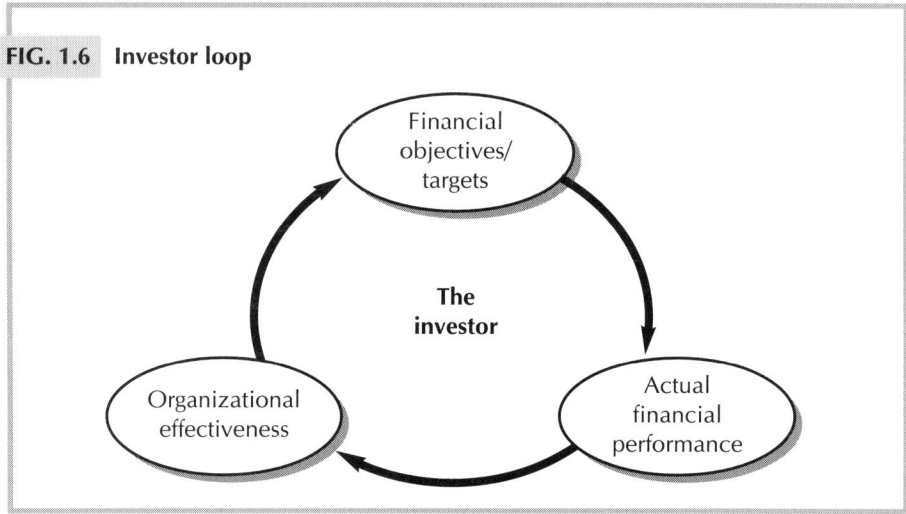

FIG. 1.6 Investor loop

These simple ideas are often forgotten when trying to make complex organizations work effectively, and we need to get back down to the basics of managerial strategy, which is to make money, that is create net value, by creating value for every element of Figure 1.7.

FIG. 1.7 Key management loops

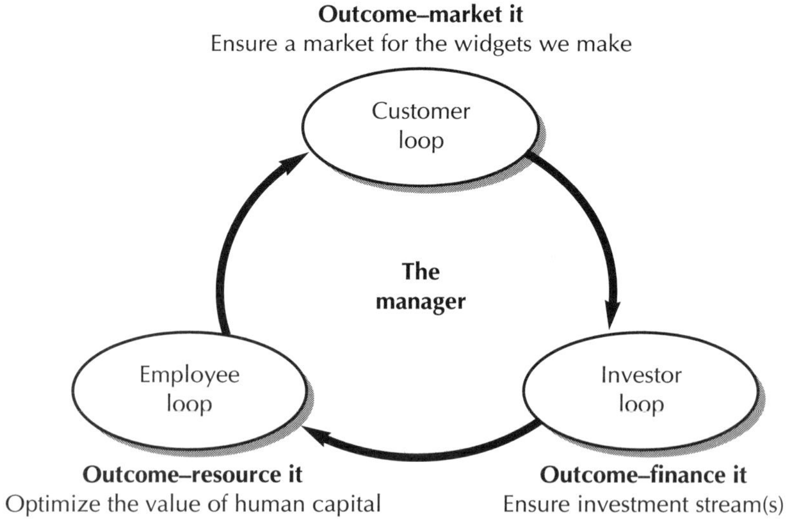

Outcome–market it
Ensure a market for the widgets we make

Customer loop

The manager

Employee loop

Investor loop

Outcome–resource it
Optimize the value of human capital

Outcome–finance it
Ensure investment stream(s)

For the 'best' companies that we have observed, success has been achieved through closing and aligning these loops, having sensibly connected systems that guide behavior, resource allocation and development. We believe this to be the essence of managerial work, and the only other important question is how to go about implementing all this. To this end, we have found the very best companies to implement these loops with highly visible, passionate and consistent leadership, which is demonstrated around a key set of axiomatic management principles sometimes (but not always) stated explicitly. We have identified 14 of these principles of management, which are explained in detail in Part 2.

Notes

1. Two knowledge platforms of the last decade were the works of Peters and Waterman, *In Search of Excellence* and the Total Quality Management (TQM) movement. Each had its own strengths and weaknesses. Neither was anywhere near complete, nor intended to be. Although Peters and Waterman's eight management principles accorded with common sense, they were narrow in focus, generally difficult to measure and difficult to action as there was no framework for implementation. TQM had solid foundations and a good measurement system (quality awards frameworks). However it was mechanistic in style and failed to address a broad range of cultural and behavioral issues adequately.
2. There are many reasons for this, of which the main ones concern the basic building blocks and the dynamics of the environments. The basic building blocks of oil refineries are molecules of raw material oils, catalyst chemicals, petroleum products, plant and equipment which more or less behave consistently and predictably, when 'change initiatives' such as temperature and pressure are applied. Molecules do not need development, support, incentives, feedback, etc. and behave rationally in a true democracy. People, the basic building blocks of organizations clearly *do* need these requirements to be met. Second, the technical operating environment of an oil refinery is relatively stable whereas the business environment for most of us is changing continuously, with the additional challenge of a few unpredictable discontinuities thrown in from time to time.
3. This could be thought of management as an 'artform', which would be fine if we were all Picasso!
4. The service profit chain (Heskett, et al., 'Putting the Service Profit Chain to Work', *Harvard Business Review*, 1994) asserts that there are causal effects between employee satisfaction and retention and customer satisfaction and retention and by getting it right for the customer, profit generation and therefore shareholder satisfaction can be achieved.
5. This is the case in all industries, from pharmaceuticals and automotive equipment to software and fast food. There are major winners and major losers in all these industries, for example, why was the US and much of the European presence in the mass markets of television set production eliminated during the 1980s? It wasn't that Sony, Matsushita and Mitsubishi had TVs that were radically different. It was 'how' they managed the design, supply chain, production, distribution, selling and servicing processes, that led to much more competitive outcomes and hence superior customer offerings and value.
6. The executives in one successful company we worked with describe this as *'Management by In-flight Magazine'*. They went on to say that if only they knew which airline their CEO next uses they would get the airline magazine and prepare for the next fad!

7. The popular press has typically been more cynical. Managers' predisposition toward introducing improvement initiatives has been attributed to other socio-psychological forces such as childlike excitement (*Business Week*, 12 July, 1986), mass conformity (*Wall Street Journal*, 6 July, 1993) and even something akin to manias or episodes of mass hysteria (*Harvard Business Review*, No 72, 1994)
8. In their landmark article 'The Balanced Scorecard', *Harvard Business Review*, Jan/Feb 1992, and subsequent articles and text, Kaplan and Norton describe how to use and create a strategic measurement system.
9. There are also numerous theories which also link employee rewards to employee motivation under various conditions e.g. reinforcement theory, equity theory, expectancy theory.

2
Towards world-class management and leadership

The best executive is the one who has sense enough to pick good [people] to do what he wants done, and self restraint enough to keep from meddling with them while they do it.

Theodore Roosevelt

COMPANY 'NEW' – WHAT WOULD IT LOOK LIKE AND WHAT WOULDN'T IT LOOK LIKE?

Imagine an organization with all the linkages shown in Figure 1.3 fully developed. This organization, 'Company New', is consistently pursuing improvement through a common, enduring approach to management and improvement, to which each and every employee contributes. Company New practices the continuous care approach to management: its model for management is nursing not medicine. This organization is not attempting to prescribe a cure for an undiagnosed illness, nor is it racing around to each and every medical practitioner searching for the latest wonder drug to cure all its ailments. It is not taking other medicines to compensate for the side effects of the latest wonder drug: it does not 'rattle when it walks' with its system in overload from everything it has consumed. Company New also doesn't spend extended periods of time in post-op recovering from the latest excision – re-engineering, downsizing, restructuring, etc., nor does it go into cardiac arrest every time a competitor makes a move!

Company New is robust and in control of its own destiny. It has a clear understanding of what needs to be done to reach 'best in class' performance, and more importantly, it has the confidence that it will succeed. Its history demonstrates its ability to establish strong and transparent links between change/improvement initiatives and business results. This company has a solid track record of actually implementing what it set out to do with minimal roadblocks or delays.

Company New has a vision that is energized through a proven set of principles, not a vision energized by faith. Consequently, corporate confidence in Company New is extremely high. Executive managers are continually seeking out and creating new business opportunities. Company New's corporate culture enables executives to focus on long-term wealth creation and competitiveness, not short-term profit maximization or survival. Senior executives are not sidetracked by short-term operational issues. Investment confidence is high. This organization actually realizes the estimated return on investment for its major projects. Engineering is developing new processes and products. Operations is investing in new systems and technology, perhaps plant and facilities. Finance is actively supporting new investment opportunities through innovative deals. Marketing is increasing existing market share and aggressively creating new markets. Most importantly, all the pieces fit together.

The activities of all these functions and the individuals and teams within them are aligned: the contribution of each and every person within the organization is supporting its overall mission and goals. There is no wasted human effort, no areas where people are working on dead projects, nor are there strong loyalties and organizational politics causing dysfunctional outcomes. A unity of purpose and extremely strong spirit of co-operation bonds all employees in a common effort. There are no status differentials.

The high confidence within Company New spills over to high customer confidence. Customer and supplier relationships are close with high long-term loyalty. Company New is internationally networked extremely well with its major suppliers and customers. Information technology spans the tyranny of distance. Consequently, suppliers to Company New organizations are closely coupled with it. Everybody knows exactly what the customer really values and everybody is actively striving to increase customer value both to protect existing customers and capture new ones. Company New, however, is not only a leader in customer service, but also a leader in industry standards, environmental policy, quality, product and process design, responsiveness, etc.

In Company New, there is little rhetoric or new age management mumbo-jumbo. Company New does not have periodic show and tell sessions that dazzle then fizzle. There is also no mindset gap between management and the broader workforce. However, there is a recognition by 'both' groups that each has a vital role to play in the company's success and to that end a common platform of understanding has evolved. The workforce understands and lives company direction, values and business direction. Management understands and is actively involved in supplier and customer issues and key organizational and operational issues. In Company New, short-term management actions are always consistent with medium-term goals, as this organization does not prescribe 'fad surfing' – riding the crest of the latest management panacea and then paddling out just in time to catch the next one – totally absorbing for managers, frequently disastrous for organizations (Shapiro, 1995). A select, easy-to-understand set of measures also helps to create common understanding and integrate the activities of all employees at all organizational levels.

The workforce actively embraces change and the challenges it brings. This workforce has a thirst for knowledge and skills, and a dedication which is second to none. All employees are fully 'switched on' and contributing to their maximum capability. Morale and trust is high, optimism and commitment even higher. Teams fluidly form and disband as problems and issues emerge and are resolved. Everyone is capable of working with everyone else. People genuinely want to work for this company as it offers a set of challenges, opportunities and rewards second to none. Employees feel emancipated by change and discontinuity and are strongly socialized to Company New. However, they do not stay with the company because of life-long employment contracts, superannuation schemes and/or a sense of company loyalty but because of their desire to learn and the immense learning and professional development opportunities that the organization provides.

Employees are responsible for their own career path planning. They are also typically very well remunerated and collectively feel in charge of their destiny. By having superior internal processes, they are better at customer value creation and productivity management, hence they earn enough to provide superior shareholder returns, reinvest in the business and pay employees well. They are leaders in the capital market, in their product/ service market and in the labor market.

AN EXAMPLE OF A COMPANY NEW: MERCK-MEDCO

Merck is one of the world's leading pharmaceutical companies, in both its size, with annual revenues of over $17 billion, and in its reputation for being an advanced, quality-focused organization.

In 1993 Merck purchased Medco, a mail service pharmaceuticals distribution company. Medco began by providing a cheaper, faster, quality service to its customers who were the sponsors of health plans, such as insurance carriers (Blue Cross and Blue Shield in the USA), unions, government departments, corporates, managed care organizations and pharmacies. Medco was created and finds its economic value in being able to be a better distribution channel than the conventional pharmacy/drug store.

The central philosophy of Medco is to supply its 50 million patients at high levels of five dimensions of performance known in the company as the 'five pillars':

- prescription turnaround time
- customer service
- quality
- cost per script
- managed care services.

These are the drivers of both customer satisfaction and performance of the Medco organization. Medco develops managed healthcare plans as well as pharmaceutical supply plans which are contracted with customers. It has a super-efficient transaction base in which it distributes 800,000 prescriptions each week, making it the largest pharmacy in the world. On top of this transaction base, which is managed from distribution centres in New Jersey, Nevada, Florida, Texas and Ohio, Medco has developed its managed care capability and constantly strives to use its employees to engage in continuous improvement in all aspects of its business.

Medco has a very high degree of *alignment* of the company's purpose with that of each of its employees, and indeed with both its consumers (the 50 million patients) and with its paying customers who are the health care plan sponsors. This alignment drives both the efficiency and effectiveness of Medco as specified by its five pillars of value listed above.

The alignment is 'hardwired' with employees through its reward system. Operating staff in Medco's high-volume pharmacies receive quarterly bonus payments based on daily through to quarterly operational performance on measures such as order fulfilment rates, productivity and turnaround time. Senior managers receive substantial bonuses dependent on business performance and customer satisfaction. These variable components of salary in the bonus system amount to as much as 35 percent of the salary base for some employees. The strong alignment and the variable rewards (based on performance) lead to a strong '*micro-to-macro*' connection in the company. Each worker identifies strongly with the company's overall performance, and the many employees we interviewed openly displayed a strong sense of pride in their contribution to those outcomes.

The principle of *discipline* is highly transparent at Medco: 'We have

SOPs – standard operating procedures – for absolutely everything. We have highly structured quality standards and our defect rate is better than twice as good as the industry standard of one error in 10,000 items, where an error might be a simple typo on an instruction sheet' (Medco executive).

Medco has a very strong focus on finding new and enhanced ways of *customer-value creation*. Based on its efficient transactional base of the distribution of medicinal drugs, Medco has developed a sophisticated information base where comprehensive patient records are kept. When a patient calls to order a script, the full record of that patient including notes from all previous conversations and transactions with Medco are automatically and immediately brought to the screen in front of the pharmacist who takes the order. Using both human skills and expert systems, the new order is checked using the latest medical technology to see whether it may react positively or otherwise with existing medications being taken.

Medco does much more than just distribute medicine. An example is in the management of diabetes, in which Medco helps to monitor a patient's health and, through the provision of latest information, helps its patients to understand and monitor the disease. By helping patients to control their diabetes better, Medco is enhancing the health and life of patients. In the case of employee healthcare plans Medco is enhancing the value that the employee can give to the corporate or government healthcare sponsor while at the same time reducing the total cost of treatment, for example hospitalization. Hence Medco has transformed itself to be much more than reacting to the need for medicine. The major area in which Medco is developing new and deeper partnerships with its clients is in measuring the total cost related to health management of its 'clients' clients', including the cost of doctors, drugs, hospitals, work-related sick leave, hospitalization and productivity loss due to poor health.

Although Medco has been based on a strong cost-reduction culture, it also places a lot of emphasis on *resourcing the medium term* through its business development and continuous improvement initiatives. It has a quality assurance review team and through its Vice-President of Quality has a focused set of quality action teams who are investigating improvements which will be lasting into the medium term. Medco's philosophy in this regard is to apply the Pareto principle to quality improvement initiatives by focusing on a vital few (about six) improvement initiatives at a time rather than dispersing its energy on a very large number of improvement possibilities. Medco has a strong focus on operational excellence and a culture of high energy to drive, improve and dynamically perform better each day than the previous. They have clearly found a formula for combining the *discipline* which is necessary in their type of operation with the *distributed leadership* and *learning* that one would expect from an industry leader. They engage in very substantial amounts of training and employ a large percentage of professionals, particularly pharmacists.

Medco has a state-of-the-art telephone center in which incoming calls are screened and orders are taken for scripts, checked, often verified with doctors, then entered into the production process. The telephone operation was designed and set up after extensive benchmarking studies (see Figure 1.3) of companies such as American Express, so that Medco could understand leading-edge standards for such an operation. Medco is at the forefront of exciting transformations from its transactional dispensing base as it moves to total healthcare management based on an acute focus on customer satisfaction. It is out front within its industry and is now automating more and more of its processes using voicemail, touchtone and forming enlightened relationships with retail pharmacies with which it both directly competes and co-operates. In visiting the Medco pharmacy operations and interacting both with its managers and operational staff, one could only be impressed by the professionalism of all of its people and the up-front style of openness and integrity within the organization. Information is prominently displayed on noticeboards throughout the organization, which are kept current such as to link clearly operational and business performance with the actions of staff. This direct linkage between strategy, action, operational and business performance and rewards contributes to what makes Medco a truly outstanding company. In its telephone centre in the New Jersey pharmacy, the measurement and publication of performance data is updated literally by the second on electronic scoreboards which inform telephone operators of the length of the queue of calls in the telephone system and the time the longest call has been waiting. Such real-time transparency of linkage between operators and operational performance provides for an impressive service centre operating at very high levels of service performance.

Medco has clearly achieved a workplace in which all of its employees are very well informed, very strongly *aligned* to the purpose of the company and very well skilled to do the job. The commitment is almost tangible and the enthusiasm is infectious. When asked why they work so hard and pursue their goals so relentlessly, a number of employees at different levels, from Vice-President to telephone operator and drug dispenser, all gave essentially the same answer: 'This is a great place to work, and when the company does well I personally do well and benefit more and more'. Customer satisfaction levels are *guaranteed* to be at least 98 percent.

• • • • • • • • • • •

Whether it is healthcare, pharmaceuticals, banking or anything else, Company 'New' is beating up on its old-fashioned rivals that try to drive improvement using the approach in Figure 1.2. The competitiveness and profitability differences between the best and the rest in most industries are large. Part 2 discusses the key principles common to the best.

Part 2
MANAGEMENT BY PRINCIPLES

●●●●●●●●●●●●●●●●●

Part 2 describes the essential heart of the principle-driven organization. First, in Chapter 3, we describe the need and value for a set of driving principles in an organization, that can be an enduring guide to action. Subsequent chapters present the key principles common to the world's best organizations we have observed. Each chapter is structured so as to provide:

- a description of the principle with some examples
- a set of questions for evaluating an organization's strength in respect of that principle
- an elaboration of the business benefits from using that principle to guide action
- suggestions as to how to improve and strengthen the organization's position in respect of that principle, with further illustrations.

●●●●●●●●●●●●●●●●●

3

Management by principles

Without principles to guide behavior and decisions, we are wandering about in circles in the desert.

INTRODUCTION

What constitutes this consistent, enduring approach to management referred to in Part 1? We have identified 14 key management principles. These principles, defined in Figure 3.1, are developed in considerable detail in the following chapters. Some of them have previously been individually described at length in the management literature. We have observed them as being common to true, 'best in class' performers.

Our observations of these principles have taken place in numerous countries[1] and in a wide variety of industries and we illustrate them in the remaining chapters with examples drawn substantially from our personal observations. These principles are not always explicit within the organizations, but are *implicit* to how leaders, managers and, in the best companies, all employees behave and organize their resources. However, although these principles are often not formally written down as such, they are often conscious in the way they are managed as part of the natural way that business is conducted.

FIG. 3.1 The 14 principles

Principle	Description
1. Alignment	There is good alignment of employee behavior with stated company values and direction at all levels of the organization.
2. Distributed leadership	Individuals and work teams are assigned, and accept, responsibility for operational decision making and performance improvement.
3. Integration of effort	The organization is focused on value creation and process management, not functional needs and hierarchies.
4. Out front	The business proactively strives to lead the pack in all industry standards and practices: safety, customer service, product and process design, environmental management, etc.
5. Up front	All employees demonstrate integrity and openness in all areas of their work and dealings with others. Relationships are highly valued.
6. Resourcing the medium-term	The business is able to balance effectively short-term operational and medium term development and growth issues and requirements.
7. Time based	Time is developed as a critical organizational value. The business practices the principles of time-based competition.
8. Embracing change	All employees demonstrate a willingness to embrace and accept change as an essential part of doing business. The organization excels at implementing new ideas.
9. Learning focus	All employees demonstrate a willingness to develop skills and knowledge and are involved in a learning/development program.
10. Discipline	The organization invests in policies, procedures and standards and applies a strong systems perspective in everything it does.
11. Measurement and reporting	The business measures and reports to all employees the financial and non-financial performance information needed to drive improvement.
12. Customer value	All employees understand the set of order winners and actively strive to enhance customer value creation.
13. Capabilities creation	Business and organizational capabilities are defined and prioritized and drive critical development and investment decisions.
14. Micro to macro	All employees know how their particular activities and individual efforts contribute to the 'big picture' of business success.

Justification of principle-guided management

Why is it useful to have a set of guiding principles? Their goal is to provide a framework through which decisions and behavior can conform to a consistent standard. We will argue that without principles it is very easy to get lost in a complex labyrinth of changing trends and shifting sands. Without principles, there is no long-term steering, or indeed if management does have some 'vision' it does not have a rudder which provides the mechanisms for getting there. A 'vision statement' or 'mission statement' often defines a desired endpoint or goal, or a sense of purpose, but is usually remote from being able to guide employee behavior and day-to-day decision making.

The principles have been found to be the common drivers of behavior in many of the world's greatest companies, and we propose that this set of principles demonstrates that management is maturing. It is salient that the many excellent companies we have observed have many and varied vision/mission statements, but in pursuing these statements of intent or purpose, they drive behavior using a common set of principles! We propose that these are therefore the 'principles of sound management' and that unlike fads, change programs and even mission statements themselves, these principles are enduring – a management constant. Indeed, we believe that they already have endured, having already been implicit to many excellent organizations for over a decade.

HOW MANAGEMENT BY PRINCIPLES WORKS

We have found that the superior organizations that we have observed demonstrate a consistent and coherent approach to management. They do not engage in unplanned and ad hoc patterns of change initiatives, routinely changing the emphasis of their organizational improvement effort, nor do they necessarily opt for the latest management panaceas. They are driven by a set of guiding principles (see Figure 3.2) which ensure that a systematic approach endures. Further, these are not just 'any old' principles, but are a set which demonstrably work in companies which excel!

PART 2 • MANAGEMENT BY PRINCIPLES

The principles do not just stand alone as separate from each other. There are many synergies between them. The reader may wish to build a picture of these connections as Part 2 unfolds. To reinforce their meaning, we provide self-assessment exercises in each following chapter within Part 2. Where does your organization fall in respect of the 14 fundamental principles of good management (see Figure 3.2)?

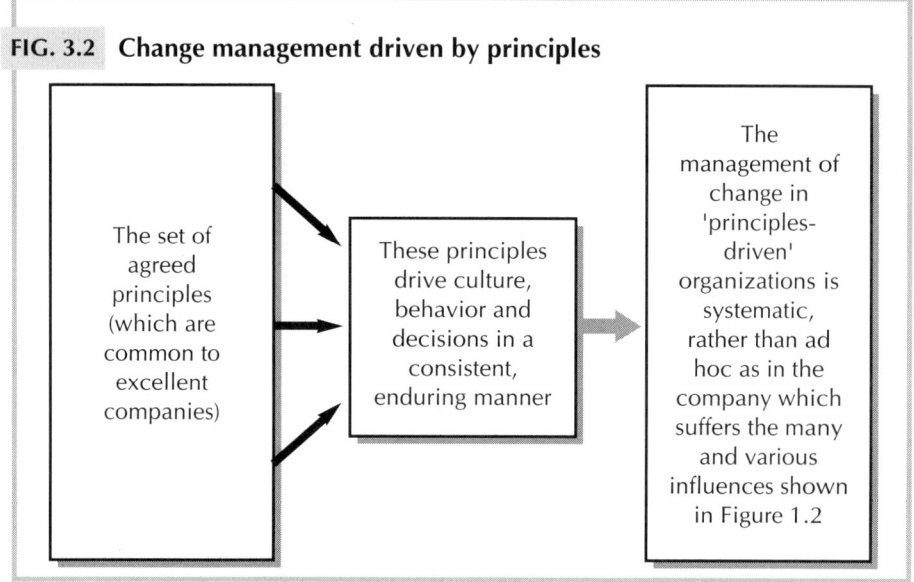

FIG. 3.2   Change management driven by principles

The 14 Principles of Management: How Much Do They Really Matter and How Well Do Firms Rate?

Summary
The results of a large research project provide very strong support for the value of the 14 principles of management as a cognitive map with which to evaluate organizational effectiveness and improve business performance.

All management principles and all management system elements are important and principles are strongly interrelated.

The research objectives
A large empirical study of management principles and business performance was undertaken at the Melbourne University. The study investigated a range of issues including the extent to which individually and collectively, the 14 principles of management are associated with superior business performance.

The research process
The study consisted of survey and broad cross-section of firms: large and small, complex and narrow lines of business, new businesses and well-established businesses, manufacturing and service sectors, public and private ownership, market leaders and market laggers, etc. After extensive pilot testing and review, a total of approximately 1000 firms received the questionnaire. Responses were received from nearly 200 sites.

The survey was seven pages in total and was mailed to the CEO of each firm. Respondents were either CEOs or members of the management team. A total of 68 questions were included that reflected various perspectives including the degree of principles orientation, principles strength and business performance. All data was analysed using tecniques and methodologies that meet established standards of academic rigour.

Results
First, consider the generalizability of the findings. For all analyses performed, we found no significant differences in results on the basis of ownership, size, complexity, sales, market share or line of business.

Second, consider the issue of principles value. When we considered the explanatory power of the 14 principles of management and the various elements of our management system, we found that we could explain approximately 45 percent of the variance in business performance. Furthermore, each principle had a statistically significant association with business performance. Alignment, bias for action, customer value creation, integration and outfront demonstrated the strongest performance associations.

Third, consider the extent of principles and management system element interdependency. The associations between each principle and the other and the various elements of our management system were moderate to high in all cases. This finding provides considerable support for the proposition that principles are highly interdependent and that firms adopting them tend to apply a structured and systemic approach to do so.

Fourth, consider the scope of opportunity for improvement. With a total principles points score of 70 (5-point response scale for each of the 14 principles) we find that the average principles strength of our test sample is 47, only 5 above the scale mean of 42. Consequently, there is a very significant opportunity for improvement. The principles of learning (mean value 2.91), out front (2.94) and measurement/reporting (3.19) have the lowest mean values and therefore provide the greatest opportunities for improvement.

Notes

1. We have observed that cultural differences can, and do, result in different barriers to overcome in order to develop a particular principle and therefore different change approaches being used, but the goals are basically the same. Consider the principle of distributed leadership in Anglo and Eastern cultures. Anglo cultures (e.g. USA, UK, Australia) frequently struggle to get individuals to accept additional responsibility due to entrenched work practices and norms and despite the fact that the individuals concerned very often demonstrate their abilities in this area outside the workplace (e.g. operator is the Head of the Local School Council). In some Eastern cultures, (e.g. Thailand, Vietnam, Malaysia) deeply entrenched societal norms e.g. 'ego', 'accepted existential inequality', 'face saving' and 'Kreng Chai'(to be considerate and take others' feelings into account) can, and do, result in individuals being reluctant to accept additional responsibilities for fear that it may adversely affect highly valued personal relationships.

4

Principle 1
Alignment

Wars very rarely break out among those who have a common understanding of goals and purposes.

Philip Crosby

INTRODUCTION

Definition of alignment

At its highest level, this principle is reflected in two key alignment elements:

- employee behavior and the set of articulated company values
- employee mindset and the stated strategic direction (sometimes referred to as the strategic intent) of the firm.

Shared values and shared strategic direction are derived from, and aligned with, customer requirements and the stated strategy and financial performance requirements of the firm as shown in Figures 4.1 and 4.2. These alignment attributes should be considered as a 'meta-principle', referring to the connection between the various elements of Figure 1.3. We have found that these two superordinate aspects of alignment (values and strategic orientation) are invariably accompanied with alignment in other key areas, e.g. goals, value chain, support processes and functions, goals, measurement and rewards.

Alignment is also reflected in the extent to which the set of employee behaviors developed, support and are reinforced, by the strategic orientation and business direction of the firm. For example, 3M is in the ideas business and its success is very much a function of the extent to which it can foster a work environment that manages ideas. The key employee ideologies of 'thou shalt not kill a new idea' and 'respect for individual initiative and personal growth' can be directly linked to business performance. Similarly, Marriot's central ideology of 'making people away from home feel that they are among friends and are really wanted' has a hard-wired connection with its central business mission. This situation is very different to many average performing firms whose core values and behaviors are fundamentally generic in kind, e.g. 'treating each other with respect', 'striving to ensure customer value and satisfaction', 'supporting change and improvement'.

KELLOGG AND ALIGNMENT

Kellogg, a leading manufacturer of ready-to-eat breakfast cereal, developed a major change initiative in one of its major businesses during the 1990s. The plan included a number of major activities including $800 million of capital investment in new plant and technology. A significant event involving all employees was convened to launch the plan, explore the need for real alignment and invite people to become involved. The CEO later remarked:

> We closed the place down and took everybody off site for a management team presentation. We talked about the big picture of doing business, what all the successful companies were doing, what competitors were doing, best practices, what we were doing, why we were going to invest $800 million in our operation, why we needed to change and why we needed everybody on board. It was a disaster, but in hindsight, it was probably the best thing that could have happened to us. It made us realize that getting 700 people to see the need to become involved, be prepared to become involved and understand the message doesn't happen overnight ... it takes time and a lot of hard work.

Kellogg's experience is similar to that of many others that we have encountered. Many firms use large, one-off presentations in an attempt to foster alignment. We have seen many of these presentations and most fall well short of the mark. Most are run by managers only and many are run by the wrong managers. Most use excessive jargon, most do not pitch business issues in words that mean something to people, many do not really tell it like it is, due to concerns about disclosure of sensitive material, and most are not followed up with discussions that provide adequate opportunity for discussion and feedback.

Apart from these observations there is a more fundamental problem. *Alignment requires an integrated strategy not a series of managerial events. Alignment is underpinned by education, not just communication.* Many managers fail to understand the magnitude of the alignment gap between themselves and the workforce. Often the problem is akin to trying to get someone who drives an automobile to understand how to drive a space shuttle. The knowledge chasm is enormous and if we want to learn how to drive a space shuttle we don't do it in one session – it takes many years of intensive instruction and we must be prepared to put the time in.

To return to Kellogg, they learned from their alignment experience. The philosophy – 'face-to-face' to align, newsletter to inform – was born. Extensive internal change management facilitation training was given to staff to increase business understanding, develop leadership skills and develop an understanding of the alignment process. A joint management/workforce committee was subsequently formed consisting of 12 people, each of whom had good facilitation skills. This committee developed a polished presentation in which each individual had an active role. Presentations were accompanied with a three-part video that discussed in detail the company's competitive position, rationale for change and change directions. Customer feedback data was included in the video. Presentations were given to small groups of not more than 15 persons and followed up with a process to test, discuss and debate the content of the plan, answer questions, address concerns and identify areas where people could contribute. Contractors and suppliers were also involved in this process. A series of follow-up sessions was also convened by line supervisors and managers.

Workshop activities were subsequently undertaken to explore employees' understanding, concerns and expectations about alignment and gain their commitment to accept responsibility to perform an activity that would contribute to alignment.

How do Kellogg know that they're on the path to alignment? In the words of the CEO:

> When we started this we said if this is what you want then you have to make it happen … it's not my vision or your vision … it's our vision. Today I find people talking about it wherever I go. It's current and it's understood. It's not just on the wall … it's in people's heads and reflected in their actions. As an example, three years ago we had a vital piece of equipment shutdown. When I went to investigate, apart from the supervisor, no-one – and I mean no-one – was onsite. I eventually found the crew in the canteen talking about football. When we had a problem two weeks ago we had 70 people down there … it's not the same place today.

●●●●●●●●●●●●●●●●●●●

In an aligned organization, if we were to ask the CEO about the organization's purpose, direction, and what he or she really believes in, we would get essentially the same answer as that obtained from front-line employees who spend their time operating machinery, computers or serving customers. This means that the organization has a focus, which is firstly articulated, then agreed and 'bought into' by the whole of the workforce. Clearly we are not gauging 'buy in' by rhetoric but by what is in the head and heart of each employee, and lived and breathed in every conversation, work transaction and decision that is made.

This true 'buy-in' is never absent in great organizations, and rarely present in low-energy or poorly performing organizations. Therefore, it is no coincidence that many of the world's greatest leaders view a major, if not key priority as being to identify and articulate a common vision, which all employees can relate to within their own domain of work. These leaders spend the majority of their time working on creating the energy in their company that comes from widespread buy-in.

FIG. 4.1 Dimensions of alignment

		Alignment group: who shares the alignment	
		Internal focus (employees)	**External focus (customers, suppliers, etc.)**
Alignment focus: what they share	**Business direction**	*Our employees understand and commit to the stated objectives of the business. They know where the business is headed and want to be part of the action.*	*Our business directions are aligned with those of our major customers and suppliers.*
	Business values	*Our employees live and breath our values. They are translated into behaviors that relate to the actual work performed.*	*Our perceptions of value are aligned with those of our key customers and suppliers. We only deal with organizations that have an operating philosophy and style consistent with our own.*

Principle 1: Alignment

ABB'S VALUES – A MANAGEMENT PHILOSOPHY

ABB managers articulate the following system of priorities that can be felt consistently through the communications of all ABB managers:

- customer focus
- teamwork and team-based management
- speed is the key
- positive managers
- what gets measured gets done
- it's OK to make mistakes as long as your batting average is high
- customers define quality
- try to make customers more competitive and successful
- everyone has internal customers
- quality results from controlled processes
- pursue zero defects.

These points of central business philosophy drive the culture and value system of ABB's leaders and managers. They also underpin the design and operation of ABB's business processes, thereby aligning all employee actions.

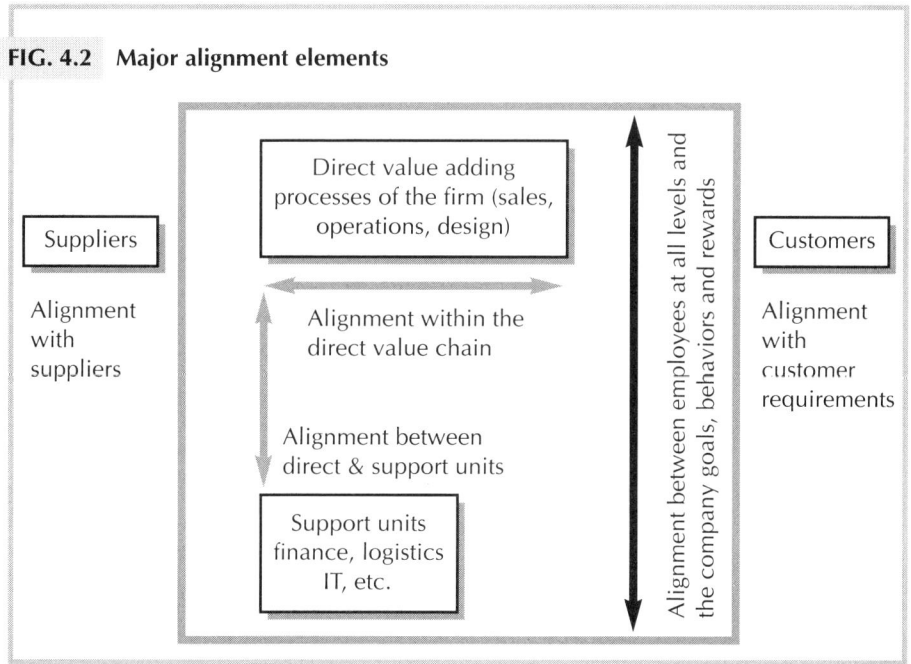

FIG. 4.2 Major alignment elements

> ### ALIGNMENT OF VALUES AT MEDCO
>
> Medco is a very successful division of the Merck Pharmaceutical organization. There are five pillars of value which are articulated at Medco, namely turnaround time, customer service, quality, cost per script, and managed care. These are seen by Medco as being driven by employees through their continuous improvement initiatives and as the creators of customer satisfaction. These five pillars are also connected to the performance measures that drive bonuses for Medco staff at all levels. They are the central operating philosophies within Medco, and they drive the priorities for decision making in all spheres of management within that organization. The five pillars affect every way in which Medco does business including the nature of performance guarantees with clients, the way employees are remunerated and the way the company's operating systems are designed and conducted.

An important part of this alignment in the organization is the Service Profit Chain (Heskett et al., 1994). This framework suggests that in order to satisfy shareholders one must satisfy customers, and to satisfy customers one must have satisfied employees.

An excellent example of alignment occurs at Uncle Ben's pet food operation. This company is part of the Mars Corporation, which has its own set of values 'principles', which are stated to be as follows.

- *Quality*. The consumer is our boss. Quality is our work and value for money is our goal.
- *Responsibility*. As individuals we demand total responsibility from ourselves; as associates, we support the responsibilities of others.
- *Mutuality*. A mutual benefit is a shared benefit; a shared benefit will endure.
- *Efficiency*. We use resources to the full, waste nothing and do only what we can do best.
- *Freedom*. We need freedom to shape our future; we need profit to remain free.

These principles can be seen as a living and breathing part of what guides behavior at Uncle Ben's. The employees in this organization, called 'associates', actively embrace and champion these values statements, behaving in a manner consistent with them. In order to achieve the alignment that exists at such a high level in this organization, the company works on communicating these five drivers of behavior in many of its processes and practices. For example in selecting new employees, a deep exposure to these drivers is given to shortlisted applicants and a fit is evaluated between individual values and those of the company. Alignment is also achieved at Uncle Ben's by having a system of remuneration whereby all associates, no matter what their level and job task within the company, have a part of their remuneration tied to the critically important performance measures of the firm, which in that case are sales growth and return on total assets. From this, it can be seen that Uncle Ben's is at least partially down the track of having made the transition from the 'old world' model of Figure 1.2 to the 'new world' model of Figure 1.3. There is alignment of the rewards with organizational performance and there is alignment of the values and guiding behaviors of employees with the articulated values of the organization.

EVALUATION OF ALIGNMENT

How does an organization rate in terms of strength of alignment? As we've discussed, it's not just values. It's also about strategic direction, and the degree of fit between the business system and values system. Alignment helps to ensure both the internal and external boundaries of the organization 'run smoothly' and generally free of the conflict that dogs poorly aligned companies.

In Table 4.1, Company Old that scores one out of five, feels 'out of sorts with itself', even on a daily basis. The various sub-systems of the company and its external interfaces just don't fit together, they grate on each other. A moderately aligned company sometimes has its sub-systems working smoothly together and sometimes not. Alternatively, some of the dimensions of alignment may work well but not others.

A fully aligned company, which scores highly on the majority of measures described in Table 4.1, runs like clockwork on most days. While no company is perfect and even the world's best have 'bad' days when a few defects are produced or some poor decisions are made, there are no fundamental misalignment problems.

Table 4.1 Evaluating alignment

	Not at all: Company Old	To a weak extent	To a moderate extent	To a large extent	To a very large extent: Company New
	1	2	3	4	5
Overall alignment: Our business has aligned employee behaviors with stated company values and direction.	☐	☐	☐	☐	☐
Subsets of alignment:					
Values					
• In our organization values are not platitudes, they are a set of deeply held beliefs	☐	☐	☐	☐	☐
• People live our values in everything they do	☐	☐	☐	☐	☐
• It is not just managers that promote our values set – every employee does	☐	☐	☐	☐	☐
• Our policies and actions are fully consistent with our values	☐	☐	☐	☐	☐
• We never compromise on our values for short-term financial expediency	☐	☐	☐	☐	☐
• Our recruitment, promotion and staff development policies support our values set	☐	☐	☐	☐	☐
• When we appoint senior managers, personal values are a critical consideration	☐	☐	☐	☐	☐
Strategic direction/purpose					
• In our organization everybody knows where our business is headed and why	☐	☐	☐	☐	☐
• At this site we all stand for the same thing – we all have the same core purpose	☐	☐	☐	☐	☐
• Our people understand the language of business	☐	☐	☐	☐	☐
• Our people want to know about the business performance of the company/division	☐	☐	☐	☐	☐
• We involve all employees in our planning processes	☐	☐	☐	☐	☐
Values and strategic direction – interconnection and synergy					
• Our values are not just 'any old' set of values – they are the key set of behaviors that we need to nurture and develop to be successful	☐	☐	☐	☐	☐
• Our business strategies might change with time but our core values do not	☐	☐	☐	☐	☐
• We pride ourselves in our ability to ensure fit between our business strategies and our values	☐	☐	☐	☐	☐

BENEFITS OF ALIGNMENT

The increasing business value of alignment is related to both the erosion of traditional structural aspects of competitive advantage (products, markets, geographical location, customer base, access to capital, etc.) and the increasing technological and organizational sophistication in the work environment. The former has resulted in an increasing emphasis on human capital sources of competitive advantage, the latter with the development of 'knowledge worker' concepts and the accompanying significant stream of investments in personnel development and training.

What benefits accrue to a company that is strongly aligned? What benefits come from the connections described above, across the full value chain, and appropriately reinforced with rewards and effective performance management? The simple answer is that an aligned organization has much more focused energy than a poorly aligned one. This energy is directed at efficiently accomplishing the activities that create value for customers and therefore for the company! The poorly aligned organization expends a lot of energy on unproductive activities, managing internal conflicts as well as those across its boundaries with suppliers and customers. To use the old adage, it might be efficient but it is certainly not effective. In a well-aligned company such as Medco, there is little internal 'friction' or resistance along the main value-adding organizational chain. Rather, there is the advantage of the synergies that come from each and every employee pulling in the same direction the same way. In other words the main benefit of alignment translates straight into efficiency and effectiveness. The link of alignment with competitiveness is clear. At Medco, the visitor can virtually smell the alignment, it is so strong. Everyone knows the organization's purpose, understands the goals and measures and gets on with it at full speed all day, every day.

The lack of internal conflict and resistance in a fully aligned company frees up the power to 'fight the good fight', namely the noble battle in the market place to get the customer's attention and consideration that achieves profitable sales. This is a tremendous benefit of course, compared to the poorly aligned company that spend so much time fighting and combating internal tensions and conflicts within itself that it interacts in the market place with one hand tied behind its back.

IMPROVING A COMPANY'S ALIGNMENT

Before addressing this issue, we note that, in isolation, no single principle is as effective in driving organizational improvement as it is when part of the overall management system (see Figure 1.3).

Given the attractiveness of becoming more aligned, how can an executive or leader of a small business increase the degree of alignment in their organization? The answer can be gleaned from watching what great leaders do. First, great leaders have a focus that is intense. Sometimes they seem so single-minded in their intensity of pursuing a focused set of behaviors and objectives that they appear inflexible. But they do clearly and frequently articulate a vision for what the organization must be and they relentlessly pursue it. They lead by example and their style facilitates others signing on and accompanying them. This strength is a prerequisite for alignment but it is not enough. The reason that it is a necessary but not sufficient condition is that other elements of alignment exist apart from values and strategic direction. Things that can be led by an inspirational leader need to be reinforced by the company's processes, practices, systems and other key opinion leaders. These include its structure, leadership capability and style, work processes, performance management capabilities, measurement systems and reward systems. As can be seen from Figure 1.3, alignment is so powerful an idea as to govern all the connections of Figure 1.3.

> *Things that can be led by an inspirational leader need to be reinforced by the company's processes, practices and systems.*

There are many different approaches to increasing alignment. The approach depends very much on the extent of misalignment and the reasons for it. Important considerations including culture, quality of the employee/employer relationship, communication system effectiveness, leadership capability and the time available.

Specific areas of activity include the following.

- A review of the extent of fit between the business system (customer needs and strategy set) and organizational system (culture, structure, leadership style etc.).[1]
- Business literacy – ensuring all employees understand the language of business.
- Development of leadership capability.
- Redesigning work processes.
- Organizational and job restructuring.
- Open disclosure of business information – ensuring all employees understand the business performance of the organization and what drives it, competitor actions and behaviors, etc. Drive out any workforce mindset of 'the boss is my enemy' and replace it with 'the competition is my enemy'.
- Introducing forums and processes to elevate the status of, and priority assigned to, alignment. Discuss desired and actual behaviors, the reasons for inconsistent behaviors and improvement opportunities.

- Having the workforce engage in processes to discover the benefits (to each and every employee) of working in accordance with the articulated set of behaviors. This typically involves work group development activities and harnessing the skills and intellect of all employees through collaborative problem solving/continuous improvement projects.

- Tying reward systems to measures that derive from the company's strategic direction and competitive position. If variable pay schemes or the values and criteria used to determine bonuses do not match corporate objectives, then a valuable driving force for alignment is missing. Consequently, consider changing the basis of rewards or changing the objectives to match the basis of rewards.

- Reviewing the effectiveness of the relationships between support functions and line functions that produce or serve customers. Are the support functions really serving the line functions with the service or product they need to maximize their competitiveness? If not, then institute formal internal service agreements, measured on criteria that are derived from strategic goals. Institute rewards for service function staff based on their achievement of goals on those specific dimensions and nothing else. Drive out any form of 'functional parochialism' in service functions, because of the devastating dilution effect that occurs and the resultant lack of alignment and focus.

- Alignment with customers and suppliers can be considerably more difficult depending upon the nature of the business, the origin of competitive advantage (e.g. cost, time, quality, product, relationship, etc.) and because of limitations in the extent of leverage you have over the activities and actions of other organizations. However, it is clear as we enter the new millennium that supply relationships that are adversarial and 'on opposite sides of the supply contract' are becoming increasingly spotlighted. Partnerships of all types are creating value along value chains, even between the fiercest of competitors. As an example, consider banks that compete fiercely for customers but at the same time share critical resources such as ATMs. In supply relationships, we now see leading companies sharing industry forecasts, jointly reviewing product designs and features and having open relationships of high integrity. The starting point for this is improved communication and understanding across the supply interface and a preparedness on the part of both parties to explore the potential of new ways. At a high level, executives should consider the degree of similarity of business purpose and basic business philosophy between companies. The supply relationship alignment is the responsibility of both parties. What does it mean to be a world-class customer? Many companies have outsourced, and continue to outsource 'support services' such as IT operations, HR support, and materials procurement, assuming that this action would address their internal operating concerns and that their problems would become someone else's problem. But that is not how it works. The structure of the outsourcing agreement is critical but so is the customer's ability to behave in a well-aligned manner on an ongoing basis as the relationship develops and operates. Equally as important is the ability to confront and address relationship deficiencies. Consequently, alignment needs to be pursued through a combination of contractual conditions and commitment by both parties to explore cultural consistencies and address cultural inconsistencies.

SUMMARY

Alignment is a fundamental of leading organizations. Its benefits are immense. It is multifaceted and pervades virtually all aspects of a company, from strategic considerations to shop floor measurement systems, and on to external supply and customer relations. At a high level, a fully aligned company has a simplicity and strength of connection between all its people, systems, strategy, and its external business and operating environment. Operationally, alignment on an everyday basis 'feels' like each employee is pulling the company in the same purposeful direction through each and every action that they take.

Note
1. We explore these connections in considerable detail in Part 3 – Implementation.

5

Principle 2
Distributed leadership

Strange as it sounds, great leaders gain authority by giving it away.
Vice Admiral James Stockdale, 1987

Over 85 percent of all problems can be resolved at the first level of supervision they encounter.
Philip Crosby

INTRODUCTION

Definition of distributed leadership

Senior managers in great companies are having less and less to do with running the organization and its day-to-day operational issues. Responsibility and accountability for these issues have been devolved to individuals and work teams who have been given, and accept, increased decision-making authority within agreed envelopes of control. Senior managers have increasingly pulled back from managing the short-term and focus on creating opportunities for business development and growth and resourcing the medium and the long-term for the organization. They have become strategists and change agents (see Figure 5.1). In these excellent companies, general managers have 'learned to let go' of the reins of day-to-day business problems, even though they may have built their personal reputation and career by being a great 'troubleshooter' over many years.

The principle of distributed leadership should not be confused with empowerment. Empowerment only enables distributed leadership – it does not assure it. For example, we have seen many organizations create an 'empowered workforce' through the introduction of structural interventions such as workteams, the redesign of roles and responsibilities, enterprise bargaining agreements (EBAs), skills development programs, etc. However, in a number of instances, these changes have not been accompanied by changes in employee behavior, and in particular, employees have not been prepared to accept the responsibility for introducing and managing improvements.

The principle of distributed leadership should also not be confused with what is typically referred to as 'team behavior'. Distributed leadership is primarily based on individuals, not teams, as the building blocks for success. We have observed that leading organizations are increasingly focusing less on the development of workteams and more on the development of teamwork. Some companies' obsession with teams has been accompanied by a failure to recognize that ultimately it is individuals that are the true source of ideas and energy. Consider what type of teams and teamwork we would achieve if we put a group of uninspired and poorly committed individuals into a team. Does common sense tell us that some magical spell would suddenly take effect and build their morale and motivation? Clearly not. This observation was reflected in the comments of a number of senior executives we worked with in researching this book. The following comment is typical.

> We don't just want a team but a team of individuals ... our team development process was initially very effective in helping us to tap into peoples' ideas and get them to work together effectively. But we've outgrown it. We've found that it discourages individual differences and ties individuals to a particular team. This team cohesiveness has in some instances led to an unquestioning loyalty to the team regardless of the demands of the situation.

In leading companies, individuals work together toward a common goal in both established and temporary teams depending upon the specific requirements at that point in time. These firms place less emphasis on team loyalty and more emphasis on the collaboration between individual employees. Organizations that are effective at practicing distributed leadership are differentiated by four key characteristics. Employees:

- are emancipated by change and discontinuity – employees enjoy the challenge of being involved in a wide range of different issues, involving different people, different business contexts, etc.
- are empowered by knowledge – employees effectiveness as 'contributors' is dependent on their breadth and depth of knowledge
- share the values and direction of the organization and their efforts are rewarded – employees collaborate because they believe in the organization and the organization recognizes the value of their contributions
- do not just perform tasks, they have assigned responsibilities with clear objectives and goals.

The principle of distributed leadership is therefore closely associated with the principles of alignment, and learning focus.

Distributed leadership specifically manifests itself as incorporating high degrees of responsibility being given and accepted by all employees. It is not just senior executives that feel responsible for outcomes and performance, because everyone is a leader in their own domain. This may be factory workers taking responsibility for the quality and efficiency of output from their own workstation or waiters being responsible for the cleanliness of the area they look after. In order to do this, the employee must be informed about what measures are important in an operational sense and must be given data about local performance outcomes so they can relate what they do and how they do it to those outcomes. In the best of all worlds, the measurement of performance outcomes is controlled by the employees themselves so they can take full ownership of the process and its measures.

DISTRIBUTED LEADERSHIP AT IKEA

IKEA started operating in 1945 and has achieved $7 billion in turnover with 30,000 employees operating 125 stores in 28 countries. It typically achieves 10 percent –15 percent market share in its countries of operation. We visited the Wembley store in London. Its UK operation turns over £90 million per year and this one store can have as many as 10,000 visitors on a Saturday. IKEA strictly adheres to the principle of distributed leadership and has a strong culture of low cost. IKEA is a very democratic organization where everyone is treated in the same way. It has few hard and fast rules and writes little down, allowing people to perform tasks their own way but making sure that they perform financially. The democratic no-frills culture of IKEA permeates from the Group CEO, who flies economy even on long-haul segments, through to the recruiting and training practices of the organization. IKEA people need to be comfortable with an unstructured environment and in keeping with this must be able to act on their own initiative. They must not be status-oriented and they must respect people for what they do and not for their title.

IKEA's marketing position, which is to take good design to the masses and 'to contribute to a better everyday life for the majority of people', fits with its overall culture and the way in which it manages its staff.

A leading example of distributed leadership and front-line employees taking on more and more responsibility and accountability comes from Du Pont's Girraween Operation which produces a range of specialty chemical products for both domestic and international markets. The notion of distributed leadership is a guiding principle of behavior which upskills the workforce and requires them to take responsibility for the design of the workplace and content of their jobs. Du Pont has organized employees into teams and equipped them with the tools, techniques and systems to analyze and improve their core work processes. Du Pont has progressed past the traditional team-based organization and developed a 'volunteer mentality' whereby employees nominate to be involved in project and problem-solving teams as opportunities arise. The formation of these teams is facilitated by a high degree of multi-skilling in the core work teams as this enables individual absences to be readily covered. Participation and contribution in team-based activities is also recognized in rewards. The formation of core work teams and the ongoing use of project teams enables middle managers to step back from direct supervision and concentrate on more strategic business and improvement initiatives. This, in turn, enables senior managers to concentrate on opportunities for business development and growth. Du Pont is an outstanding example of how distributed leadership can simultaneously achieve ownership for the core work, develop a shop floor engine of continuous improvement, and a mechanism to continually enhance employee skills and

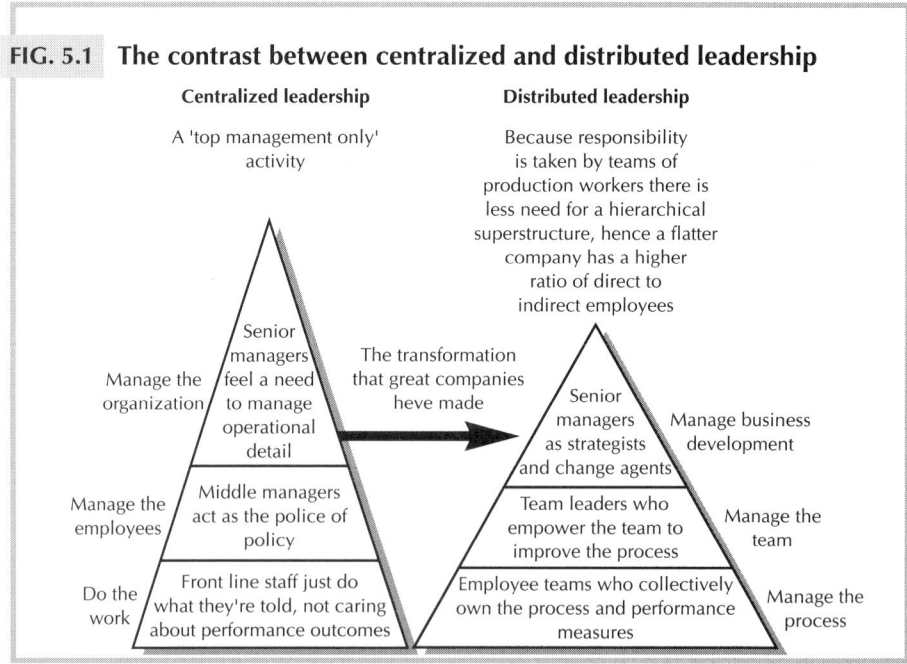

FIG. 5.1 The contrast between centralized and distributed leadership

Principle 2: Distributed leadership

capabilities and in so doing free other organizational resources to concentrate on the more strategic, long-term business and organizational activities that are generally recognized but typically under-resourced.

So when pondering the question 'Why do continuous improvement initiatives sometimes work and sometimes fail spectacularly?' we say question the existence of alignment and distributed leadership and we will have the answer!

DISTRIBUTED LEADERSHIP AT ABB

ABB is so keen to ensure that all of its key business managers are given responsibility and accountability for decisions and performance that it has broken itself up into a matrix-like network of local businesses. Even though this company is a $34 billion (revenue) global giant on which it earned $3.3 billion of profit in 1995 employing over 200,000 people around the world, ABB really has implemented the 'think global, act local' maxim. As a matter of core operating philosophy and organization, ABB employs local managers in its 140 countries who run a total of 500 operating profit centres. ABB operates a very flat, highly decentralized business, such that its Zurich-based global head office has less than 100 people in it. Control of the ABB businesses is achieved by monthly reporting and aggregation of financial and operating performance information and through its mission and values and company policies. Distributed leadership at ABB is built into the very structure of the way businesses are broken down to small building blocks such that the local entrepreneurs have profit and loss responsibility within their business. This is supported by corporate resources and excellent developmental and management systems. It represents a very advanced approach to distributed leadership.

EVALUATION OF DISTRIBUTED LEADERSHIP

To evaluate the extent of existence of distributed leadership in an organization, we can decompose it into the five major elements outlined below.

Responsibility is widespread

To what extent does a whole workforce act responsibly? Do workers treat the company's resources as carefully if they were their own or is it a 'we don't care' attitude that prevails? Unfortunately the latter is still all too common in organizations today. An assessment of the degree of widespread responsibility can be made:

> **Responsibility:** to what extent do employees care and accept that the company's assets and outcomes are their individual and collective responsibility?
>
> | 1 | 2 | 3 | 4 | 5 |
> |---|---|---|---|---|
> | Not at all | To a small extent | Moderately | To a large extent | To a very large extent |

Accountability is distributed throughout the organization

This means that performance of tasks and the measurable outcomes that are expected and set around those tasks are hard-wired into the company's culture. For managers, this means that if a strategy is set and an executive or manager is given responsibility for implementation, there will be a day of reckoning! If the implementation does not occur or the benefits are not derived, this does not go unnoticed in excellent companies. Managers take accountability for their objectives and tasks, and the conversion of actions into value. This can be contrasted with poorly disciplined companies where accountability may or may not be high at the top of the company, but it is certainly low at the shop floor. Accountability throughout the organization involves a discipline that comes through performance appraisal, management by objectives and a culture of performance.

Just as distributed leadership means distributed responsibility, it also means, and goes hand in hand, with distributed accountability. To assess an organization's distributed accountability, consider what actions occur when things that were supposed to be done just slipped away and weren't done well, completely or possibly at all. Is this acceptable, or is there a review process with accountability for non-performance accepted that leads to remedial action and possibly penalty? Or do individuals just keep on getting away with poor performance?

> **Accountability:** to what extent do employees at all levels take on accountability for their performance, particularly for under-performance?
>
> | 1 | 2 | 3 | 4 | 5 |
> |---|---|---|---|---|
> | Not at all | To a small extent | Moderately | To a large extent | To a very large extent |

Managers can pull back from everyday tactics and concentrate on strategy

In mature companies, trust and skill exists throughout the firm so that general managers do not have to micro-manage their functional managers and department supervisors. Because of the very fact that these folks down the line, all the way to the employees who actually add the value and deliver service and product to customers, work with an acceptance of responsibility and accountability, managers can let go of some of their interfering ways! No-one can know the detail like the person who is closest to it, whether it's a machinist, or a bank credit officer or a sales manager, so the best thing a more senior manager can do is ensure they are properly skilled, place objectives around them and manage to those objectives in a well-balanced, controlled and monitoring role, but don't do their job for them! This is obviously easier to say and write than it is to do. Perhaps the hardest thing for managers is to delegate and let others who report to them have control of sub-systems, but this is a characteristic quality of all advanced companies and cultures.

At one of Kodak's most competitive plants, the most senior manufacturing executive put it beautifully: 'There is nothing that can happen on the factory floor that is serious enough to need me to intervene and make a decision. Not even a fire. I have truly let go and our workers run the factory in every way.' This led us to the question about just how that executive justified his keep, including a large salary and luxury car, etc. His answer was just as lucid: 'My job is to look three years, not three days out. I plan, strategize and ensure we have the capabilities in one, two and three years to be competitive.'

Compare this with the general managers we spent time with in a large packaging company. This second company had grown rapidly and managers had been promoted from specialist roles in sales, marketing, manufacturing and finance and administration to be general managers who ran national and international businesses. The CEO pointed to one of his biggest challenges being to have these GM's assume their real GM duties, because they typically retreated from their GM responsibilities, much preferring personally to go back to being heroic troubleshooters down the line where they had made their name as functional specialists. So, compared to our Kodak example, this packaging business was strategically underdeveloped, because the GMs were spending their time on micro-managing daily tactics. This of course causes the young 'up-and-comers' in functional areas to resent the interference and lose interest. Some leave, and these are usually those with the highest potential who are most marketable. The rest lose their motivation and senses of responsibility and accountability, and the businesses basically unravels. From these contrasting examples, it is clear that distributed leadership and the ability to manage but also allow and encourage others to assume responsibility is central to maintaining an organization's thrust and energy.

> **Managers focus on strategy and do not 'micro-manage' their subordinates:** To what extent do managers pull back from micro-managing lower-level tactics and actions that are best controlled and conducted by others?
>
> | 1 | 2 | 3 | 4 | 5 |
> |---|---|---|---|---|
> | Not at all | To a small extent | Moderately | To a large extent | To a very large extent |

All employees work in processes and have the potential to improve them

This improvement requires a distribution of leadership or else the potential does not get unlocked. Process improvement has been a wonderful area of focus for many companies, yet others have tried and failed, and this variance in effectiveness is strongly related to the extent of ownership that occurs throughout the company. Process improvement is a higher-level task for employees and if they have not bought in to the organization and its purpose, they will just run their processes and not engage in questioning and improving how things are done.

> **Improvement:** to what extent do all employees act as leaders in the sense that they strive not just to run their processes but to find ways to improve them?
>
> | 1 | 2 | 3 | 4 | 5 |
> |---|---|---|---|---|
> | Not at all | To a small extent | Moderately | To a large extent | To a very large extent |

These aspects of distributed leadership need higher level skills than just task-oriented skills. High-performing companies have invested in switching their workers on to behaving at work just as they would at home, which typically means being responsible and accountable for money, co-workers as respected people, physical assets and economic performance.

Distributed leadership also is best viewed like all the principles within this pattern of excellent companies, as an integrated component of this excellence rather than as a stand-alone piece. It is clearly linked to fundamental principles such as learning, resourcing the medium term, alignment, and embracing change.

BENEFITS OF DISTRIBUTED LEADERSHIP

We once asked a bank executive who controlled the operations of 50,000 people, how many brains out of the 50,000 were being utilized in improving the business. The answer was 'About 500, which is up from the 25 of two years ago.' She went on to explain that slowly but surely leadership was being distributed around the organization, whereas it had previously been limited to a very few elite executives. She said that the benefits of even getting partially there were remarkable. In moving from about 1.5 to 3 on the boxed scales above, she pointed to the success of continuous improvement initiatives, transfer of best practice programs that did not work previously, and the fact that she now had some 500 change agents working to improve the business processes of the bank. We mused that sheer hell could break loose if we extrapolate this from 500 to 50,000! But to her credit, this executive did not shrink back from wanting to go all the way with distributed leadership, once she recognized the connection with the principle of discipline. When we have everyone fervently working on improving systems and processes, chaos would result if not for a structured change process that must be in place. When we acknowledged this, this wise executive resolved to accelerate the spreading further of distributed leadership behaviors and when asked why, she said 'Money, professor, money!'

The bank was more efficient and productive than it would otherwise have been and if everyone were allowed to be fully responsible and accountable even more productivity would arise. The bank was also more nimble as a result of the spreading of leadership and it was more robust to changes in its environment. The extra commitment in the organization improved the service quality, and this executive was convinced that this all translated to the bottom line, and she had the data on profit improvement to back it up.

IMPROVING DISTRIBUTED LEADERSHIP

The banking executive told us of her plans to spread the leadership further through the company. Her plan was very sound. It involved a major 'culture change' in all levels. Senior and middle management need to be prepared to 'let go' and create the work environment for their subordinates to 'have a go for themselves'. This means helping to make sure people are open to new ideas, prepared to help each other out, supported to learn and prepared to contribute. Some managers had resisted for a variety of reasons, including fear of the unknown, fear that employees would not run with the ball and it would fall back on them, reductions in personal power and status and the personal satisfaction and organizational importance of being a troubleshooter.

The structure reinforced a low level of distributed leadership by having an excessive number of layers. Middle management also required development of a new leadership capability and appreciation for the difficulties in changing to a distributed leadership culture. Leading companies know that distributed leadership involves changing the type and style of power, from power by coercion to power through co-operation.

Employees need to have the skills, confidence and encouragement to try new ways and push the boundaries. New ways mean that improvements and failures will occur. This means that the organization needs to reassess how it manages failure and risk and the signals that it needs to send to employees to support them in a distributed leadership approach.

> *The organization needs to reassess how it manages failure and risk and the signals that it needs to send to employees to support them*

The bank executive also realized the need to ensure that distributed leadership has some discipline and structure. This typically means establishing processes and contracting roles for key areas, e.g. relationship maintenance, setting targets and measures, setting work priorities, measuring and managing performance, transferring skills, allocating work, etc.

In relation to major skills upgrades and disciplines of accountabilities being pushed 'down the line', the bank executive knew from experience that this needed a firm evolution, rather than a revolution-like approach.

Other companies have used the customer satisfaction imperative to achieve gains in distributed leadership. Even if employees dislike the notion of working co-operatively with management at first, they may well sign on to being individually and collectively more accountable for serving customers better. Similarly, many managers are reluctant for their employees to have close customer contact for fear they may be irresponsible and damage extremely important relationships. If these two-way concerns can be worked through there are major improvement gains possible in this area.

We often see companies where management acts with responsibility and care, but shop-floor workers do not. In some of these instances, could it be that management has chosen not to share the responsibility? One view is that most workers want to care and be responsible, if only management would let them in! Whether this is an accurate description or not of any particular situation, the principle of distributed leadership is a powerful one for managers to use to break through the impasse.

SUMMARY

Distributed leadership means delegation that folds every employee into the company's vision and objectives. It provides the means for people to get properly and deeply involved in driving the organization forward. It allows people to get real meaning and satisfaction associated with achievement from their work and therefore it is associated with commitment and high performance. Distributed leadership can be observed as the extent of responsibility, accountability, appropriate delegation and control, and contribution to improvement in a company. More particularly it embodies the degree to which these elements of a high-performance company are widespread.

Most workers want to care and be responsible for their work outcomes, if only management would let them! The corollary of this logic is powerful: in companies where management holds responsibility and accountability very close to their chest in a small circle only, one must question whether they are really acting responsibly. Ultimately, it is clear that they are not, because by using their structural powers to keep leadership behaviors to themselves, they are foregoing the large potential that is available through the application of distributed leadership.

6

Principle 3
Integration

So much of what we call management consists in making it difficult for people to work.

Peter Drucker, 1978

INTRODUCTION

People put their local loyalties to teams and departments ahead of the whole organization so often and so pervasively that it is grossly dysfunctional. There is only one balance sheet! Shareholders care only about the overall result! We should banish the practice of sub-optimizing for ever.

Leading companies have broadened the scope and span of all employees' mindsets and their cycle of objectives, performance and responsibility. Functional barriers and parochial mindsets (the 'silo' mentality) have been largely overcome and replaced by a unity of purpose and spirit of co-operation. This change is supported by a high degree of interdependency and interaction between employees and teams. To achieve an integration of effort and purpose across all areas, firms are often restructured, from a functional hierarchy to a value chain and process focus (see Figure 6.1). Leading firms systematically manage by using processes as the unit of management. Business processes, capabilities processes and operational processes are typically used. The adoption of principle 12 (driving customer value) insures that the adoption of a process focus does not inadvertently adversely affect the set of core capabilities that underpin current and future success.

Integration does not stop at the organization's boundaries. Leading firms are also involved in integrating their activities, values and goals with those of customers and suppliers including material and technology suppliers. They focus

Principle 3: Integration

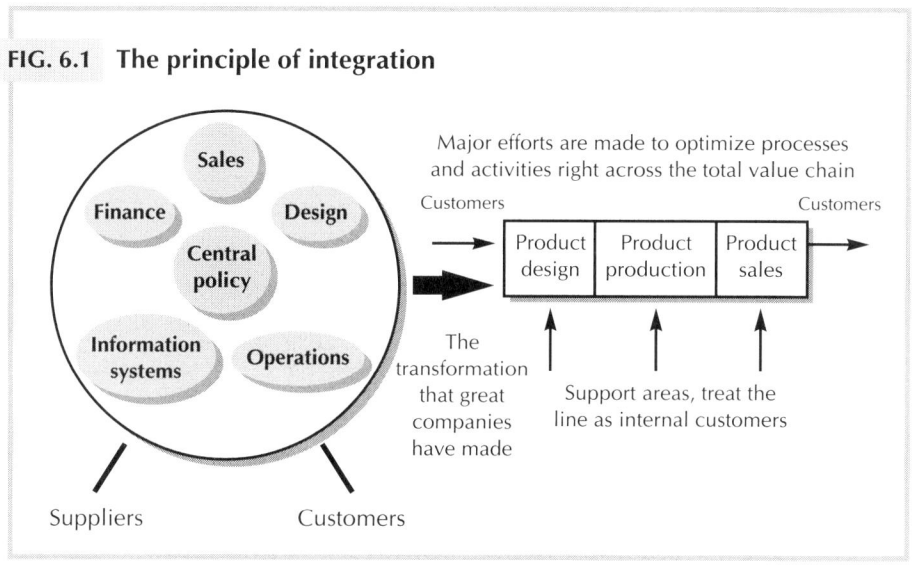

FIG. 6.1 The principle of integration

on making all relationships partnership-like and the commercial arrangements between suppliers and customers reflect this paradigm shift (from 'us and them' to partners). These firms have often taken a leading role in catalyzing relationships with their suppliers, customers and even with their suppliers' suppliers and customers' customers. This provides for the optimization of investments and co-ordination of supply, delivery and production schedules across a complete value chain, allowing the ultimate consumer of the products and services which come from that value chain to achieve a higher level of benefits and features per unit price. In many of the leading companies we have visited, the talk and action is about 'adding value to our customers' customers', or of 'getting into our customers' revenue stream'. Hewlett Packard, and Dun and Bradstreet are leading exponents of this philosophy.

The same partnership-like behavior applies to suppliers. Integration back through the supply chain causes great companies to address the question 'How can I be a leading edge customer?' Uncle Ben's, part of the Mars Corporation, is an excellent example of this in that it has worked closely with its suppliers such as Gadsden who supply it with many millions of cans per week. Joint development in this packaging realm has provided advantages both to Gadsden and to Uncle Ben's. The supplier of offal to Uncle Ben's has also benefited from a partnership-like relationship with this leading-edge customer, in respect of design specifications, delivery schedules and the implementation of quality systems.

In another excellent example, Kellogg has worked closely with its suppliers, its suppliers' suppliers, its suppliers' suppliers' suppliers and various government departments to improve the characteristics of hybrid corn seeds. The new seeds developed have substantially increased farmers' yields (return per hectare), millers' yields (return per kilogram of product milled) and Kelloggs' cooking yield (cereal yield per kilogram of corn used).

Definition of integration

The most important practice of the company that practises integration is a focus on 'horizontal' value-adding processes, as against 'vertical' organizational silos. The starting point for this is at the customer interface. Leading companies like GE ensure that the 'voice of the customer is brought pervasively into the company. Once the customer requirement is known, it should, in theory, be relatively easy to respond to this shouldn't it? However, this is generally not the case in practice. This very element is the cornerstone on which an integrated company can be built. If the external customer requirement isn't well known to our company, then we don't have a basis around which to integrate our activities!

Consider how an ideal company organizes its activities so as to achieve high levels of integration. First, we should take the company's customer requirements as being well known. Leading companies do whatever it takes to achieve a close understanding of their customer's requirements. These requirements, once identified, are not just known by the marketing and sales departments, but are disseminated throughout the company in terms of how they contribute to external customer value creation and ultimate customer satisfaction. This is often done by defining internal service relationships as a service or internal value chain. Since most people in most companies do not directly interface the customer, we need systems that allow this key data to be communicated around the organization. This can be done through a variety of communication channels, from newsletters, circular e-mails, reports, meetings and arranging for direct contact between 'back office' or factory people and end-use customers. The key point is that to encourage co-ordinated activity across the company, people need a central theme and set of goals to pursue, and what could be better than customer value maximization? This is exactly what leaders such as GE, HP, Medco, Avis and British Airways do.

Once everyone understands the customer requirement, the next task is how to organize various functions and activities in order to meet or exceed it. Figure 6.1 shows the 'value-chain' approach to this that leading companies have achieved. Essentially, product/service design activities *serve* product/service production with designs that are 'do-able'. Many companies use the phrase 'design-for-production'. The idea is obvious once we see a great company do it, namely that a close working relationship between designers and operations managers achieves two important things:

- Designs will not be impossible to produce, but rather designers will carefully consider the 'manufacturability' of the product when designing new services or products.
- The capabilities of the operations function will be known to designers, who can take advantage of them in their designs. If a company has an advantage through its 'operations excellence' or process technology, this should be exploited by ensuring that the products are designed to maximize this advantage.

In great companies, this is a two-way street. Designers want to specify services and products that can be relatively easily mass-produced, as against designs that make life for operations people a constant struggle. Clearly, the operations people need to inform the designers of both the capabilities and limitations of the company's production function.

Consider a leading bank in Canada that made the following change. In their 'bad old days', marketing executives in their ivory tower offices used to invent products based on seemingly good ideas, then 'roll out' these products across their branch network. Often, branch managers did not hear about these products until after customers did, because the marketing department wanted to keep the designs secret from competitor banks. Products were often announced or launched via TV advertising campaigns on weekends. On Monday morning, customers came to bank branches to buy the product and if they were lucky the branch manager would have received the documentation by that time, however this was often not the case. Exasperated service staff realize that the product design might seem conceptually clever and innovative but cry out 'We can't service this', 'Our systems can't cope with this' or 'The product has a fatal flaw'. This phenomenon is all too common and occurs through lack of integration!

Some companies observe 'communication breakdowns' and address this directly by setting up meetings and forums, such as 'town meetings', whereas poor communication may be the symptom, not the problem. If integration is poor, effective communication needs to be addressed at the deeper, 'integration principle' level.

No matter what the industry, from banking and retailing to the heart of manufacturing, poor integration has been everywhere. Now consider an example that drives the other way, from operations capability to design to improved customer value. When Western companies designed and built cars, poor fabrication capabilities led to the need for complex parts that allowed for all sorts of adjustments to be made in assembling. For example, the door latches and hinges in Fords, GMs and Chryslers were made to be adjusted. In contrast, some Japanese manufacturers were able to build car frames and doors with such precision that no adjustment was needed. The doors hung square, making for cheaper, easier designs, cheaper components and easier assembly. In addition, Japanese components didn't fail or lead to problems once in operation, because they could not go out of adjustment! Designs took great advantage of this superior manufacturing capability.

To achieve these benefits for the external customer, internal co-ordination across functions is a must. When Chrysler got into serious trouble in the 1980s, its way out was via a new set of automobile products which had been the result of a great deal of *integration* of effort. Purpose-built facilities were constructed that led to frequent contact and communication between designers and manufacturing engineers. With new products that were 'designed for manufacture' and with all this based on an acute understanding of what customers want and value, what is the result? Chrysler bounces back and is reinvented. We should not be fooled, however, into thinking that this somehow happens magically as a result of a CEO speech in which he or she suddenly 'sees the light'. The speech may be a good start, but the revitalization occurred because the company reinvented itself and reorganized from a bunch of vertical silos to a fully integrated, value-chain focus.

> **Integration does not come at the expense of dilution and fragmentation of core functional capabilities and skills**

In leading companies, integration does not come at the expense of dilution and fragmentation of core functional capabilities and skills, but rather connects them across processes, departments and functions in ways that maximize their value to the business.

To summarize this, leading organizations start with the customer requirement, try and lead this requirement then organize to fulfill that requirement better than anyone else. They typically organize their value-adding activities, sales, production and design (see Figure 6.1) as a service/value chain, carefully co-ordinated and linked to maximize the overall result, not the individual organizational pieces! Support functions such as accounting, corporate marketing, human resources and information systems, all realize that their role is to serve those who serve, and they act accordingly.

For many companies, success in this realm has meant having formal service relationships, even contracts between departments such as IT and operations. These specify service levels and are a great opportunity to transmit the voice of the customer from the 'skin' of the company throughout its internal systems.

Principle 3: Integration

EVALUATION OF INTEGRATION

How strong is the integration in a particular company? On a five-point scale, from poor or no effective integration, to fully integrated, this can be assessed:

1 .... 2 .... 3 .... 4 5
Poorly integrated   Fully integrated

At the fully integrated end of the scale, people have given up local departmental empire building as an objective. They realize that the company only has one balance sheet and they act accordingly. Departments' activities and processes are co-ordinated. There is an internal service ethic. As one executive has put it 'Either you are directly servicing a customer or you better be servicing someone that is!'

The organization should also consider the extent to which it is or has used these levers to work towards improved integration as against separation and sub-optimization of functions and work:

Company structure and roles:
  Drive separation   Drive integration
    1 .... 2 .... 3 .... 4 5

Work processes and systems:
  Drive separation   Drive integration
    1 .... 2 .... 3 .... 4 5

Rewards and recognition:
  Drives separation   Drive integration
    1 .... 2 .... 3 .... 4 5

Behavioral norms:
  Drive separation   Drive integration
    1 .... 2 .... 3 .... 4 5

Work environment and layout:
  Drive separation   Drive integration
    1 .... 2 .... 3 .... 4 5

Objectives and goals:
  Drive separation   Drive integration
    1 .... 2 .... 3 .... 4 5

BENEFITS OF INTEGRATION

Firms that have poor internal integration suffer from poor linkages, poor internal quality and therefore low reliability and service externally to their clients/customers. Things seem to forever fall into cracks, even chasms with these companies. Output is usually not timely and flexibility and responsiveness to changing customer requirements are often too hard to achieve.

Similarly a lack of external integration, such as with suppliers, causes even bigger problems. From this, it is easy to understand the benefits of integration to the company. Integration is really about having the organizational glue to ensure that work processes link together smoothly and effectively. The benefits from being really strongly integrated are therefore immense. There is essentially no downside to drive the integration principle hard as a guide to organization and action. Quality goes up. Responsiveness improves. Innovativeness can be more effective in its implementation. And integration has essentially no capital costs! If there is a 'cost', it is of spending a little more time on communications; however leading companies have certainly found that such costs are strongly made up for by savings in rework and the fixing of problems.

IMPROVING INTEGRATION

Moving from positions one, two or three on the five-point assessment scale towards four or five can be achieved in many different ways. These include, but are not limited to, identity development, values development (alignment), organizational restructuring, job redesign, process re-engineering, supply-chain mapping, application of integrating information technologies, introduction of decision-making forums and processes, introducing interfacing forums and/or forming interfacing roles, developing customer service agreements, revising goals and measures, improved management and use of performance information, rewards, recognition, etc. These approaches can be thought of not as alternatives but as complementary levers. We discuss some of these below.

Identity development is concerned with defining the mission, purpose and scope of responsibility of a particular work area and exploring the connections with neighboring work areas (work group to work group, function to function, etc.) and the business as a whole. Behaviors, myths and norms that encourage or inhibit integration are explored. The total core value-adding process is reviewed to identify key business issues and improvement opportunities, highlighting integration and interfacing areas. The specific contributions and activities of the various work groups and functions that contribute along the value chain are then analyzed to understand their needs, concerns and expectations. Through this process the alignment between group identity and activities and business vision, values and goals is enhanced which in turn facilitates improved integration and co-ordination.

The structural lever is associated with changing departmental structures towards either product-family-based or market-segment-based concepts, that typically have higher levels of delegation of authority to facilitate integration by giving those who do 'the real work' the responsibility for it. Structural changes may also result in less off-line or 'corporate' departments such as 'corporate human resources', and reassigning functions and resources to line managers. Instead of perpetuating functional silos with their own objectives, leading companies encourage departmental managers to look and manage outwards, to serve their department's internal and external clients as the first priority and to organize themselves and their departments internally in order to do this well. An example from the service sector is professional consulting engineers and architects. These have traditionally organized themselves by discipline such as mechanical engineers, electrical, civil, architects, etc. They form project teams to do jobs but often struggle to work together and fight hard over resources and how to cut the cake and return value to their 'home' discipline. The core problem is that they are strongly socialized to their base discipline, which they see as 'home', rather than the real needs of the team and job.

Leading firms have formed powerful multi-disciplinary teams. And the breakthrough occurs when the mindset changes from 'loyalty to discipline' to 'loyalty to the project team'. Ultimately the performance responsibility and accountabilities change too, from discipline to project team, and resources, decision making and power shift away from silo department to the unit of customer value delivery, the project team. The example of structural change lays the groundwork for the other levers of change. In some work systems, the adaptive nature of the organization makes it hard to build in integration into organizational structure and roles. Here, decision-making forums and gating processes are often employed to make sure that the right decisions are made at the right time in the value chain and the parties making the decision take responsibility for the consequences of the decision made. This is explored further in Part 3.

Work processes frequently need to be changed too. Too often, we find processes with an excessive number of hand-overs and different roles involved which blur accountabilities and cause delays and mistakes. Cross-functional work teams involving designers, engineers, marketers, accountants, etc. are far superior to sending these people off to do other work independently. Ultimately, the company and its value chain should work as a 'seamless' or 'boundary-less' organization. We first heard this term in 1990 mentioned by John Young, CEO of Hewlett Packard, who said that Hewlett Packard had done a lot of work on process improvement but now needed to move the formal structures of Hewlett Packard to support the horizontal process focus that had been achieved. Hewlett Packard had changed its work systems, beginning at one major production facility in Vancouver, spreading through all its factories, then right across its other business processes. The mechanism originated with the Hewlett Packard just-in-time manufacturing concept, expressed by one manager as 'Never make nothing, nowhere, no how, unless and until the customer ordered it'.

The grammar may not be world-class but the idea was one of integration, that is a connection of customer need to the production schedule. Hewlett Packard spent a decade (the 1980s) getting lean and mean in production, then reorganized its whole business centrally around the principle of integration, or in their terms 'boundarylessness'. They integrated this with a decade-long quality improvement initiative that was equally effective. This meant establishing cross-functional teams and having broader spans of responsibility defined across middle management throughout the company's functions. However, Hewlett Packard found that the best way to do this was not to *mandate* the change (i.e. force it on people). Having tried this, the preferred method was found to be based on 'enlightened self interest'. The principle of integration guides actions that lead not just to win-win for the two executives or departments that integrate and co-ordinate their work, but also to win-win-win, because the customer wins too! A marketing manager at Hewlett Packard's corporate office in California whom we interviewed in 1997 explained this:

> Cross-functional work is critical in a fast-moving industry like ours. We would be dead without it. Our product lifecycles are so short that when we release a product such as a laser printer we have already designed and prototyped the next model that will supersede it. To complete on time the way we do, we must have terrific integration right across all our functions, including our support areas. It works by enlightened self interest. It's just a plain fact that once you give up your local allegiance to your little fiefdom, you can start contributing more to the overall goal. The 'give up' is key. Its best for everyone to get past the local sub-optimization we all used to do and buy into the greater goal. We're far from perfect, but after all there is only one balance sheet. We now try to optimize our big picture together rather than separately sub-optimize our individual bits and processes. But make no mistake, we're not forced into this: everyone must justify how their function adds value. Even my own department, corporate marketing, is used and consulted by marketers in our business units based only on the value we add to their activity. Enlightened self interest again. And we add co-ordination and process integration.

Rewards and recognition are also often a key lever. Do individuals receive variable rewards based on their personal (or their department's) performance, or on a broader performance set? When we visited a division of the UK company ICI, managers were given rewards based on the overall business outcome. The functional activity heads, of marketing, production, research and development, etc., did not even have separate performance appraisals, but were appraised by their general manager as a team. They received their bonuses based on this team-based appraisal. The behaviors fostered by this are to help the other functions achieve the team goals. If one function or process is falling over, everyone pitches in to help. Cross-functional integration abounds. And this ICI business has now extended this philosophy to its suppliers and partners in the industry-wide value chain. This was seen as just an external extension of the integration ICI had achieved inside the company. It worked. Productivity went up 240 percent over three years, service standards rose dramatically and DIFOTIS (the percent of orders delivered in full, on time, in specification) went from 55 percent to over 98 percent in two years.

The reward and recognition systems were powerful. They were strongly aligned to other elements of behavioral change. Workers were previously not trusted with performance data, told to 'park their brains at the door' and not expected to do anything except minimally comply with detailed work commands. These attitudes were changed, leading to a workforce ready to take on the challenge of lifting their heads, and working in an integrated manner, across internal work processes and even across the organization's formal boundaries, to suppliers and customers.

SUMMARY

The integration principle is, simply put, a winner for all concerned, and when implemented well, there are no losers from improved integration. Key levers for achieving improved integration include:

- identity development
- structural change
- work redesign
- process re-engineering
- rewards and recognition
- behavioral change processes and practices.

7

Principle 4
Being out front

Good leadership must be for the future, not for the past or the present.
J. Arthur Urciolli

INTRODUCTION

Leading organizations, perceived as such, get a premium in the marketplace. Being 'out front' means *leading*:

- customer requirements
- environmental policy and practice (rather than responding to regulations)
- industry standards
- supplier partnership development
- quality
- responsiveness to customer requirements
- product design and features
- technology management.

Leaders generally make extensive use of information technology in order to look and act global: they develop international networks, understand the big picture of international business and benchmark their operations on an international scale. These firms have learnt to be industry leaders (see Figure 7.1) in every sense of the word. They are not reactive but are strongly and forcefully proactive and often use their leadership position in an industry to their great advantage by being able to take industry practices and standards to places and levels where competitors cannot follow or find it difficult to do so. An example is a large oil company which was able, through the early development of a technological edge which allowed it to reduce drastically the lead content of high octane petroleum grades, to influence government policies and standards on this issue such that it obtained a substantial competitive advantage over its rivals. In another example we observed a petrochemical company which was able to demonstrate the superior integrity of production processes and equipment to regulatory authorities. It was subsequently able to negotiate a relaxation of government inspection requirements leading to reduced plant downtime and increased plant profitability.

Another example is from Uncle Ben's pet food operation where environmental policies are far from minimalist (those which comply with regulations only) but are proactive. Through staying well ahead of regulations and minimum standards, the company has been able to reduce its cost of waste and improve its productivity while at the same time being a good corporate citizen.

Being out front provides these leaders with marketing advantages of brand and image value.

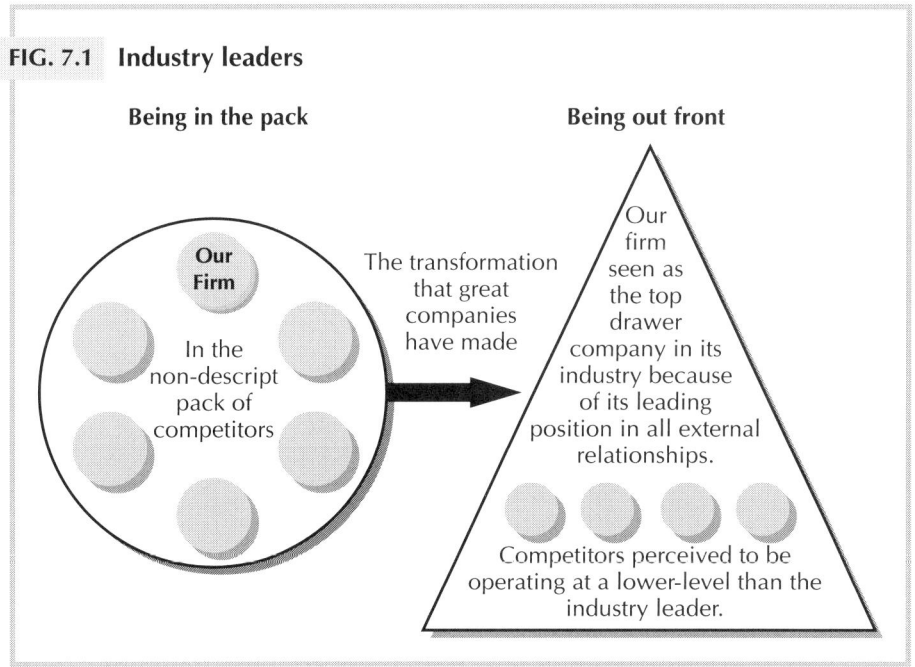

FIG. 7.1 Industry leaders

> **IKEA – OUT FRONT AND UP FRONT**
>
> IKEA has positioned itself in the market place such as to have a unique selling point. The executives of IKEA have conducted exhaustive research of customer tastes and purchasing behaviors and determined early in the life of the company that quality, service and price are not enough to grow and be successful at the rate at which they desired. The organization as well as its products must be perceived of in the marketplace as likeable or as one executive said: 'Nice stuff'. IKEA's market position in the UK for example is very different to that of department stores and existing traditional furniture manufacturers. IKEA's position is with modern design at low price and their UK mission is to change the taste of the average citizen from a preference of traditional-style furniture to modern-style furniture with an efficient or economic design and matching price. This strategy connects to IKEA's design and to its store operating philosophies. IKEA sells furniture, large and small, through a self-serve distribution system. IKEA does not assemble its manufactured furniture products for customers but asks customers to buy furniture in a box and take it home and assemble it themselves. Customers can also use IKEA's advanced telephone system to see whether a particular item is in stock via an automated inventory enquiry system.

Definition of out front

The leading company that drives to be out in front in the industries that it participates in achieves this as a matter of strategy not 'happenstance'. Microsoft is clearly such a company. So is General Electric in most of its industries. McDonalds held the out-front position in its industry segments, globally, for nearly three decades. Our study of these companies leads to the conclusion that there are very few or no out-front companies, that is industry leaders that are unprofitable. Further, most out-front companies achieve superior financial returns to the industry average, often with very high premiums relative to their competitors. So it is clearly worth considering in detail what the nature of out front is, how its achievement provides benefits, and how to get it and sustain it.

The potential areas in which a firm can lead its industry is vast. Further, the notion of being a leading firm in an industry can be considered as being 'the best' in some manner, or being the leader in terms of the time dimension. This means being first and perhaps most innovative, in the sense of fastest to adopt or introduce new techniques, services, products or distribution

Principle 4: Being out front

channels. We found out-front leaders to employ a combination of these.

The out-front factors include leading in:

- brand position and value
- technology
- service and product design
- distribution and supplier partnerships
- government and community relations
- developing all its people
- quality
- innovativeness
- occupational health and safety, and environmental practices
- customer satisfaction and value creation
- operating efficiency
- cost
- delivery reliability or agility
- market share
- financial performance and other elements.

The above list is not supposed to be exhaustive, but rather illustrative of some of the desirable characteristics that many companies would like to be 'out front' on. Some of the items on this list are practices, some are performance outcomes.

We have not yet found a single company that is well and truly out front on all these dimensions, but there are clearly some out-front companies that have defined a focussed set of elements that they want to be leaders in and pursued these with vigor.

The most common set of factors we have seen can be considered in two sets, namely practice and performance sets.

The practice dimensions of many leaders tend to include:

- brand/market position
- occupational health and safety, and environmental issues
- leadership and human resources
- technology
- customer value focus
- community and social responsibility.

Note that these companies are very careful about establishing their leading positions as a matter of conscious strategy, and this includes being careful not to go too far! It is possible to over-invest in brand positioning and development and it is possible to take the idea of being at the leading edge of product or process technology too far. This can be thought of as going past the leading edge to the bleeding edge! Most companies have painful 'bleeding edge' experiences of going too far in attempting to achieve an out-front position. It may be a technology, product or brand, but most executives can recognize over-investments that led to pain and loss. Even in those rare cases where there may have not been a recent problem with a product, service or technology, there are very, very few that have not had a major management initiative that went astray, or at best did not deliver the expected benefits. We believe this is fundamentally because of the lack of strategy in these improvement initiatives and hence their fad-like adoption (see Chapters 1 and 2).

So those who wish to be out front decide in advance on the things they wish to lead on and then allocate resources internally to optimize their position as an out-front company in the ways they specify. One of the companies we visited and studied as part of our applied research, State Farm Insurance, has a focus on brand and drives this 'good neighbor/trustworthy' brand position using its unique distribution system. Its dedicated sales and service agents, spread through every town and city in the USA, are all deeply involved in local community activities. State Farm sponsorship banners are seen everywhere from the local soccer team to the school fundraiser. Further, the State Farm agent will be often seen at these events, cooking the hamburgers. This grass-roots community service supports the brand and indeed drives it out to the front of the pack.

STATE FARM

State Farm is an insurance giant, and as a leader in general insurance, particularly automobile and housing and a major player in life insurance, has not changed its basic business philosophy in over 50 years. However, the fact that its basic philosophy is old and its head office has remained in a small town in Illinois, Bloomington, has not stopped it from steaming ahead of many of its competitors. This has substantially been accomplished through its agency distribution system and its use of information technology as an enabler of its out front position.

When many insurers pulled back from offering insurance in Florida after a series of huge losses through hurricanes, State Farm did just the opposite. It saw this as an opportunity to further drive its 'out-front' differentiation as a trustworthy 'good neighbor' by sticking with its customers, at a potential loss, through tough times.

Principle 4: Being out front

> State Farm also differentiates on customer service. For example, in automobile insurance it was a leader in reorganizing claims processing in order to maximize service value to clients. It threw out the traditional approach of getting the client to obtain three competitive quotes, fill out forms, etc. Through setting up a series of pre-qualified repairers, the policy-holder simply arranges for the automobile to be taken to the single most convenient place for repairs. State Farm measures customer satisfaction at the time of claim and benchmarks itself against competitors that it tries to stay in front of. State Farm also can use its scale to advantage, having set up a national network of these repairers to service policy holders who travel. The network of agents, who are electronically hard-wired to the core operations in Bloomington Illinois, is a key and the information, analysis and communications infrastructure achieved through State Farm's scale is used to keep it out front by ensuring that the local agent, out in the far reaches of local markets and communities, is extremely well informed and well trained, with leading-edge practices and modern products. Performance is carefully monitored and managed. Agents see a range of performance benchmarks. And finally, State Farm stays out front by using a powerful incentive system, that allows the best of its agents to earn as much as six times the average. State Farm is clearly operating many of the elements of Figure 1.3 to great effect.
>
> • • • • • • • • • • • • • • • • • • •

Out-front companies are often so because they seem to be able to see the future. When changes occur in their business environment, they seem better equipped to meet the future when it happens than their competitors. No doubt there is sometimes an element of luck in this. However some companies have been out front for too long to ascribe this to chance or luck. What do these companies that are consistently out front, such as Citycorp, American Express, Toyota, Dun and Bradstreet, British Airways, and Microsoft do? They invest in understanding the future by creating the future. British Airways first put showers in for their arriving high-value customers at Heathrow, redesigned their arrivals halls to improve customer value and then when competitors copied these things, dramatically upgraded their first and business class fittings to keep them out front. In order to know the value of these investments and to ensure these initiatives are the right ones, British Airways go to great lengths to bring the voice of their key customers into their service design processes. They employ creative people, carefully selected, to scan their environment and look for points of differentiation with real bite in the market.

The British Airways call center does not merely take bookings and respond to enquiries. It captures market intelligence very systematically from travel agents, corporate travel managers and other key industry players. This is genuine value added from its information technology platform. British Airways' call center provides live data on customer choice and preference to marketing analysts and operations managers.

The final element of description for companies that are strongly out front is cultural and behavioral. Out front companies have a deep-seated dissatisfaction with the status quo. Some of them have an irreverence of the present and past, a healthy skepticism that drives change. Conversely we rarely see a truly out front company in which executives spend much time reflecting on the past glories of 'the good old days'! Such companies would not stay out front for long.

EVALUATION OF OUT FRONT

We can assess the extent of the out front principle for a business unit in holistic terms as follows.

To what extent is a particular organization in an overall out-front position in its industry?

1 .... 2 .... 3 .... 4 5
Very low   Very high

Further, the out-front principle can be decomposed into its constituent elements or driving forces. These are the extent to which we are out front in:

- customer value creation and product/service offerings

    1 .... 2 .... 3 .... 4 5

- social responsibility, environment, community, etc.

    1 .... 2 .... 3 .... 4 5

- employee management and development

    1 .... 2 .... 3 .... 4 5

- process and technology

    1 .... 2 .... 3 .... 4 5

- investors' and financial performance

Principle 4: Being out front

From these constituent element assessments, executives can diagnose their organizational out-front strengths and weaknesses, then plan to use this principle as a guide to change.

BENEFITS OF OUT FRONT

There are many benefits to being out front in your industry. True industry leaders such as Microsoft can create enormous value for customers and shareholders through their strong market position. In such cases, they can actually shape and reshape their industry (as against just participating in it).

To illustrate this in detail, we examine the out-front position and policy of Bank A, a Canadian financial services institution with extensive operations, both domestic and elsewhere. This bank is radically reinventing itself and tearing down its traditional, highly vertical, integrated approach. It is also abandoning many of its traditional market segments, products and even distribution channels as part of this. Bank A came from a 100-year history of stable, branch-outlet-based banking across all segments of retail and business markets. This bank did it all! It took deposits, had lots of checking accounts, mortgages, credit card products, etc. and a full range of business loans and associated services. For 100 years, it was in the pack of banks that made mediocre returns on investments, gave mediocre service and had reasonably dissatisfied employees. As of 1999, it has decided to reinvent itself. The threats of new competitors and new distribution channels have lit fires in its marketplace that it can no longer ignore. Its strategy is summarized as follows.

- Decouple processes and hold them all up to the light of external competition. Uncompetitive processes must be fixed or outsourced.
- Rationalize products, eliminating duplication and abandoning unprofitable services.
- Closely examine all market segments and abandon unprofitable areas, customers, segments, geographies, etc.
- Invest heavily in becoming the leader in electronic commerce, Internet and telephone banking.
- Lead in private banking.
- Develop new suites of financial services, to become wealthy customers' 'wealth manager'.
- Cut costs through process re-engineering.

The decoupling and associated requirement for each step in the value chain to justify itself economically will eliminate major cross-subsidizations and inefficiencies that previously existed in the vertically integrated structure.

Migrating customers aggressively to new, low-cost channels or else migrating them out of the bank is a radical move. Indeed the whole strategy is bold and risky. Huge IT changes are needed. A massive new sales and service ethic is required. The old static culture of 'open the doors on time, everyday, and take their orders' must be overturned. Old, generally failed attempts to cross-sell will be abandoned and holistic asset-management products will replace them. These brave strategies are aimed directly at taking the company directly out front of the pack of traditional banks, using the latest technology and distribution systems and shedding a lot of baggage and cost. The aim is to reposition the bank out front of the market and take valued customers to places that competitors cannot go.

The benefits for the bank are clearly articulated to be at both ends of the income/profit statement. Revenue will be significantly enhanced through new value-added products that market research showed would be very attractive to customers. Costs will be shed through moving customers to lower cost channels, losing unprofitable customers and products, then disinvesting from expensive assets. Less staff will be needed because of the higher efficiencies and lower complexity of the product/service range. Further, fixed costs will be replaced by variable costs, providing flexibility. Finally, the bank's brand and image will be transformed from staid and old to innovative.

To summarize these benefits, powerful gains will arise from revenue *and* cost gains, brand image, productivity, flexibility, and innovativeness! Indeed, for companies that are truly out front, *super-normal* profits may well be available. This is because many customers will pay significant premiums for offerings that are truly differentiated. As the economists say, being differentiated and truly out front produces economic surplus, and price will determine how this is shared between producer surplus and consumer surplus.

Other benefits that are more directly internal to the organization drive these marketplace and business benefits. These include improved decision making, better use of information technology, and investments in teams of people. These benefits do not relate to customers directly, however they clearly take the organization forward so that higher levels of customer value can be created.

IMPROVING OUT-FRONT STATUS

Value can be created through better understanding future market trends and other environmental changes facing a business. Companies that aspire to lead their industries need to take a combination of incremental and bold decisions to establish that positioning. This requires standing out from the pack and can be achieved in any or a combination of ways as outlined at the beginning of this chapter. So how is an industry leadership (out-front) position established and sustained? The answer, like for many other types of organizational initiatives, comes down to strategic leadership, discipline in implementation and accountability. As an example, we cite a world-class insurance company, TAC Insurance, that specializes in personal injury insurance only from transport accidents. TAC is government owned and has a mandated local monopoly in its region of operation. Wouldn't it be easy for its leaders to sit back, relax and enjoy the ride? A series of CEOs and management teams has taken exactly the opposite path as a matter of choice. A decade ago, this company saw rising claim rates as a result of the high levels of car accidents that were occurring in its jurisdiction. It formulated a bold strategy of advertising on TV, newspapers and magazines, that safer driving would save lives. So it set up a series of very graphic TV advertisements showing very realistic car accidents that were really alarming to viewers. It showed dead bodies including children, fiery car wrecks, surgeons amputating limbs, people being hit by cars. It lobbied legislators to bring in lower blood alcohol limits, radar speed detection, random breath testing (of alcohol) by police and a variety of other incentives. The end result was a more than halving of the road toll! This was of course associated with much lower claims rates, low severity of injury in claimants and a much lower burden on society.

Is this a demonstration of the out front principle? We believe so, relative to two bases of comparison. First, there was no compulsion to do this. Second, it was bold and there was risk involved in going where no-one had previously been. Fatalities per million miles driven in the TAC's region of coverage are now at the world's lowest levels. In a neighboring region, where this insurance market is fought over by eight private sector competitors, the incentives were not in place to engage in accident prevention to nearly the same degree and many lives have been lost that might well have been saved if the same out-front approach had been taken.

A further example from TAC is to buck the general trend towards outsourcing non-core activities, and to insource a major service. This was in spite of enormous resistance in the industry and many so-called experts who said the initiative would fail. TAC contracted many law firms to defend against civil damage suits, of which it had thousands per year. However these external law firms were not as effective as desired because they came to work on cases too late to be effective and were not integrated with TAC claim officers. So TAC did something radical. It set up its own captive law firm of in-house specialists to work on critical cases from early stages, closely integrated with claims officers. Significant benefits have been won, in direct costs of operation and in claims cost. These examples of bold measures and a host of others have established this company as a worldwide industry leader. It has been asked for advice by insurance companies from all around the world who wish to understand how these initiatives were formulated and implemented. What is really extraordinary is that such an out front capability and position was established by a government-owned monopoly player! One could argue that given the context, if this company can successfully be so differentiated and bold, so can everyone.

The steps towards increasing the degree that a company is out front involve:

- investing in scanning the environment and working in defining the future
- outlining alternative strategies that take the company down a different, 'industry-leading' path
- evaluating these paths and checking their implementation feasibility
- making strategic choices, then communicating these to all stakeholders
- making key decisions based on fact, but also making them quickly, i.e. being dynamic
- using the discipline of project management to ensure the benefits are achieved.

Out front means creating an environment where the enemy is complacency. Essentially, the first critical step is to identify the domains of potential opportunity to get and stay out in front. Most of the world's great companies have found ways to achieve such positions.

Sustaining a position out front means continually moving forward, because out front is a relative thing. It is usually relative to the position of competitors, and all competent competitors are moving forward. This includes technical standards, service standards, efficiency, product/service design, indeed all aspects of business in which differentiation is possible. It also includes the other stakeholders of the firm such as shareholders and employees.

SUMMARY

Being out front is a key principle of most leading organizations, whether it is in their markets, in technology, or in organizational factors. An analysis of most industry leaders shows that it is clearly possible to identify the areas in which they have used the out front principle to drive their investments and behavior, whether it is GE, McDonalds, Toyota, Sony, 3M, Hewlett Packard, IKEA or British Airways. Their out-front actions and position are usually directed at providing them with a superior customer value offering, leading to more value for customers, which also will boil down to some superior value being created for shareholders.

8

Principle 5
Being up front

The measure of a man's real character is what he would do if he knew he would never be found out.

Lord Macaulay

One of the more disturbing aspects of this problem of moral conduct is the revelation that among so many influential people morality has become identified with legality. We are certainly in a tragic plight if the accepted standard by which we measure the integrity of a man in public life is that he keeps within the law.

Senator William Fulbright, US Senate speech, 1967

The sun may cool off and the moon may heat up, but all the bedevilments there are cannot destroy true speech. What is true speech? Ninety percent accuracy is not as good as silence.

Yeuh-lin, 13th century

INTRODUCTION

Being 'up front' means being open, honest and acting with integrity in all areas of business and operating activity. Leading companies do not make promises to customers that they cannot deliver. If they are unsure about whether they can comply with a request from a particular customer, they let the customer know and give the reasons for it. Managers in leading up-front companies tell employees the truth and encourage employees to tell the truth in return. This is typically demonstrated by the use of performance appraisals employing effective, 360-degree feedback processes. If downsizing/job loss is imminent, leading organizations do not confront the issue with a soft message – they tell all their employees 'the way it is'. Managers in leading up-front companies place an extremely high value on the quality of their working relationships.

Up-front organizations have a transparency about them, which pervades their culture of openness and their sharing of information. In one leading service organization we visited, no information is held sacred apart from that on possible acquisitions (which needs to be kept secret from the market until the appropriate time) and some information on new product developments (which is commercially sensitive and needs to be kept out of the hands of competitors). The accounts of this company in all respects are fully open and all performance information is available and shared with all staff. This openness provides the feedback loops for staff shown in Figure 1.3. People become involved because they are consulted and are well informed.

When an accident occurred within another leading organization, a 'flash-note' was issued to all employees in 2 hours, a preliminary report in 24 hours, and a full report within the week. This company also provided the two external regulatory authorities investigating the incident with copies of the full report. Incidently, this full report concluded that certain company policies had, to some extent, contributed to the accident. In the words of a senior executive 'We were in part responsible ... the best way to learn from it and move ahead was an open process not a litigious one.'

At its Botany site, ICI has made substantial changes to the way it manages information and company culture. The previous practice was for managers to keep information close to their chests, especially data on productivity and profitability, because management knew that if any gains were made and the information was shared openly, the workforce through its union would serve a 'log of claims' for increased pay and benefits on management. From this difficult and tense position in the past, managers in the propylene plant at ICI's Botany site now share all performance information with its workforce at all levels. Further, all management team members are given the same performance assessment and bonus assessment based on a single set of plant indicators and performance measures. This openness has led to developments in which the plant operators themselves deal directly with customers rather than leaving this to management. Everyone works towards the good of the business. Everyone is involved in increasing customer satisfaction and plant efficiency. Everyone is aligned because the style of management is up front.[1]

In another manufacturing example, a large integrated paper mill, we observed the application of this principle in the management of employee relations issues. Through a series of discussions, representatives of management and the (unionized) workforce have identified the common ground

Principle 5: Being up front

between them and the issues, both ideological and practical, that separate them. Through these discussions an 'understanding of difference' and openness has evolved which assists in the resolution of issues.

In two other service organizations with which we have had extensive working relationships over nearly a decade, a bank and an insurer, formal employee opinion surveys have been conducted over the past four years and the results have been openly shared with staff. In both these organizations, culture and climate surveys had been performed previously, having been commissioned on behalf of management. Because the results were highly critical of management, they were essentially buried and few people across the rest of the organization saw them. A big change in these organizations, driven by the principle of being up front, was that the more recent employee opinion surveys results were shared publicly with everybody.[2] As a result of this, focus groups were held with a high degree of employee participation, and improvement suggestions were made which are continuously being actioned. Targets have been set in both these organizations in pursuit of improvement of the organizational culture and working relationships in each company. In one of these companies the principle of openness has led to a substantial improvement in the closeness of the employer-employee relationship, improved morale and therefore higher productivity and profitability.

UP FRONT: MEDCO (MERCK) AS AN INDUSTRY LEADER

The up-front nature of this excellent company is reflected in the way managers and other employees relate to each other, as well as in the 'equality' expressed in the very nature of all its systems.

Medco, part of Merck Corp., has transformed itself from being an efficient, high-volume pharmaceuticals dispenser to being a value-added managed health care organization. It is leading its industry in the way in which it works with regulators in setting standards. It is also developing new forms of client relationships and sharing best practices around the organization from client to client and from pharmacy to pharmacy. It is being benchmarked and emulated by other organizations around the world, again indicating its leadership position. In its internal processes, Medco is automating more and more of its routine systems such as through the use of voicemail, touchtone telephone for automated script ordering and using other forms of taking the human operator out of the process for repeat scripts. It takes a lead with its prescribing doctors by keeping them

▶

> informed through its expert systems and intelligence gathering of the latest treatment systems which are available.
>
> Medco is up front, open and professional even with the retail pharmacies with whom it directly competes. Medco provides services to these pharmacies and deals with them in a very professional manner just as it does with its paying clients, measuring satisfaction levels and acting to improve these relationships.
>
> ●●●●●●●●●●●●●●●●●●●

Definition of up front

We did not anticipate finding the up-front principle when we set out to observe the common characteristics and principles of leading companies. But indeed it is a joyous thing that it exists so strongly in these leaders. Up front essentially means telling it like it is, that is having a high degree of integrity and openness in communication. It drives behaviors of honesty, trust, information richness and sharing, mutual respect and trust. It fosters the building of teamwork and goes hand in hand with the principle of alignment and distributed leadership.

Importantly, being up front does not mean creating a soft, 'touchy-feely' or 'be nice' style of management and leadership in business. Up-front companies tell it like it is in both good news and bad. They do not hide bad news from senior management or employees. This aspect of being up front is consistent and reinforcing of the principle of discipline. Up-front companies face into their challenges and ailments early, before they fester and grow into advanced organizational cancers.

The mutual respect aspect of the up-front principle is important. Genuine mutual respect is evident when employees can say they respect their line manager, his or her supervisor and so on up to the CEO. People at different levels in the company can have a discussion that focuses entirely on business issues with no-one feeling threatened in any way. In other words the discussions between employees can be as adults to adults, regardless of formal authority levels, because of the mutual respect that exists.

Bosses do not treat their workers as children in an up-front company. We have nearly all worked in companies where a dictatorial or tyrannical boss did treat employees like children, or worse, as if they were all idiots. The lack of trust is terrible for morale, destructive to productivity and stifles creativity and contributions to improvement. To summarize the extremes of these dimensions, Table 8.1 quotes workers we have talked to and interviewed over the past two decades.

Referring to Table 8.1, which organization, up front or backwards, would win in a competitive battle and by how much? How about pay and benefits?

Table 8.1 Typical responses from a 'backward company' and 'up-front company' worker

Item	'Backward company' worker responses	'Up-front company' worker responses
Attitude to work	Today is just another day and I'll do the same as yesterday	Today is an opportunity to improve on past performance, to do better than yesterday
Why you work	To get paid	To achieve rewards, including money of course, but there is also pride and satisfaction from contributing and achieving
Problem solving	It's not my problem	We all use our problem-solving skills to contribute in a proactive way
What the company thinks of you	I am a cost burden and they haven't yet found a machine to replace me	I am an asset and the company invests in my skills, knowledge and contribution. I receive regular feedback on my performance
How you contribute to competitiveness	I don't know, presumably someone else does	I understand how my work contributes to the big picture as follows ...
What is your commitment to stay here	Anytime I can find a better job I'm out of here	I feel part of a team and would only leave if a much better job came along
What is your commitment to quality	Quality is the inspector's job	We all monitor our team's quality of output, always striving to get it right the first time
How do you feel about your time spent at work	As little as possible – I try not to care at all	Since I spend so much of my life at work, it is important to me to achieve a sense of satisfaction and achievement

How can one or a team of shop floor workers discuss – as equals – the business issues of the day, when the CEO earns between 10–100 times that of the service or factory worker? This is not a problem in up front companies, because of the mutual respect. Everyone realizes that the market for CEOs 'clears' at a different price to that for waiters, laborers, bank tellers and plant operators. In the up-front company, people respect each other for what they do in their different domains, fitting beautifully with the principle of distributed leadership.

CEOs in strongly up-front organizations understand that they cannot know all the detail of production processes, and appreciate this notion, therefore they will listen, and will try to use influence to help with the workers' problems and opportunities. In addition, executives in up-front companies do not take unfair advantage of or abuse their authority, and they set up symbolic and tangible signs of democracy and equality. Up-front companies do not operate either a class system or an 'us versus them' culture. Up-front companies have often dispensed with the perks that workers resent such as reserved parking spots. They recognize that people at all levels and functions of the business are just that – people. We have certainly met many senior executives who behave as if they come from a superior gene pool to their employees – this is far from best practice in leadership style.

All this is to say that up-front companies are human and humanitarian. But let us make no mistake, they are still steel-edged and tough in their insistence on disciplined approaches to work and achievement of stretching business targets. When people make mistakes, they do hear about them and they expect to be accountable. But the occasional mistake is tolerated and used as a learning experience 'as long as your batting average is high' (as told to us by an executive of ABB in Europe). This approach shows a maturity of the up-front principle, although clearly one has to wonder about colleagues who repeat the same mistake or have a generally low batting average. This leads to another characteristic of up-front companies, namely that everyone knows that a good team cannot carry passengers, and that under-performing behavior must be fixed or else even tougher decisions must be taken. A backwards company (see Table 8.1) carries lots of poor performers, lacks accountability and is only as good as its weakest link. The up front company is transparent, and there is basically nowhere for underachievers, at any level, to 'hide'.

Leading companies are up front in their external relationships too. They tell governments if they are helping or hurting their competitiveness. They tell suppliers about their supply performance, good or bad. They admit to customers when there are delays or mistakes. Indeed, referring to Chapter 1, which described management's major tasks as successfully interacting in three markets, capital, labor and product/service, leading companies are up front consistently across all three markets.

Principle 5: Being up front

Inside these companies, they may use the up-front principle to guide mentor schemes, in which senior, experienced people mentor 'up and comers'. Indeed we have acted as external mentors for executives in companies that are sufficiently up front to identify the development needs of its executives. Up-front companies also conduct regular employee opinion surveys.

EVALUATION OF UP FRONT

To what extent do employees at all levels 'tell it like it is'?

1 . . . . 2 . . . . 3 . . . . 4 5

To what extent is your organization 'open' in its information sharing with employees at all levels?

1 . . . . 2 . . . . 3 . . . . 4 5

To what extent does your organization articulate and display high standards of business ethics?

1 . . . . 2 . . . . 3 . . . . 4 5

To what extent is there mutual respect in your organization between employees at all levels?

1 . . . . 2 . . . . 3 . . . . 4 5

To what extent is there a foundation of trust throughout your organization?

1 . . . . 2 . . . . 3 . . . . 4 5

To what extent is there an up-front approach to dealing with external stakeholders, such as customers, suppliers, government?

1 . . . . 2 . . . . 3 . . . . 4 5

BENEFITS OF THE UP-FRONT PRINCIPLE

It is clear from our observations of high-performance companies that they are almost invariably strong on the up-front principle. What is not clear from our survey work is which is the cause and which is the effect, and indeed, we believe it is some of both.

Put simply, companies that practice behaviors that are strongly up front perform better. In addition, high-performance companies are able to resource the communication and investment in people that embody up-front strength. It is a virtuous circle (see Figure 8.1).

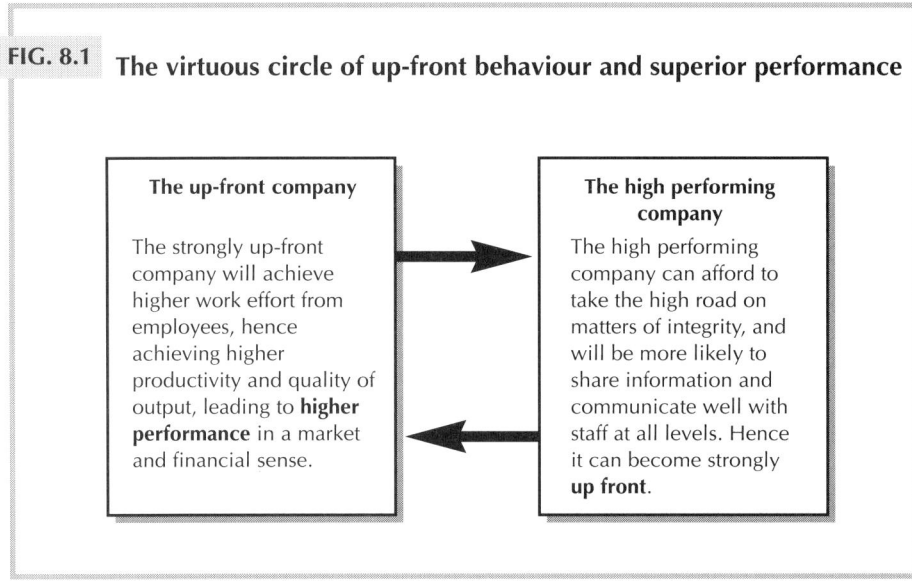

FIG. 8.1 The virtuous circle of up-front behaviour and superior performance

The trust and involvement achieved in a strongly up-front company with all stakeholders leads to better outcomes for all concerned. This certainly includes outside stakeholders such as customers as well as all staff. At ICI Botany, once the up front principle was used to guide managerial style and action, staff started to buy into the plant's operational and business performance, and this performance really started to take off. As it did so, the virtuous circle powered up and management became even more strongly up front in their behavior. Before long, there was a strong increase in alignment and distributed leadership, and the employee relations nightmare that had previously characterized that site for 40 years was broken.

IMPROVING UP-FRONT STATUS

If there is just one key to unlocking the up-front principle and strengthening it, it must be a trusting respect of all stakeholders that an organization deals with. If this is negative, then information will not be shared and performance will always be limited. Secondly, there will be no empowerment. There will always be 'us versus them'.

If trusting respect can be shown, communication both up and down the line can be free of fear, and will be strengthened for the common good of all stakeholders. Once the communication improves, based on respect, work processes can improve, alignment will improve, and everyone can get on with combating the real competitor, namely rival companies, rather than wasting effort on internal battles, either vertical or horizontal (e.g. across departments) within the organization.

Many executives who have been relatively low on up front have been very pleasantly surprised at the positive power and resultant benefits unleashed when they show respect, trust others and 'open up', even if they have been 'organizationally constipated' for years.

Ultimately, where does the sense of up front come from? Our observations of leading companies such as ABB and GE clearly indicate that it is the CEO who sets the standards in this regard.

SUMMARY

The up-front principle is a strong performance driver, going hand in hand with the principles of alignment, distributed leadership, and micro to macro in particular. Apart from the relationship that up front has with stronger organizational performance, it intrinsically leads to higher job satisfaction for all employees.

Clearly, up front is a compelling principle of leading companies, being associated with strong ethics, integrity and high qualities of behavior in all organizational domains.

Notes

1. By this point, the reader may have noticed that the principles described so far which are common to great companies act together. They are not independent. They support, enable and reinforce each other. Great companies work in a holistic sense on initiative which relate to the principles of alignment, integration, distributed leadership, up front …
2. One of these successful companies is a bank called The National, which employs some 50,000 people in seven major retail banks across three continents and conducts global wholesale bank operations and insurance businesses. This organization has increased its profitability by 15 percent per year over recent years, to over $2 billion in 1998, and is making major efforts to further improve its workforce morale and participation. The first step is to measure and report (see Chapter 14) these items comprehensively so that executives can compare across business units and local managers and team leaders can set targets and relate actions to outcomes. After two years, there was a much heightened awareness and priority of these issues, and people throughout the group are now up front about issues which were previously not well measured, not well understood, therefore not clearly discussed and debated, therefore not clearly managed.

9

Principle 6
Resourcing the medium term

Most managers are so concerned with today, and with getting their own real and imagined problems settled, that they are incapable of planning corrective actions more than a week or so ahead.

Philip Crosby

INTRODUCTION

While being lean, excellent organizations do not cut so close to the bone so as to stop their development. Compared to the average firm, significantly more attention is paid to the long-term health of the company than just the short-term wealth of the shareholders[1]. Leading organizations have enough professional resources to engage in key strategic projects. Managers are able to balance their time between business development, organizational improvement and self-development. Operators are able to balance their time between operating, improving processes and learning. Resources are provided to make the continuous improvement initiatives and investments work properly. When times get tough, these companies somehow still manage to invest in their future, rather than cutting back on their improvement initiatives which is a common practice of more short-sighted companies. Moreover, they do not get caught in the 'numbers/cost reduction trap'. We have frequently observed short-term resourcing policies driven by aggressive labor reduction targets that result in the introduction of supplementary labor (e.g. contractors) to assist with workload peaks. However, over time, this supplementary labor becomes de facto staff labor, which undermines employee morale, management credibility and organizational effectiveness. In particular, it frequently results in a conflict between espoused values and practiced actions and it undermines the principle of alignment.

This is not to say that cost reduction is not a driving focus in 'best practice' firms, as it invariably is, but by investing in learning and improving today, great companies build cost reduction and other capabilities for tomorrow. Cost reduction does not result in core capabilities depletion in great companies because it is not taken to the extremes where it does harm (see Figure 9.1).

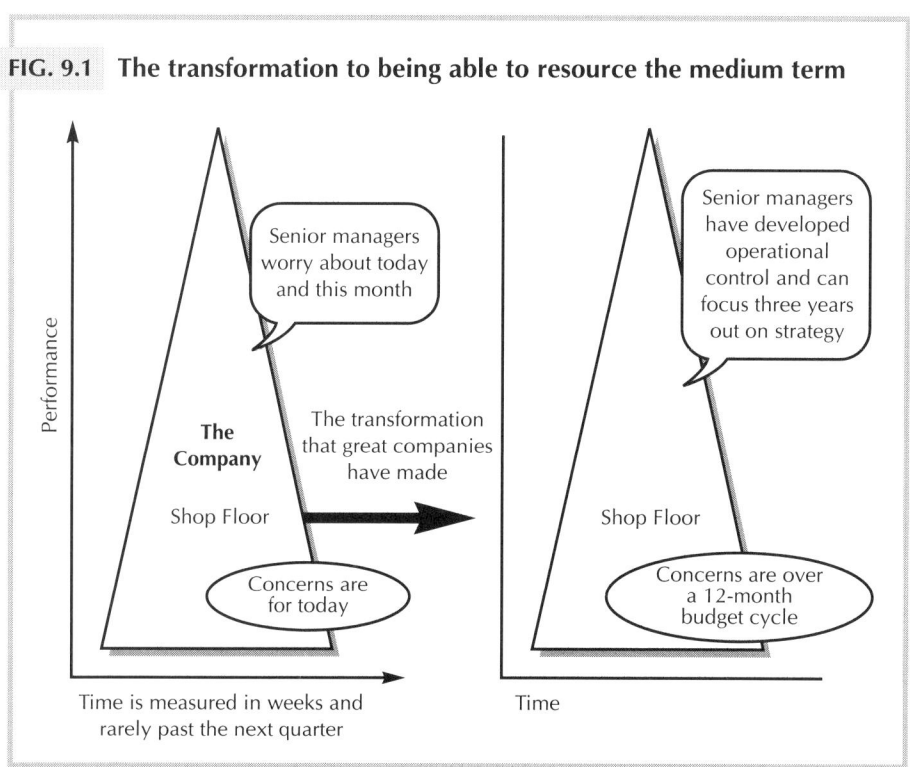

FIG. 9.1 The transformation to being able to resource the medium term

General Motor's Holden plant assembly plant in Elizabeth is an excellent example of this. The company provides the time and facilities for production operators to work on improvements outside of their rostered production shift times. It also invests heavily in training operators and in new technology with a long-term view. It has a very successful suggestion scheme, comparable to the Toyota production scheme, which is well resourced and delivers tangible improvement benefits. The upskilled workforce operate a visual factory, own the performance measures and leave managers to plan for and resource the medium-term (three-year) future.

RESOURCING THE MEDIUM TERM AT ABB

ABB makes very significant investments on the sales and marketing sides of its business as well as in product development and manufacturing. The sales and marketing initiatives are not just short-term sales push exercises – major investments have been building capabilities and infrastructure to make ABB an excellent selling and market-focussed company. ABB documents its customers' needs which clearly vary across the country and the customer. Indeed even for a given multinational customer such as a large chemical or automobile or paper manufacturer, the order-winners vary across operating divisions, countries and sites. ABB has documented on its worldwide databases the customer's decision-making criteria based on:

- performance
- reliability
- value for money
- local support
- delivery
- ease of installation
- being environmentally sound
- ease of use
- quality
- service.

These systems are available to 60,000 LotusNotes users, all of whom are actively contributing and using the knowledge on specific customer requirements from the same information system. ABB carefully manages its distributor relationship as well, because its distributors are key to its customer relationships. In resourcing for the medium term in its sales and marketing processes ABB has disciplined processes for sales management.

Step 1 Raise awareness
Step 2 Present to customers
Step 3 Trial its products by supplying one unit
Step 4 Migrate the customer to regular use
Step 5 Become the sole supplier
Step 6 The customer becomes an advocate

ABB has invested in creating and disseminating structured processes for each of these.

Principle 6: Resourcing the medium term

> ABB uses its global networks and power through its customer and prospect databases to segment its market by area, industry, size, relationship status, step in the sales process (see above) and a variety of other parameters. The database allows ABB to use the power of its global contacts network to be comprehensively used. As one senior executive from ABB told us 'Nothing is more expensive than a cold call'.
>
> ABB is very focussed in the way in which it has invested in its medium term. It focuses on the key products and services which are to be sold and delivered to its key accounts and customers into specific segments in the value chain. Its key order winners are efficiency, quality and speed and it aims not to be all things to all people in the marketplace and to be very focused in its medium-term investments.
>
> ●●●●●●●●●●●●●●●●●●●

To be able to engage in key strategic projects looking three years out, senior managers in these companies have avoided being swallowed up in solving day-to-day issues, hence there is a strong connection between this principle and 'distributed leadership'. This may be the formal approach of Hoshin Planning at Hewlett Packard, or a less formal approach as at Kodak, where senior people have stepped back from the details of 'running operations', in order to focus on bigger, longer-term challenges.

It is worthwhile for the reader to ask the question: 'What do our senior people, say general managers, spend most of their day doing?' Is it managing operational details, or being a strategist and change agent? Our experience shows that it is very easy for managers to fool themselves in considering these questions. Of course, there is nothing wrong with spending some time on operational issues, and indeed it would be a poor manager who is out of touch with the details of a business's operations, but we know of companies where senior people are simply more comfortable working on details than on the medium term, because that's where they come from and what they are good at. Imagine a ship where even the senior people, such as the captain, are working in the engine room, doing a hard day's work getting the coal into the boiler, or oiling the engine parts. Who is steering? Perhaps nobody, and that is a problem which pervades even some large companies today who have not embraced the 'resourcing the medium term' and 'distributed leadership' principles.

Common sense tells us that the captain should determine direction and steer, and the engine room people should be free to load the coal, in an agreed best way (that is, to a specified standard). The captain should generally keep their eyes looking all the way out from the bow to the horizon, and not manage the details of every shovelfull of coal! In organizations, like in ships, this principle is really about letting the shop floor run the shop floor (to agreed standards), letting team leaders lead teams and therefore giving general managers the time and space, through staying out of the minutiae, to look out at the horizon (one–three years?), and plan, resource and steer.

Definition of resourcing the medium term

'Resourcing the medium term' is a principle shared by leading companies, that also-ran companies have not stepped up to. Many mediocre companies concentrate almost solely on the short term, that is on doing business effectively and hopefully at a profit today, this month and this quarter. These mediocre companies have annual plans and may even have three or even five-year business plan projections, but this is not the same as resourcing the medium term. This is simply because these business plans are aspirational statements of:

- how many we plan to sell
- how many we want to produce
- resource needs
- financial projections.

Leading organizations plan ahead in terms of how they are going to improve their resources, develop capabilities and drive their competitiveness. They do not assume that today's 'status quo' will necessarily hold into the future. They carefully plan and forecast future trends and set out to create their future, knowing that it may mean changing direction and strategy. These leading firms aim to connect external events and forces to internal resource development. It is substantially about being proactive about the future, as against being reactive and allowing oneself to be carried along by the tide of external forces acting on the organization.

> **Leading organizations plan ahead in terms of how they are going to improve their resources, develop capabilities and drive their competitiveness**

Consider the types of external forces acting on a banking group we have worked closely with over the past decade.

- Industry consolidation and restructuring. Banks are merging, with over $300 billion of mergers taking place in 1998. Banks and insurers are also getting together, and these trends will accelerate.
- New players are entering the industry. Some of these have successfully picked off profitable businesses and are achieving large, efficient scales of operations. These included AT&T, GE Capital, Fidelity, Schwab and a host of others, who are able to establish a 'greenfield approach' when they enter the industry.

Principle 6: Resourcing the medium term

- Technological change and new channels of distribution have never been more prevalent. Staying still means going relatively backwards as many players make massive investments in new hardware and software.
- Customers are discerning, always looking for value, for a better deal expressed as a more competitive offering.
- Loss of power as 'the' money exchange. A banking licence used to be highly valuable, being a licence to operate payments systems and be the financial intermediary between lenders and borrowers. Alternative savings schemes and increasing direct contact between lenders and borrowers have reduced the traditional power of banks.
- The economic environment in which banks lend money seems to be increasing in volatility and is very unforgiving to those that do not exercise real prudence and careful risk management.

Let us compare and contrast two organizations' approaches to dealing with these issues, one that is low in resourcing the medium term and one high.

The company that is poor in resourcing the medium term pretty much has its head in the sand in respect of these issues, reacting to them only when they become critical as threats. Unfortunately, it is the 'boiled frog' syndrome – a frog in a saucepan of cold water will remain in it, die and be cooked if the saucepan is slowly heated, even though it is physically capable of jumping out. These companies are low on strategic acuity, often a little sloth-like. The industry creates value by restructuring, developing new products and channels and shedding cost, while it plods along until it finds itself in the 'dinosaur position', uncompetitive and ripe to be taken over and become someone else's brand. This company's lack of competitiveness is due to its myopic view of the world. It is short-sighted in its consideration of market forces, regulatory regimes and product development. This company is not necessarily inactive, in fact it may be furiously active, but everything is founded on today. This company may have engaged in downsizing, possibly a number of times, and indeed may have eliminated important resources such as experienced staff, in order to drive current period profitability. This company may have driven its revenue stream unwisely too, pursuing profit today, but perhaps not in its long-term interest. To summarize this position, this company is too short-term focused.

All organizations must make trade-offs between performing well in the short term versus in the medium and longer term. The company that is too short-term focussed will always struggle to make sound investments, always scratching to catch up and forever in 'scramble' mode. Consider Figure 9.2 in which we illustrate the relationship between the short versus long-term focus of an organization and its business performance.

We have just been describing company A (Figure 9.2). Company A may be tactically proficient, but it is short on 'big-picture' competence. Very often these companies seem to be good at cost reduction and little else. Company A focuses relatively too much time and effort on doing things well today, and not enough on doing the right things for the future. It's a self-fulfilling approach, because company A is able to survive for a long time by concentrating on optimizing its position today and being tactically sharp. However Company A is unable to break out of a limited 'follower' position, so its position and existence becomes not only self-fulfilling, but also self-limiting, unless it breaks out of its position on Figure 9.1 and moves towards position B.

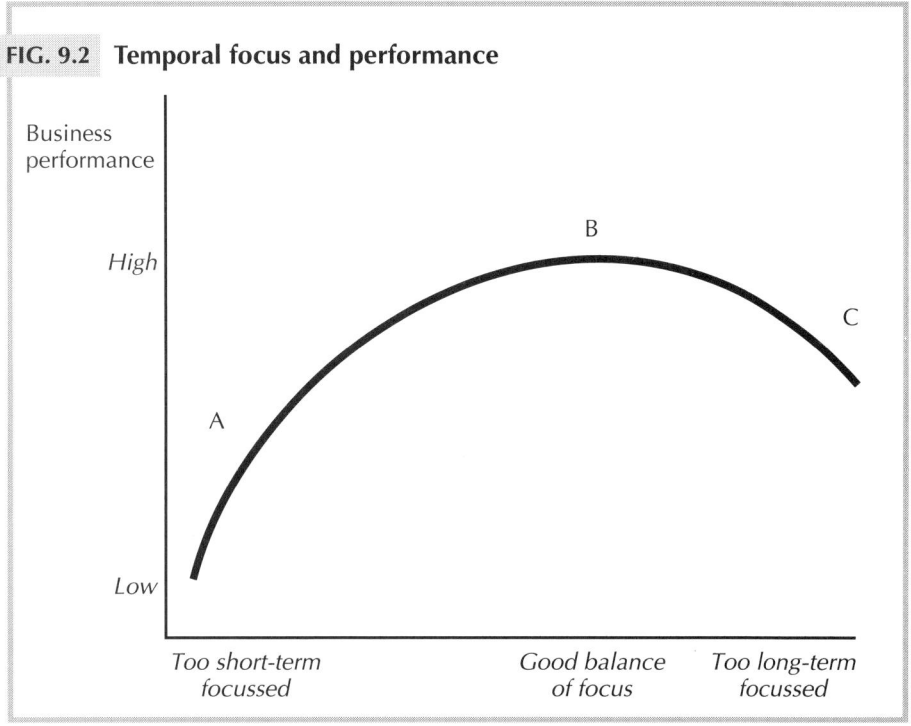

FIG. 9.2 Temporal focus and performance

Company B (at position B on Figure 9.2) has superior business performance to company A. The higher profitability comes from it being better positioned, earlier, and hence able to participate more competitively in its markets. This is also a self-fulfilling position, because the higher profitability creates more resources for reinvestment in the continuing medium term.

Let's return to the banking industry to compare and contrast the positions A and B on Figure 9.2. Company A reacts to the challenges in its environment primarily by cutting cost. It may try to do some other things, however due to its lack of real commitment to anything other than short-term performance, these other initiatives do not succeed. These could be technology initiatives in which projects of the order of $100 million often come to nothing. They may be service quality initiatives, which spark short-term energy but then die the death of all fads. Company B, the bank we have worked closely with for years, is smart enough to have learned that there are limits to cost cutting and that after one has cut away almost all the fat or 'organizational slack' then we start cutting into muscle, and this weakens, not strengthens, competitive position. This realization causes it to examine other options. Now it may have some false starts, go down some blind alleys, but eventually it develops a capability to undertake the magnitude of change required to leap ahead, which will keep it ahead of competitors. It may look for easy, low-effort solutions first. A common example is to do some sales training and tell line staff to push additional products at existing customers. This strategy, known as cross-selling, suffers from one major flaw, namely that there is little or no incentive for customers to cross-buy! Ultimately these exercises can become frustrating for both staff and customers, leading to a typical comment a senior banker told us of, made by a retail customer who came in to a branch 'I'm here to deposit a check and before you start, I still don't want the mortgage products you have already offered me three time this month!'

What has this industry-leading financial services group done that is far-sighted? Nothing less than a three-year plan of complete reorganization to globalize, standardize products, processes and technologies, and reassign responsibilities and work structures to specialist salespeople, servicing departments and support areas. This transformation also includes developing a whole new suite of products that change the organization from one of 70,000 pure bankers to one of broader financial services. Further, the organization is investing in properly segmenting its markets, which has rarely been done before in its markets, and even more rarely with success. This strategy is medium-term focussed, and will be expensive and involve trading off some short-term performance in order to fund its implementation. It involves breaking the existing mould, which is a daring move for a highly profitable market leader.

Companies at position B in Figure 9.2 have vision, a sense of medium-term purpose and they perform well. This 'breakthrough' is that focussing on the medium term does not mean large short-term profit trade-offs, because the company that spends money and other resources on the medium term achieves competitive superiority in the short term.

Position C involves being too 'far-sighted' in focus. This organization is pretty rare relative to the As and Bs, and we have not seen any large companies we would classify as C. However, some smaller companies are so 'vision' oriented in their early days, they seem to be much more focussed on the medium term than the short term. Perhaps this explains why some of these smaller start-up companies based on single products and service ideas go broke so regularly. These companies are not grounding their development sufficiently in today's realities.

PART 2 • MANAGEMENT BY PRINCIPLES

EVALUATION OF RESOURCING THE MEDIUM TERM

> To what extent is the organization generally sufficiently focussed on resourcing the medium term?
>
> 1 .... 2 .... 3 .... 4 5
> Too low   Strong focus
>
> More specifically, does it allocate sufficient resources to ensure competitiveness in the medium term in terms of:
>
> Financial resources?
>
> 1 .... 2 .... 3 .... 4 5
> Very low   Very high
>
> Human resources?
>
> 1 .... 2 .... 3 .... 4 5
> Very low   Very high
>
> The right strategic projects?
>
> 1 .... 2 .... 3 .... 4 5
> Very low   Very high
>
> Is there an appropriate balance of measures, incentives and rewards in order to focus managerial attention the medium term?
>
> 1 .... 2 .... 3 .... 4 5
> Very low   Very high
>
> What batting average has the organization achieved in its medium-term development initiatives?
>
> 1 .... 2 .... 3 .... 4 5
> Very low   Very high

BENEFITS OF RESOURCING THE MEDIUM TERM

The company that successfully and sufficiently resources the medium term will outperform those that are short-term focussed, almost by definition in everything except the very short term. Some examples of benefits that accrue to medium-term resource allocation are outlined below.

Next generation product leadership

Company A can only ever hope to be a fast follower whereas company B will be able to reap the harvests of product and service innovation. Sony, Hewlett Packard and its 3M are examples of product leaders. Sony led with the introduction of its Walkman so successfully that it sold some 20 million units at high margins by the time the followers drove supply up and price reduced. Sony then reinvested by plunging resources into other bold medium-term investments in products such as Discman and Watchman.

Distribution channel leadership

Whether it is www.amazon.com, Internet banking or mail order clothing purchases, those companies that strongly resourced the medium term over the past five years are usually the leaders in developing and taking advantage of new and better distribution systems. At IKEA in Europe, customers can dial in on the telephone to check for availability of items by store and reserve those items for pick-up or delivery. That may not sound all that fancy until a customer tries doing it at one of their competitor's stores and finds they generally cannot.

At Medco, it was the efficient, effective purchasing and distribution system which began as the value-add for the company, but investments in the medium term developed the business in a new direction of 'total health management'. This required major investments in technology and expertise, upgrading skills of all employees, a world-class telephone center and a number of other components of a medium-term strategy. The key point is that a company with a predominantly short-term focus, Company A on Figure 9.2, would not have been able to step up to these developments. They often involve 'hard' technology investments and upgrading of organizational 'software', culture and skill sets.

Attracting and retaining great people

Organizations that have too strong a short-term focus, at the expense of properly resourcing the medium term, just will not be able to get and keep the best people. At job interviews, no matter what the level of job, really go-ahead people want to know what the company's development plans are. They might ask 'Where is the company going over the next few years?' and further, 'What role might I be able to play in that development?'

When we interview someone and they have virtually no questions about the organization's hopefully exciting development plans, then we have to wonder about their personal development plan. Are they just happy to occupy a job? This boils down to a fairly obvious but powerful truth – that the company that invests and resources its medium term will be populated by people who do the same personally, and vice versa for the company and people that are going pretty much nowhere. There is a pretty efficient market out there in terms of matching the caliber of people and the organizations they work in. If we want people with vision, who want to shape and create the future rather than just arrive or be taken there, then that philosophy must be an inherent characteristic of the organization. Strongly resourcing the medium term is a major element of achieving this in all industry leaders we have observed.

Dynamic organizations tend to partner with dynamic suppliers and customer organizations. It would be relatively unusual, for example, in automobiles, computers and electronics, for a leading edge company such as Toyota or Dell to partner with a supplier that was low on the principle of resourcing the medium term. Toyota and Dell just cannot afford to rely on partnering such suppliers. Similarly, for a components manufacturer that wants to stay at or near the leading edge, such as Denso in Japan, it makes little sense to partner with an assembler that is not investing strongly in new products, technologies and process improvements. It may still supply such a company, but do so just to drive its cash flow stream and not to drive it forward in improving its business.

So what is the answer to executives who say:

> Business conditions are tough and our competitors are trying to eat our lunch today! If we don't focus almost exclusively on the short term, we won't have a next year much less a medium term, so don't tell me about resourcing the medium term.

We ask whether these executives would like to still be in business in two and three years, not just fighting the good fight of competitive survival, but growing and prospering. The answer is generally yes.

Question And if we go forward three years, will you still be happy to be on the knife edge of survival as you are now, or would you prefer to have a buffer of competitive edge keeping the wolves of bankruptcy from the door?

Answer That's easy. Of course we want to be out of our difficulties.

Question Is your short-term focus ever going to allow you to build the capabilities needed to break the cycle.

Answer No.

Question So what is the answer?

Answer Somehow, we have to find a way to develop some 'strategic' projects and capabilities, while we must focus on today, we must also accomplish those developments. It's a case of both, not choosing. Since our resources are limited though, it will have to be a small number of carefully chosen, strongly managed initiatives. We have to watch them carefully. Clearly, not doing these is not an option, because it will relegate us to always being in 'struggle' mode.

To summarize this, those who effectively sow seeds for the medium term usually get to harvest, while those who are too busy as hunter-gatherers, foragers or scavengers to sow seeds for the future, will have to live with higher uncertainty of returns. Being too busy managing today to invest for tomorrow is an understandable reason but not an acceptable excuse. Leading companies are somehow able to do both well and achieve a balance over time of managing 'bread and butter' and 'jam' projects.

IMPROVING ON RESOURCING THE MEDIUM TERM

One way of forcing an organization to improve from a low position of resourcing the medium term to a position more like company B (Figure 9.2) is to explicitly choose a resource level. First, as a matter of business strategy, how much money, or what percentage of sales or budget, should optimally be allocated to projects that do not pay back during this next 12 months?

The second question is what are the opportunities that should be resourced? What mix of processes, products, technologies, markets, skill levels and other factors do we aim for two or three years out? Then, leading companies construct a plan and a schedule for execution, with review milestones and performance expectations, that they use to guide actions.

Some companies set aside 20 percent of sales for all this, some as little as 1 percent, and there is certainly no universal formula or generally applicable ratio. The point is that of taking control of those precious 'free cash' amounts that the company worked so hard to generate, and optimizing the time schedule of budgeted allocations, to some short-term and some medium-term investments. This is a vital part of a company's strategic make up and will be a key determinant of future competitive position and performance.

SUMMARY

Companies that are strong on resourcing the medium term usually have a firm set of plans in place such that they are less prone to falling prey to fads, simply because they have relatively better control over their destiny. These companies won't over-react to change in the marketplace either. They are better at choosing winning strategies because of their 'consciousness' and focus. Their people view resourcing the medium term as essential work.

The principle of resourcing the medium term has strong links to distributed leadership, in terms of using all staff to effectively pick medium-term projects. Strong distributed leadership enhances strength of resourcing the medium term. Strong distributed leadership also clearly frees up executive time from day-to-day issues, to enable focus and effort on the medium term.

Strength in the out front principle is also good for building the medium-term focus. It is the out front capability that raises the organization's ability to pick medium-term projects that are likely to have winning outcomes. Finally, the micro-to-macro principle is related to resourcing the medium term because the cascading of medium-term strategy and projects into effective operational actions and outcomes is an implementation effect. Micro-to-macro strength leads to the whole organization being signed on to these strategic thrusts, and ready and willing to implement, hence once again lifting the probability of success.

Note

1. These companies have senior executives who have the fortitude and vision to be able to tell analysts and shareholders about building a future, not just optimizing profits for today.

10

Principle 7
Being time focussed

Work expands to fill the time available for its completion.
C. Northcote Parkinson, 1955

Time is money!

INTRODUCTION

Leading companies have time itself as a critical value and set of measures, whether it is the order-to-delivery time, the product development time or precision itself. These organizations' relentless drive to reduce time is analogous to many organizations' efforts to improve quality during the 1980s. Moreover, it became clear during our visits to world-class companies that focussing on reducing time requires these firms to have excellent cost controls, quality and flexibility. If quality is not right because processes are out of control then it will be impossible to manage efficiently and compress cycle times. So a focus on the management and compression of time requires the organization to have previously developed a quality improvement and process management capability (see Figure 10.1).

As with many of these principles, the exact manner in which the principle manifests itself in driving behaviors depends on the strategy, position and preferences of the organization:

- for a process-focussed organization, time means processing efficiency and throughput speed
- for a relationship-oriented company, time-focus often means time to respond to customer requests

- for a market-focussed leader, time focus means speed to market of new value creating ideas
- for an innovative product leader, time focus is around the commercial value of ideas and intellectual property.

SPEED AT ASEA BROWN BOVERI (ABB)

ABB operates in 140 countries, employing 210,000 people in the business lines of power plants and transmission, industrial and building systems, transport and financial services. ABB and its executives have won many prizes and awards for being the most respected company both in general terms and in respect of technology and innovation management.

Critical to ABB's success and integral to its core operating philosophy is the notion of speed. At one level this has manifested itself in its core operating philosophy 'The cost of delay usually exceeds the cost of mistakes'. This translates into the way people work at ABB and as one of its business units CEOs told us 'The worst thing you can do is nothing!' Speed of decision making combined with accountability are hallmarks of ABB. In response to questions about the downside of acting fast, the response was 'We tolerate some failures. It's OK to make mistakes as long as your batting average is high.' This neat statement of business philosophy is common to many of the world's best companies but nowhere is it articulated and implemented more positively on a worldwide basis than at ABB.

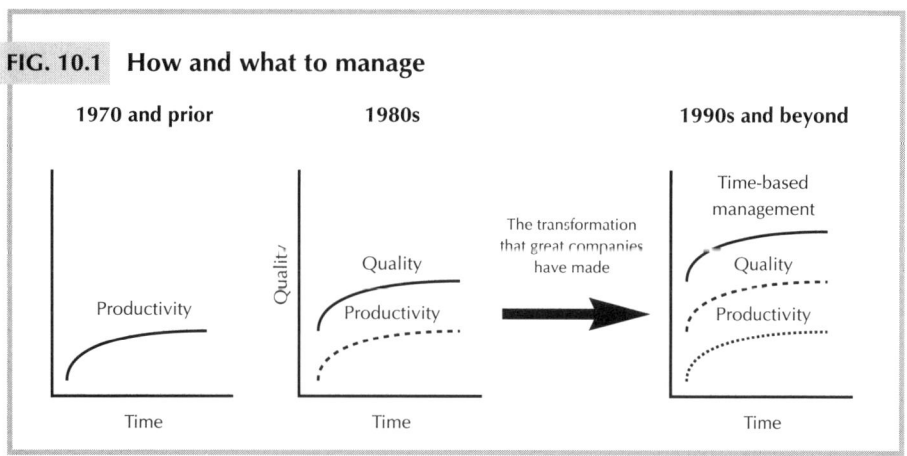

FIG. 10.1 How and what to manage

KODAK

Kodak has a make-to-order system which is 'lightning fast'. In its film operations, its speed-based approach achieves low inventory, excellent responsiveness and cost savings for its local and Asian customers. By being able to respond to the demand of its export market place across South East Asia, Kodak from Australia has been able to sustain its competitive advantage in supplying that market relative to other Kodak plants.

SOUTH PACIFIC TYRES

A second example is South Pacific Tyres based in Melbourne which is a joint venture company owned by the Goodyear group and Pacific Dunlop Limited. This company has achieved, along with many others in the auto industry, a degree of precision through just-in-time manufacturing and delivery which requires them to co-ordinate their deliveries to the minute to match the requirements of automobiles being produced. All this is monitored by a real-time electronic data interchange (EDI) system. There are thousands of similar companies around the world who have used the time principle to drive their precision of delivery forward so that they can be effective as just-in-time suppliers.

Definition of time based

'Time management' has existed as a concept for decades. 'Time-based competition' (Stalk and Hout, 1993) is also not a new concept. Managing time in project environments, using tools such as Gantt charts and network sequencing diagrams (PERT, CPM) etc. are also well known.

In our observations of truly leading companies the 'time management' concept goes deeper and is a fundamental principle guiding actions. In these companies, time itself is an important, valued dimension, a resource to be allocated, measured and proactively managed. There are many elements in which time impinges on organizational effectiveness, and the principles of being time-focussed can include any subset of these.

Speed of responsiveness to customer enquiries and orders

Often known as order-to-ship time or lead time in some countries, this measure can define competitiveness and advantage in some industries. By its very name, an example is 'fast-food' in which advantage is usually not the gourmet quality, but the fact that the order-to-delivery time of suppliers like McDonald's is measured in seconds.

Another instance of time-based positioning is in the printing business. In our work of running short courses and professional seminars at the University of Melbourne, we switched printers for our color brochures because of the speed of responsiveness of our new supplier. This company does in three days what our previous supplier did in two weeks. Cost and quality were factors that were similar across a number of suppliers (we call these 'qualifiers' to be in a business or industry) and the 'order-winner' is speed of response to our requirements.

Product development cycle time is another competitive 'speed' dimension

In the 1980s, Xerox found that its Japanese competitors could develop new products such as photocopiers in half the time it took Xerox. General Motors, Ford and Chrysler encountered a similar situation. Generally, the Japanese automakers were completing the 'concept-to-customer' cycle in under three years, while US companies needed five. More recently, while the Western companies have compressed their cycles to below three years, the Japanese companies are well below 18 months. The differences have traditionally been caused by concurrence of processes. Whereas some companies sequence their processes, others manage to deal more and better with the complexities of conducting major processes in parallel. It could be argued that life is generally simpler in the context of product development if we robustly design the product first, specify it completely, then take the finished design through a process/tooling/manufacturing design. However the sequential path takes significantly longer in total, and the resulting product is generally no better, and often not as good as those in which major product and process development occurs in parallel.

This time-based principle also manifests itself in major projects such as building construction. Known as concurrent engineering, the idea put into practice is that major design activities (structure, electrical and mechanical systems, etc.) can be overlapped with construction. The traditional method that takes much longer requires essentially sequential phases of design, various sub-system designs with construction occurring after the final design is frozen.

In other contexts, time focus relates to responsiveness and commercial information value. Kodak's lightning fast reaction from one of its plants to serve its Asian markets has become its clear competitive weapon.

In product development and project management, where significant amounts of money are invested well before the revenue stream begins, it is certainly true that 'time is money'. Consider infrastructure projects such as roads, water and energy supply systems or telecommunications networks. Time compression in project development and implementation brings the dual benefits of starting the revenue stream earlier, hence reducing the time and perhaps the size of the financing costs, as well as increasing the total revenue quantity and bringing it forward.

In pharmaceuticals or aerospace product development, enormous amounts of money are invested years in advance of any potential revenue stream. Here, there is another benefit associated with time compression, namely the probability or likelihood of success. Two major elements are technical success and marketplace success. Is technical feasibility enhanced or reduced in a 'time-compressed' or 'time-expanded' project? Although there are no universal laws, there is evidence that the 'tight' management of 'time-compressed' projects is associated with focussed project management in general and solid management of quality. There is much less uncertainty about the relationship between speed and market uncertainty. Time-compressed product and service developments lead to a variety of first-mover advantages. Just ask Sony, 3M or Hewlett Packard. These advantages are less in industries with stable base technologies such as coal mining, and are very substantial in industries with rapidly developing technology such as telecommunications.

Reliability and time punctuality

This element combines general ability to deliver on promises with the time dimension. It has both internal and external organizational benefits. Internally, there are clear efficiency and productivity improvements in a company that 'runs like clockwork'. When things mostly happen on time, such as reports, analyses, designs, components and facilities, then internal customers can be more effective in their planning and work. Some companies tend to have a high degree of internal reliability and time disciplines, while in others the staff always talk of being held up by late delivery of something they needed from their colleagues. This phenomenon manifests itself all the way down to the most micro level of the company, such as punctuality at meetings and the extent to which individuals and work teams arrange their day such as to use time most efficiently and effectively.

Further considerations

External reliability and punctuality, in meeting due dates and delivery to clients, is a competitive dimension of time. Just-in-time production and delivery use techniques such as Kanban systems, which are aimed at achieving

To what extent does the organization manage time as a critical resource?

1 .... 2 .... 3 .... 4 5
Very low   Very high

To what extent does the organization have in place the basic productivity and quality platforms (see Figure 10.1) that a true time focus can be built on?

1 .... 2 .... 3 .... 4 5
Very low   Very high

Consider the dimensions of time-focus in more detail:

To what extent does the organization achieve relative speed of responsiveness to customer requirements/orders?

1 .... 2 .... 3 .... 4 5
Very low   Very high

To what extent does the organization achieve rapid new product/service development relative to its competitors?

1 .... 2 .... 3 .... 4 5
Very low   Very high

How capable is the organization on time-based reliability and punctuality:

- in its internal activities?

1 .... 2 .... 3 .... 4 5
Very low   Very high

- in its external activities?

1 .... 2 .... 3 .... 4 5
Very low   Very high

To what extent does the organization have a 'sense of urgency' culture in its workplaces?

1 .... 2 .... 3 .... 4 5
Very low   Very high

Principle 7: Being time focussed

waste-free precision. The punctuality of a just-in-time system is based on high levels of process reliability. Customers want their service suppliers to be punctual as well, whether it is a plumber, doctor, hotel service or any other form of service.

A further category of time is a general sense of 'urgency to get the job done'. This translates directly into productivity, and even as consumers we can all tell the difference intuitively between a 'high-performance workplace', a mediocre or average workplace, and a poor, unproductive workplace. This 'sense of urgency' factor can be seen in things like the speed of walking (and working). Imagine two branches in a bank, one in which staff spend only a little time chatting and generally focus on attending to their work efficiently and courteously. Now consider a branch where staff seem to move in slow motion. Given all the same products and systems and technologies, how much difference in productivity does the human factor, 'sense of urgency', make? We have found it to be as much as 35 percent. Most consumers say that the differences are not just in pure productivity. In the urgent culture, staff are generally eager to serve customers. In the slow-motion culture, staff try not to serve customers, try to keep their heads down avoiding eye contact and pretending to be processing paperwork while customers wait.

> *Given all the same products and systems and technologies, how much difference in productivity does the human factor, 'sense of urgency', make?*

The time-focussed organization then, concentrates on managing some or all of these aspects of timeliness proactively, driving them for competitive advantage. These may combine time compression of lead times, product development, punctuality or a general sense of urgency.

EVALUATION OF TIME FOCUS

Yet another dimension of time-focus is the speed of organizational change. Some companies can implement a variety of changes rapidly while others seem to take forever to achieve the same things. We refer here to business process changes, organizational restructure, cost exercises, downsizing initiatives, implementing outsourcing contracts and many other tasks. For nearly all such tasks, speed of implementation is an important dimension of implementation effectiveness. In one large insurance company we know, senior executives complain that it can take literally years to accomplish major changes that should only take months. This aspect of time focus is clearly related to the 'embracing change' principle.

> How effective is the organization at achieving rapid change?
>
> 1 .... 2 .... 3 .... 4 5
> Very low   Very high

BENEFITS OF THE TIME-FOCUS PRINCIPLE

Apart from the fact that the fast-response organization delivers greater customer value than the slow-motion or slothful organization, a number of other powerful benefits exist for the time-focussed organization. First, let's acknowledge some of the first-order benefits.

Responsiveness is a form of value that drives volume and/or the ability to command a premium price. Would McDonald's be as popular if they took 10, 20 or 30 minutes to fill an order? If a supermarket checks customers out very quickly every time while others force them to wait, would this affect consumer choice? In a market with say five major banks, having similar products, with one able to have faster service, shorter waiting queues and quicker response to inquiries, what would happen to market share? There is evidence to suggest that consumers take significant account of the published statistics concerning help-desk waiting times when choosing personal computers and software. And when we are buying insurance or a plane ticket or choosing a hotel by telephone and get put on hold, do we wait forever or choose another supplier? Response time counts for consumers as a valued dimension.

Service levels are often the key to success and timeliness is a big part of this.

As to product or service development cycle time, which company is more likely to be able to incorporate new features, new technologies and new fashion trends or aesthetics, the fast developer or the slow-motion company? First-mover advantages have been demonstrated repeatedly in most industries.

In terms of delivering reliably and on time, the story in many industries such as retailing is that if a supplier misses a 30-minute delivery time window, it bears the enormous costs of either rescheduling, missing the order and the sales entirely or paying a contract penalty fee that is based on time. If product differentiation is not a big order-winner, then service levels are often the key to success and timeliness is a big part of this.

As individual households consuming repair or maintenance services from plumbing to gardening and cleaning, does punctuality count? Imagine the word-of-mouth recommendations for a plumber who consistently arrived on time and did a speedy, efficient job.

The benefits that accrue from being able to rapidly effect major organizational change can be significant. If an economic downturn occurs or a technological breakthrough occurs, the firm that can rapidly adjust its workforce size or skill base is able to capture value and possibly market share. Companies such as Hewlett Packard that did a fast and efficient job of globalizing the business, a very complex big-change exercise, captured great advantage from their speed of doing so. Similarly, companies like Hewlett Packard, which reorganized from functional silos to value chains quickly and effectively, gained substantial benefits.

IMPROVING TIME FOCUS

One very important point about 'speeding things up' is that great companies do not trade off on cost or quality to achieve speed. Quite the contrary. Quality, meaning process control, customer focus and continuous process improvement driven by company wide involvement, is a foundation for building the truly time-focussed company. And reducing time, such as order-to-ship lead-time can reduce cost through process improvement and simplification.

If time is money, then clearly wasting less money on non-value-adding activities also wastes less time. Saving time and saving cost go hand-in-hand in leading companies. Even a university department can provide a time-focussed example of compression. For 40 years, the MBA program at our university's Business School ran for two semesters of 13 weeks each year, meaning that full-time students did their 20 subjects, five at a time over just under two years. The introduction of three teaching semesters per year brought the elapsed time of the program down to 16 months, hence substantially reducing the opportunity costs for students who leave the workforce to do their MBA. What happened to the productive output of that Business School, that gains its revenues from fees charged per student per course? Annual capacity went up by 50 percent, and demand was able to rise to this new level! Individual teaching loads remained unchanged. There were no quality trade offs or reductions but clearly a time, productivity and unit cost gain.

Time-focussed activities include those listed below.

- Doing tasks in parallel, such as concurrent engineering products.
- Communicating effectively so as to enhance speed.
- Using technology that is fast such as electronic commerce, e-mail and Internet, intranets, extranets, etc.
- Speeding up decision processes. This is a major focus worldwide at ABB, one of the world's most respected companies based in Europe. ABB's phi-

losophy on decisions is that occasional mistakes are OK, as long as decisions are rapid and the worst kind of manager is one who delays decisions.

- Remove or reduce bureaucracy that slows things down. In this regard ABB has a very small corporate headquarters, receiving and monitoring monthly financials from its hundreds of profit centers around the world, but being careful to avoid interfering and imposing delays on successful line managers. This is very different to a large paper manufacturer we know, where delegation levels are ridiculously low and line managers spend their life waiting for questions from head office bureaucrats who then rubber stamp a myriad of documents. Is it possible to be truly time-focussed while fighting a losing paper war inside the company?

- Sticking to process standards. Would McDonald's be almost lightning fast if they did things different ways on different days? Process standards can be honed, sharpened, speeded up, but we must first have them and be disciplined in sticking to them in order to achieve any of this. What other food supplier has the processes to accurately tell customers how many seconds it will be till they get their order when its system is overloaded? That is a 'precision capability'.

- At the micro-level, leading companies often have protocols for conducting meetings so as not to waste time. These disciplines signify time focus.

- Establish time standards and measures. One integrated measure is 'the percentage of orders delivered in full, on time, in specification' (DIFOTIS). Another is simply turnaround time. This certainly is the case at Medco in their pharmaceutical mail-order operation, where turnaround time of order-to-ship is carefully measured, closely monitored and connected to people's pay.

- Create a sense of urgency by using all opportunities to motivate staff to push the time theme, the time measures and the time performance. At NASA, the terms 'faster, better, cheaper' are often used. Time and timing are high-profile measures of focus.

- Aim before firing. The returns to effective planning are usually solid, resulting in implementation that is more likely to get it right the first time, hence saving monetary resources and time. However it is clear that too much planning is possible too, so where is the middle ground? Although we can not universally generalize, consider the construction of a residential home. The market leader we work with in this industry is certainly into time compression to increase asset turnover, and does not wait till every brick is planned for before starting construction. This experienced and successful builder gets the concept and overall design right, the aggregate material measures assessed, then has the confidence to start building in the knowledge that the detail will work itself out as the job proceeds.

- Valuing punctuality, dependability and reliability as key personal and organizational values.

SUMMARY

The time-focussed organization achieves many advantages in its marketplace. Through time compression and precision, value is created for customers, market position is enhanced and efficiency is improved. The 'time is money' adage has a lot to commend it, and most leading organizations manage time effectiveness because it is just that – a business effectiveness issue, including all the elements of 'faster-cheaper-better'. For many organizations that have done good work and made gains on improving their organizational processes, the next big opportunity may well include their potential to improve their process speed.

11

Principle 8
Embracing change

It must be considered that there is nothing more difficult to carry out nor more doubtful of success, nor more dangerous to handle than to initiate a new order of things. For the reformer has enemies in all those who profit by the old order, and only lukewarm defenders in all those who profit by the new order, this lukewarmness arising partly from fear of their adversaries ... and partly from the incredulity of mankind, who do not truly believe in anything new until they have had actual experience of it.

Niccolo Machiavelli, *The Prince*

INTRODUCTION

Leading firms are as good at executing ideas and strategy as they are at formulating them: they have an action orientation and they strongly embrace change. They recognize that there are times for consultation and times for action – they have not fallen prey to consultative overkill. They have developed change management capabilities and project management disciplines as core capabilities themselves.

Leading firms recognize the 20/80 rule of change management i.e. spend 20 percent of total effort on design and 80 percent of effort on implementation. This behavior is in stark contrast to what we have observed in many mediocre companies. Many of these are far more interested in the problem than the solution and they grossly underestimate the complexity of moving from identifying the answer to fixing the problem. Hence they take many years to achieve any real movement on major strategic or cultural change.

We have also often worked with organizations and found it possible to formulate, during a business retreat with a group of senior managers, ambitious change management plans. Then nothing happens! These managers go back to their businesses and the enthusiasm and sometimes even desperately strong commitment to change which is expressed at a conference or executive retreat gets diluted by the necessities of dealing with the day-to-day business. Some managers seem to lose the courage to implement change, even though they fervently committed to catalyze some change initiative at the business retreat. The issue is that courage is not enough! It is a necessary but not sufficient condition.

Really excellent companies differentiate themselves from the rest of this pack by being able to manage change in a disciplined way (see Figure 11.1). A good example of this is the National Bank's use of taskforces to conduct strategic projects. Once proper accountability for milestones and project completion is given to the executives who lead these taskforces, action occurs. Through a network of such groups, a multitude of strategic initiatives can be attempted in a relatively focussed manner. This organization has also found that using leading edge information technology, taskforces can operate with members from anywhere in the world. The reason for this success is that managerial courage to change is combined with a rigorous project management regime and strict accountabilities for achieving project goals.

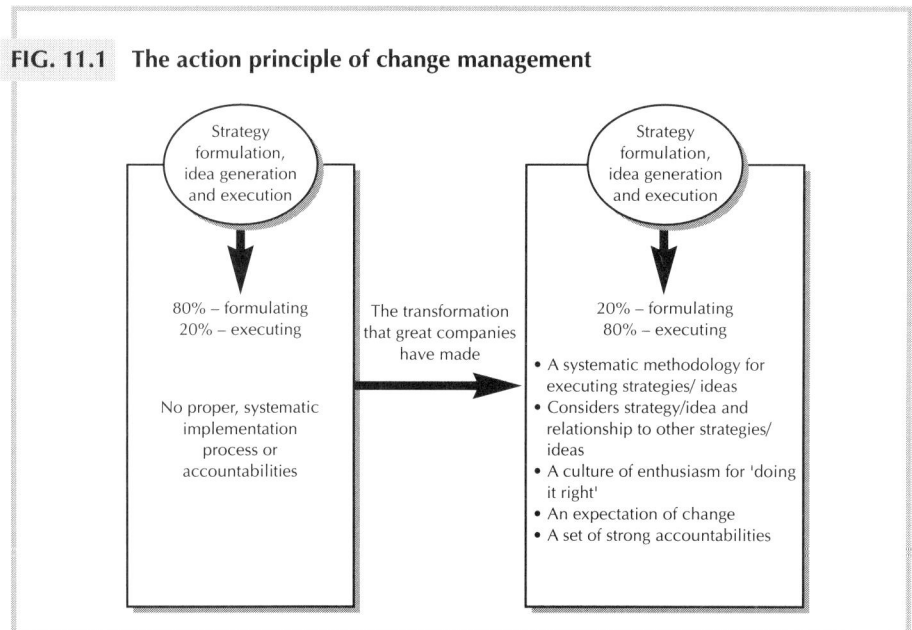

FIG. 11.1 The action principle of change management

Definition of embracing change

The adage that comes to mind about organizations' ability to implement change effectively is that 'The only constant is change itself!'

In recent years, the volatility in business markets has continued to grow.

Turbulence in markets is caused by many factors – elements in the environment in which business is conducted – which we briefly review below.

- New technology. Whether it is information technology, or advanced manufacturing, or process equipment, or telecommunications, these factors are pervasive in reshaping companies and industries like never before.
- New players in industries and new or redefined industries. Manufacturers such as GE and GM are going into financial services.
- New channels of distribution such as electronic commerce.
- Globalization of suppliers and markets, including not only product markets, but also financial markets and labor markets.
- Competition for customers becoming fiercer as industries go into 'over supply'.
- Government regulation is changing character. Some industries are moving towards self-regulation, some to less regulation as companies become larger and more powerful and regulators lose control over currencies and fiscal measures.

In the light of all this pressure we see companies that have hardly changed their basic products and processes for a hundred years having to completely reinvent themselves. Organizations such as banks are spending unprecedented amounts on technology, shifting investments from branches to call centers and electronic media, and coping with new specialist competitors.

For manufacturers, the 1970s, 1980s and 1990s were periods of quality improvement, where superior competitiveness through differentiated quality was possible for most. Although this factor will never fully disappear, there are now many industries where many, or all, players are very good at quality. In these, new dimensions such as speed (see Chapter 10) and mass customization are becoming important.

In the services sector, including retailing, financial, hospitality and others, particularly professional services, quality (as demonstrated by the 'best practice' car manufacturers) has not fully been achieved and the opportunity is still in front of them.

The principle of 'embracing change' is, at a personal level, about behavior and attitudes. Let us again consider two contrasting companies, the first of which comprises mostly people who seek a brave new future, who like the challenge of change and see themselves as being able to cope with and control change. The second is made up mostly of people that shun change, seek stability and avoid uncertainty. Before anything else, how did they arrive at such different positions? The answer must be put down to leadership, not just the distributed leadership principle (see Chapter 5), but first to executive management and the CEO's approach to business life. The CEO can have an

Principle 8: Embracing change

enormous influence on the character of a company. At Hewlett Packard, John Young's '10x challenge', of reducing all process errors and waste to one-tenth of their existing level, transformed the company completely. Jack Welch has remade GE. This is not to mention those who created and built corporations from scratch such as Fred Smith at Federal Express, Steven Jobs at Apple Computers and Bill Gates at Microsoft. These CEOs set the scene entirely. Is the company going to be static, cautious and ultra-conservative, or dynamic and constantly reinventing itself, or most likely somewhere in between? In this regard we have observed two key things about the truly leading organizations we studied.

- It is not possible to be ultraconservative in the year 2000 and beyond and survive. Business conditions are changing too fast. Leading companies embrace change as a fundamental principle of their existence.
- Leading CEOs do take bets but they analyze carefully first and work the odds in their favor. It's not change for change's sake at GE, ABB, HP, Toyota and Sony. It is deliberate, considered, rapid evolution. It is certainly not revolution either, for this is too risky. It is project managed, disciplined (see Chapter 13) movement to a prescribed next stage in a planned multi-year initiative as described in Chapter 1.

While the CEO, Board and executive management are often the authors and leaders of this change plan, it will not be successful unless it takes hold in middle management and at ground level, too. This is where the principles of alignment and distributed leadership come in and drive the company's ability to embrace change.

How do great organizations achieve excellence at implementing new ideas, whether they are innovative new products, management philosophies, business structures or anything else? It is a question of motivation, in this case making it easier, or more attractive, for everyone to move to the new state than to stay put. We observe that the best managers, be they CEOs or middle managers, use both carrot and stick, exercising careful judgement about how and when to use these. These managers spend most of their time giving direction and giving positive strokes and encouraging feedback to those who are moving in an aligned way. However all really competent leaders, like their companies, also have a 'steely edge' of toughness and when the carrot just isn't working, they occasionally must be prepared to wield the stick.

Asking and motivating a single person to change behavior and motivating even a large organization to change are fundamentally the same in principle, although the inertia seems to rise exponentially with company size, due to 'group refuge' and politics factors. In a 70,000-person company we know well, change was very slow even though the business logic for changing was compelling and had been communicated often. The inertia was so extensive because people saw it in their own best interests not to change. After many conferences, speeches, newsletters and debates, the time came for the CEO to get serious and publicly state that anyone blocking the change initiative would be shot at dawn for treason (which was a dramatic term meaning retrenched). It seemed incredible, but many senior executives still didn't sign on, presumably because the company had never ever taken such dramatic action and the blockers had spent over 25 years as colleagues and friends of the CEO. There are no surprises in this case history. The CEO had to fire about a dozen senior executives who simply were not complying with the change initiative. What a great example of the 'boiled frog' syndrome. The retrenchments got everyone's attention and the alignment of the organization improved rapidly. Change was then successfully achieved.

The key question is 'why?' Why does it have to be so hard to dislodge some people, often key people, and lots of them, from their existing positions? We believe it can be best expressed in terms of comfort zones. When the executive management group in a company want to achieve change, individuals will ask 'what's in it for me?', in order to understand whether to move to the new state, or resist change and try to preserve the status quo. In leading companies, the executives who are championing the change initiative work hard to reduce the comfort that people have with the status quo.

> **Executives who are championing the change initiative work hard to reduce the comfort that people have with the status quo.**

It is also important to articulate the attractiveness of the new position being sought. The idea is to make it powerfully more attractive for people at all levels to move rather than resist the change. So leading company executives mount the forces of change, make it clear that not changing is not an option. They continually articulate the personal and organizational benefits of changing. Amazingly, there is still a significant proportion of people, even senior people, who want to resist change and cling to the past. That is when even really good CEOs and executives can be excused for losing patience and getting tough. The resistance seems irrational and from a shareholder value perspective, it really is. The organizational forces required to overcome such resistance must be such as to make it less attractive and ultimately unsustainable to stay put than to embrace the change.

Leading organizations often find that they do it best by working first on the 10 percent of people who are natural 'change embracers', then working on the next 40 percent of the workforce who have been sitting on the fence watching, but not actively resisting. Then the very best of these companies have achieved the ability to have almost all their employees embrace change, collectively and therefore individually. The culture is that change can be of benefit to all, rather than something to be afraid of. This is not to say that these leading companies engage in frequent or continuous change just for the sake of doing it, for that is not true and would not be sensible. Rather they carefully plan, strategically analyze and calculate the costs and benefits first. Leading companies realize that there is risk involved in change, however they take on these calculated risks and explicitly work to manage those uncertainties in their favor. They often use analytical techniques, such as decision analysis, risk analysis or scenario planning. Once the analysis is done and a considered decision is taken, they execute the change with discipline and with professional project management driving the implementation.

For the major change initiative referred to in Figure 1.3 (see Chapter 1), accountabilities for achieving the change are assigned and accepted by the senior team. The broadly based commitment to change is so strong that resistance is futile. Resistors, or those who cannot personally go along with major change, will feel so uncomfortable that they leave. Peer pressure begins to make them feel uncomfortable. The organization then increases its 'embracing change' capability as it loses the 'no' voters.

The notion of organizational focus is strongly related to the principle of embracing change. Simply put, those companies that try too many different initiatives usually lack the focus to make any of them work properly. This is so fundamental as to be a major component of the difference between the ad hoc approach to management (Figure 1.2) and the systematic approach of Figure 1.3. The leading companies we have observed focus on embracing change using the Pareto principle (focus on the vital few things, not the trivial many). They then resource these initiatives properly rather than diffuse resources over too many varied initiatives.

Further, leaders tie their change initiatives to results. They are bottom-line oriented, but also know how to work on the drivers of bottom-line performance too. These clearly include revenue drivers and cost drivers, customer satisfaction and employee satisfaction, as well as the effectiveness of asset utilization. The focus on results connects strategically to the major change initiative providing the motivation for 'embracing change'.

EVALUATION OF THE EMBRACING-CHANGE PRINCIPLE

First consider the organization's overall propensity to embrace change.

> To what extent does the company embrace major change initiatives?
> Low   1 .... 2 .... 3 .... 4 5   High

It is also possible to assess related aspects of the principle of embracing change:

> To what extent are the blockers of change able to 'survive and prosper' in the organization?
> Low   1 . . . . 2 . . . . 3 . . . . 4 5   High
>
> To what extent is the organization focused on a small number of 'vital few' strategic change initiatives?
> Low   1 . . . . 2 . . . . 3 . . . . 4 5   High
>
> To what extent does the organization analyze and carefully plan its change initiatives?
> Low   1 . . . . 2 . . . . 3 . . . . 4 5   High
>
> To what extent does the organization properly resource its key change initiatives (as against expecting them to magically occur for free)?
> Low   1 . . . . 2 . . . . 3 . . . . 4 5   High
>
> To what extent does the organization connect its change initiatives to driving forward on organizational performance?
> Low   1 . . . . 2 . . . . 3 . . . . 4 5   High
>
> To what extent does the organization assign and explicitly use accountabilities for change in order to ensure implementation?
> Low   1 . . . . 2 . . . . 3 . . . . 4 5   High
>
> To what extent are senior managers used as 'champions of change'?
> Low   1 . . . . 2 . . . . 3 . . . . 4 5   High
>
> To what extent are project management disciplines used to plan and execute implementation of change initiatives?
> Low   1 . . . . 2 . . . . 3 . . . . 4 5   High

From these assessments, an organization can understand its strengths and weak spots in terms of the embracing-change principle, and hence use the principle to guide the actions of improvement in change management.

BENEFITS OF EMBRACING CHANGE

As we start the new millennium, the dynamic nature of most markets and economies and the downright instability of some of these mean that the benefits of embracing change should not be considered relative to the status quo base. Rather, consider the consequences of not engaging in major change over the next five years. Will competitiveness stay the same or diminish? As a rule of thumb, improvement rates in competitiveness for most industries increase by at least 5 percent per annum, whether in cost competitiveness,

Principle 8: Embracing change

quality, service, delivery, customer satisfaction, or any other aspect. In really dynamic industries and for industry leaders, rates of improvement exceed 5 percent. So the status quo, of not changing, leads to line 2, not line 1 in Figure 11.2. Those companies that are successful through embracing major change do so by moving, sometimes jumping, to the new curve (line 3 on Figure 11.2). This major change may be new product or services oriented, new process technology, new market or region or segment, new forms of organization such as moving from regional to global focus, a new quality or service initiative, or any of a number of other moves.

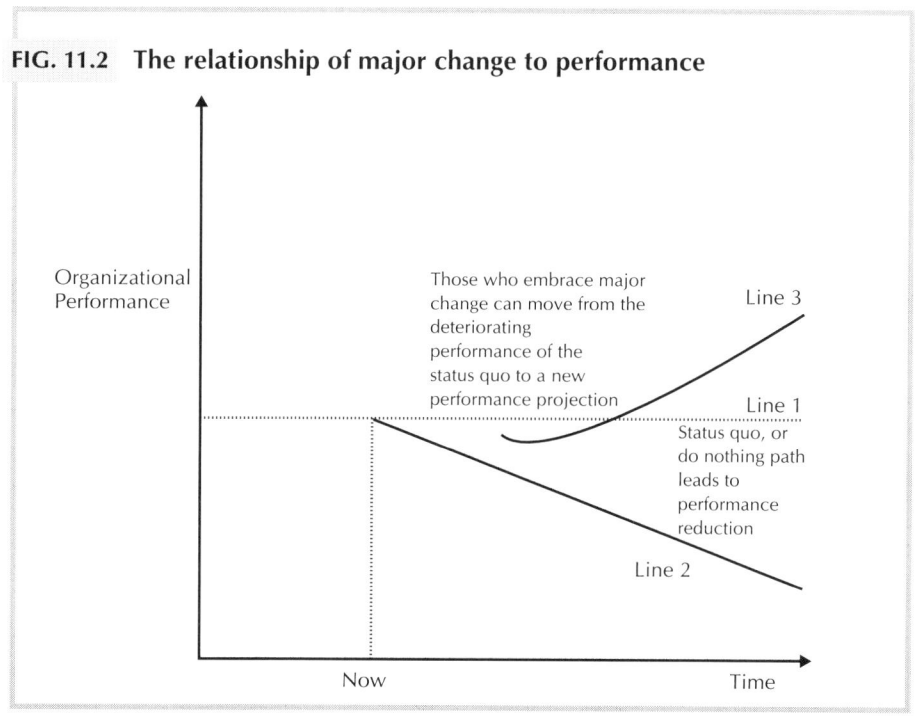

FIG. 11.2 The relationship of major change to performance

Just to achieve and sustain industry parity implies changing as quickly and effectively as your competitors' average. The real benefit comes from being able to embrace change more quickly and effectively than competitors. And it's not just any old change. The single integrated improvement (see Figure 1.3) must be formulated and designed correctly or else changes in accordance with it, even if vigorous, can take you backwards. So it's clear that the wrong strategy, strongly implemented, is not going to get us there, however our experience is more that most companies are not short of good strategy formulation, but rather of implementation. They lack the 'bias for action' that Peters and Waterman described nearly 20 years ago in their path-breaking book *In Search of Excellence*.

The benefits of being strong on the embracing change principle are therefore primarily in terms of competitiveness, whatever the order-winners are for the organization. There are second-level effects that are powerful too, in terms of employees, customers, processes and suppliers. Using the comparison of two companies, 'A' which is very strong on embracing change and company 'B' which is poor on this principle, consider the following questions.

- Which one, A or B, will be better able to anticipate and adapt to customer requirements or competitor offerings?
- Which one, A or B, will be able to take advantage of new product or process technologies?
- Which one will be able to adapt its organizational form and structure more effectively?
- Which one will be better able to enter new markets or even new segments?
- Which one will be better able to implement new business strategies?
- Which one will be able to attract more dynamic people at all levels of employment?
- Which one will be more able to form effective joint ventures or partnerships with suppliers and leading-edge customers?
- In aggregate, which one will be better able to effect planned, disciplined implementation of its single integrated improvement initiative (Figure 1.3) and hence drive its competitiveness?

IMPROVING ON THE EMBRACING-CHANGE PRINCIPLE

Two key questions for every organization are:

- How can the principle of embracing change be strengthened in the company?
- How can improved ability to embrace change be used to improve the organization's adaptability, strategy implementation effectiveness and hence performance?

On the first question, we refer to the discussion on motivating people (Chapter 1) and suggest that again, appeal can and should be made to the three great leverage points of the human body as they apply to work – the heart, the mind and the wallet.

Leaders in great companies go to great lengths to articulate the focussed future state, often two to three years out (see Chapter 9), then they provide the plan for getting from 'here and now' to 'there and then'. However, this is not enough. Even poorly performing companies articulate grand plans of improvement. The difference between true industry leaders and the rest of the pack is implementation effectiveness. Leaders make it happen, laggers see their strategies disappear in a puff of smoke. The leaders do it by appealing to hearts, minds and, where appropriate, wallets, and they are also really tough on 'non-compliance' with the change initiative.

To make it work, responsibility for implementation in leading organizations is assigned to senior executives who sponsor projects and initiatives. These executives accept these responsibilities with zeal and take on the accountability of achieving the result. They monitor progress of the change process, leading from the front and unblocking points of resistance across the organization. They know that the best way to do this is to create 'win-win' outcomes for those who are affected by the change initiatives, including those who may lose local power or whose local empire may be reduced in scale or importance. In those points of resistance, the conflict is between the short-term interest of a divisional, country, or local manager, and the company as a whole. Common sense usually provides the best guide to resolving such conflicts, but astute executives do not shrink back from resolving the issue. This is a key differentiator of good leaders and leading companies in terms of implementation effectiveness. Real leaders will generally step up to such difficult issues, whereas lesser executives tend to put them in the 'too hard' basket. Our experience is that the issues don't go away but rather fester, and they destroy value while doing so.

> *Leaders make it happen, laggers see their strategies disappear in a puff of smoke.*

Leading companies remind themselves frequently that there is 'only one balance sheet', meaning that we should not 'sub-optimize' but rather, using the principle of alignment (see Chapter 4), they are prepared to give up on local loyalties to contribute to the big picture. In great companies, such actions do not go unnoticed and may well lead to personal recognition, promotion or reward down the road. In mediocre and poor companies, people resist change of all kinds unless there is 'something in it for me, today'. Where the concept of win-win, or 'enlightened self-interest', works, that's fine, but sometimes there are local give-ups needed today for overall benefits tomorrow. These situations are the ones where really good leaders show their mettle.

Finally, to achieve a high level of embracing change, leaders lead and others follow a visionary approach of wanting to create their destiny rather than just getting there by chance. They are opportunistic but also careful in calculating which risks they want to run. They plan for the future but also realize that strategy and change emerge as a set of real-time opportunities. And even when they are in leading positions in their industry (see Chapter 7), they are never complacent or vain. Just as elite athletes in most sports are humble about their achievements and talk about further improvement rather than gloat, so do leading executives. Both the outstanding athletes and executives have the same fierce, burning desire within to change and improve.

SUMMARY

The motivation to change in successful companies is normally accompanied by a well-researched plan that is stretching but achievable. The plan works best when it can be connected directly to demonstrable benefits, and some early wins. Successful pilot projects, where time permits, are often a good way to achieve widespread buy-in to change initiatives.

To summarize the 'how-to' of embracing change, successful companies achieve movement through:

- motivation of hearts, minds and wallets – this is done substantially with carrots, but sticks are used where necessary;
- non-compliance equates to treason. It is OK to have debates about the merits of a change initiative, but once the decision is taken, resistance or even passive non-compliance is not tolerated in great organizations;
- responsibility is assigned and accepted;
- accountability for performance outcomes is non-negotiable;
- the organization is led by people who create and foster positive energy in the culture, i.e. 'can do' attitudes;
- dynamic individuals and teams succeed and passive people don't;
- project management disciplines are the platform and structure through which change is successfully managed;
- the benefits of change are won, in other words, the cycle is completed;
- in the very best of companies, learning cycles are in place such that a review of each change initiative is carried out to enable the quality of embracing change to improve as a result of every experience. In these companies, the embracing change principle is consciously and actively managed;
- making the future state desirable and the present state unsustainable;
- making the change effort relevant to the key organizational issues of the day.

12

Principle 9
Learning focus

Never tell the people how to do things. Tell them what to do and they will surprise you with their ingenuity.

George S. Patton, 1944

INTRODUCTION

Learning for all employees is seen as critical to best practice firms. This is born from being always dissatisfied with performance and processes and realizing that improved knowledge translates into improved processes and then performance. We have noted that employees in leading companies work actively to transfer knowledge to others. They do not feel threatened by knowledge transfer, but rather, acknowledge the value of this activity in securing future firm prosperity. Ranging from multi-skilling to management think-tanks, excellent firms invest in the brains of all of their employees.

This learning is not necessarily confined to employee development. Leading companies also have a focus on collective learning, for the company itself. The organization actively manages learning at an organizational level as well as an individual or team level. The organization realizes the importance of its knowledge base, ultimately above and beyond that of any individual, but closely tied to that of all its people's intellect and skills. For example, General Motors uses technology alliances to stay up with a variety of new process technologies that pertain to its manufacturing and assembly systems as well as to automotive components technologies. This is an investment in learning and knowledge at an organizational level.

Another characteristic that differentiates leading firms is that learning requirements are driven by their need to develop their core capabilities set – those things that make a difference to business performance (principle 13). Learning is not driven by external agendas (national training and workplace reform agendas, awards, union influences, etc.).

In another example, a paper manufacturing company has embraced open learning concepts to encourage employees who want to develop skills but who may be unable to attend conventional study courses for reasons that include irregular working hours, family commitments, distance, etc. Employees are able to learn wherever and whenever they choose (see Figure 12.1).

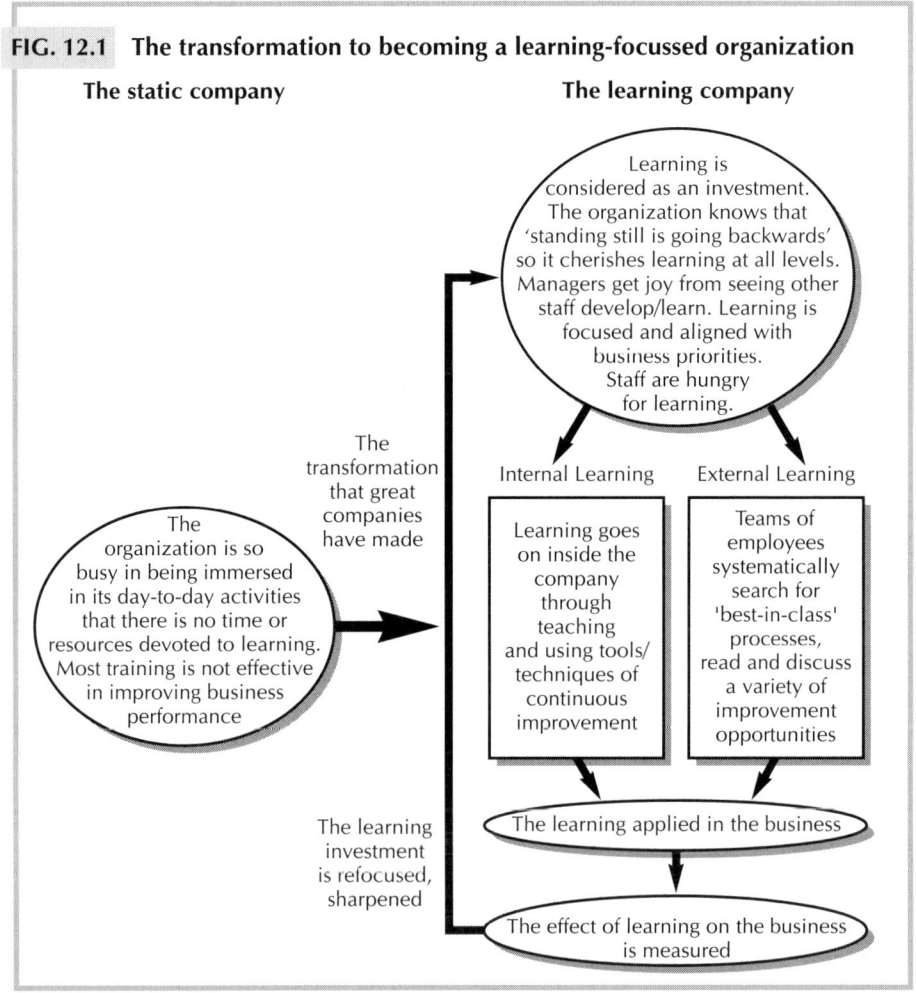

FIG. 12.1 The transformation to becoming a learning-focussed organization

Definition of learning focus

Name one organization that leads its industry, that stands out from the pack in any substantial, sustainable way, that hasn't invested in a big way in its people and their knowledge, skills and capabilities. Sony, Xerox, Toyota, 3M, GE and HP all got to where they are through making major investments in human resource development. It is particularly true in the information age that learning and knowledge throughout a workforce are key to competitive advantage. The principles of distributed leadership and measurement reporting provide both the delegated responsibility and the data for staff at all levels to excel through 'Job 2' (see Chapter 13), with the remaining element being the emphasis on knowledge and learning. We have seen this principle applied in large organizations such as NUMMI (Adler, 1992) and in small companies, particularly high technology or professional service firms.

FLETCHER CHALLENGE

A company with a real investment and commitment to learning is Fletcher Challenge. This New Zealand based company has as one of its divisions its Building Products Sector, which regularly sponsors substantial teams of people to visit the best companies in the world and to hungrily and systematically learn through benchmarking their systems and processes. Everyone in this company is on a learning curve and these learning curves are both individual and collective. The company has actually formed a subsidiary 'learning company', focussed entirely on the development of its human resource, which it sees as critical to its future. This focus on 'learning from the best' comes from an inspired leader who knows that the growth and development of his 1,500 people is critical to the growth and development of the businesses he controls.

Investments are made in the knowledge of employees at a number of levels as described below.

At its business conferences a mix of managers and workers present on their accomplishments and discuss how to improve further. A 'best practice' instance of this was an employee who stood up in front of 150 people, including all the company's managers and the CEO, to tell her story of being 'digitally challenged' (unable to switch on a computer) when she joined the company 12 months previously. She was a press operator with little formal education, but her attitude was right in that she hungered to better herself, and in so doing, contribute more to the company that just running the press the same way each day. She took the opportunity to do a series of computer courses, sponsored by the company but mostly in her own time, and in 12 months had become a spreadsheet wizard. During a three-month period, she had used this knowledge to produce spreadsheet models of the press and its performance. This work was supported by the maintenance and engineering support functions of her business. The project demonstrated that under certain operating conditions the press performed better in terms of both productivity and quality and she was even able to relate this 'optimal operating schedule' to differences in the properties of raw materials coming in to 'her' press. Business benefits resulted. While not all of the 1,500 personal stories in this company were as dramatic as this one, in terms of skills and knowledge, essentially everyone in the company was on a strong and powerful personal learning curve of some kind.

Another learning investment that the company made was in study tours. Comprising senior and junior people (including production supervisors and operators), these tours involved teams of between 5–25 people going to wherever in the world there was significant learning to be gained. Having organized and participated in some of these, we can hardly find the words to describe the power and intensity of learning achieved during these exercises, that were typically of about 7–10 days duration. As structured learning exercises, small teams of (usually) three people within the larger group focussed on assembling knowledge about how the world's best companies go about their business, whether it is sales, value creation, production/operations, leadership, customer service, quality (get it right the first time!) or any other aspect of importance to the business. These series of visits involved a lot of professional pre-reading and research on the companies visited, intensive 16–18 hour work days during the process of visits, and a series of debrief meetings, reports and dissemination seminars when back home.

Each business unit was then expected to use the knowledge gained to implement improvements in the business that had a demonstrable performance lift. Although they did not go so far as to measure a direct return on the investments made in knowledge and learning from these study tours, it is clear to us that these investments, of between $100,000 and $600,000 per study tour, were very worthwhile, based on the changes that resulted. The benefits came not just because of the learning but also due to the company's ability to embrace change (see Chapter 11).

These direct benefits of adopting what was seen in global leaders were not the only ones. For years after the visit, participants used the knowledge gained to enhance their business processes. The impact on staff morale at all levels was impressive, too. Participants were personally and collectively invigorated by the opportunities given to them. Through the internal

Principle 9: Learning focus

> conferences and workshops that followed the study tours, this energy spread around the whole business group.
>
> Further, follow-up visits were arranged of small groups of the company's staff to return to some of the companies that were visited and studied, and reciprocal visits occurred as well. Some ongoing business information exchanges developed. These 'secondary' or indirect benefits lasted for years, as did the direct business improvements that resulted from adapting the practices employed in the great companies we visited and implementing them.
>
> Another benefit of all this activity and investment in personal and collective learning was in positioning this company in the labor market. The CEO was clearly of the view that to become and remain a superior performer in their industry, it was critical to be able to attract and retain the highest caliber of staff at all levels. Where would talented, energetic people who thirst for bettering themselves want to work? Clearly in a company that is strong on the principle of learning!
>
> ●●●●●●●●●●●●●●●●●●●

It is interesting and not surprising that this company was the subject of some turnover, essentially at all levels during this period, which we ascribe to a number of dynamics:

- knowing of the high skills and dynamism of culture in the company, some key managers and shop floor people were, purely and simply, poached by other companies, often being offered significantly higher levels of responsibility in their new company;
- along with the business learning, all employees, from CEO to every employee, were given a chance to examine their alignment with the company's values through a very comprehensive leadership workshop that everyone took part in. Comprising between one to three days of workshop sessions, these sessions made some employees realize that their values did not fit those of the company very well and some of these staff chose to set themselves free;
- as a result of the study tours, the company found that it could operate on a much leaner basis in terms of indirect and overhead staff, and reorganized to eliminate many processes, and some people, that were not adding net value.

Although we can say from close, first-hand knowledge that some of the people who were lost were truly outstanding individuals, the losses and turnover were turned into opportunities for further change, improvement and the introduction of fresh ideas and approaches.

Whatever the approach, whether it's the GE workout system, or conventional staff and management development, the best, most effective learning occurs when directly embedded in business improvement. In a GM engine plant we are familiar with, learning centers were built right in the middle of the plant. Teams of workers undertake a week's intensive learning in which they review business imperatives, quality improvement and just-in-time supply and production. The principles of learning, discipline, embracing change and distributed leadership are all intertwined in this process, such that the ideas presented in the learning center are immediately applied by the natural work teams, to improve their 'QCD' (quality, cost, delivery) outcomes.

One very powerful technique used by GM is to micro-analyze the time spent (in seconds) on tasks and classify these as either 'value adding' or 'non-value adding'. Value adding tasks are essentially those that customers are prepared to pay for. For example, customers would be prepared to pay the reasonable cost of inserting the piston assemblies into the engine cylinders, because they want their automobile delivered that way. However, considering the totality of activity conducted by the team of workers who are responsible for 'pistons into cylinders', there are many non-value adding tasks that customers would rather not pay for, and the business opportunity is to reduce or eliminate these. These include inefficiencies of walking (e.g. to get parts), waiting and re-doing work.

The learning center accomplished an amazing thing in this workforce. The tools and techniques of 'time and motion' study, once the domain of industrial engineering specialists and hated and sabotaged by workers, were now being placed in the hands of those very workers. Further, through the principle of distributed leadership, these workers have accepted these tools and the responsibility for using them to improve QCD outcomes. These tools have become the method and structure through which 'Job 2' is accomplished in such GM plants. This learning was spread throughout some 2,000 people and the productivity and quality lift was impressive.

Next, this company realized that these techniques and this approach is not 'just a factory thing' and considered whether a similar approach would work in the sales force, the design office, the finance and administration departments, human resources, even in the executive suite! The answer was a resounding 'yes'. This example of 'world class learning' is so not because of the investment in learning itself, but because of the integration of learning and business improvement, producing at least four major benefits.

- The knowledge itself is of lasting use, of being able to distinguish value from non-value adding activities.
- The learning is more effective and more likely to 'stick' with employees because of the way that learning is integrated intimately with real applications that are close to the people's work place. Learning new things and using the knowledge is seen as one entity in this initiative.

Principle 9: Learning focus

- The payback period to the company that makes learning investments in this way is anything from ten minutes to a couple of weeks. The substantial benefits from placing the tools of 'industrial engineering/process improvement' in all workers' hands and applying them immediately to real work processes are fast pick-ups in productivity and quality.
- The effective learning and associated process and business improvement helps create a virtuous cycle of improving morale, pride, commitment and employee satisfaction, that can be further harnessed and energized towards even more business improvement work. In the world's leading companies, the learning principle is intertwined with those of embracing change and of discipline and distributed leadership. In these organizations, it is 'cool' to be strong on personal business alignment of values and on having a strong connection between individual and team 'micro' contribution and the 'macro' big picture.

EVALUATION OF THE LEARNING PRINCIPLE

To what extent is:
Individual development for all employees a strategic business objective?

    Low   1 .... 2 .... 3 .... 4 5   High

Learning and skills development linked and focussed towards business strategies and change drivers?

    Low   1 .... 2 .... 3 .... 4 5   High

The organization skilled and capable at idea capture and management of its important knowledge areas?

    Low   1 .... 2 .... 3 .... 4 5   High

Accountability for learning taken by all employees?

    Low   1 .... 2 .... 3 .... 4 5   High

Accountability for learning shared by the company?

    Low   1 .... 2 .... 3 .... 4 5   High

A solid resource base (budget) allocated to support learning?

    Low   1 .... 2 .... 3 .... 4 5   High

The workforce aware that learning leads to a win-win positive outcome?

    Low   1 .... 2 .... 3 .... 4 5   High

BENEFITS OF LEARNING

In the present and future world where competition is fierce and getting fiercer, markets are turbulent, customers are demanding and choosy, and shareholders aggressively seeking success and high returns, with low switching costs in all the three markets (labor, products and services, financial) that managers must compete in (see Chapter 1), improvement through learning is a must.

Companies like Fletcher Challenge, GE, GM, Sony and Toyota are seen by many as an 'employer of first choice' because existing and potential employees know they will get skills and knowledge from the employment relationship, as well as pay. A selection process will eventually lead to a matching between companies with a strong desire for learning and improvement and similar individuals, who want to better themselves and 'get ahead' through better skills and knowledge.

At the other end of the scale, those individuals who work only to exchange labor hours for dollars will find matching companies. The clear benefit is in the rate of business improvement that is achieved. If 5 percent improvement per year is an average for an industry, then 'best' companies are probably improving (through learning, knowledge and application of these) at double that rate, or 10 percent per annum, whereas the 'ordinary' companies are not changing at all, indeed they are going backwards in relative terms.

Xerox used a major learning initiative to drive its business improvement initiative when it was fighting to restore its competitiveness and market share in the late 1980s. Xerox gave all its 100,000 workers a minimum of 40 hours each of behavioral and process improvement learning programs. The programs involved a carefully conceived LUTI (learn, use, train, inspect) system, in which the knowledge was passed 'down the line' from top management, through middle management, to production or sales office, etc. The system involves a manager learning the material (such as a standard way to identify and solve problems, improve processes, etc.) using the material in daily work, then training others such as direct reports with the same techniques. The manager then 'inspects' the use of the techniques in their department. Learning and training are thus a line activity rather than something for specialists. There is quite a lot of support needed for this to happen from professional trainers and program designers.

GE have similarly invested large amounts of resources in staff at all levels, and this has been a distinguishing feature of that company. Having been involved in workshop processes in GE, we can certainly attest to the powerful thirst for 'learning combined with business improvement' as suggested by a GE executive when discussing their approach. The present GE focus on 'six-sigma' quality requires incredible discipline and very real knowledge-based improvement all the way up and down the line.

In sum, the benefits of all this learning are that employees and their work processes will be better able *and* better motivated to do things better for customers and do things at lower cost. This drives both ends of the profit and loss statement. The learning focus is a very powerful principle in any organization and the benefits do not have to be far down the road at all, because any company can do as GM and GE do, namely integrate learning and improvement.

IMPROVING ON THE LEARNING-FOCUS PRINCIPLE

The good news is that at the turn of the millennium, we have a solid two decades of experience as to how effective learning occurs in the work place. First, leading companies make a serious commitment of resources. How much money should be spent over the next 12 months on the learning investment in the organization? $200 or less, $500, $1,000, $1,500, $2,000 per person?

Second, we would argue that there is no need to reinvent the learning wheel. There are many excellent systems and processes including LUTI (learn, use, train, inspect) systems, self-paced systems, multimedia systems and education establishments that can help.

Third, there are no universal answers as to what should be the focus of learning and how it should occur, but there is a lot of information around as to how the best companies go about learning. It will be very different in large companies to small ones. It also depends on the strengths/weaknesses that the company has on other key principles such as alignment and distributed leadership.

Fourth, despite our view that there are no universal solutions, we do hold strongly that the most successful learning involves connecting it directly with business improvement.

Fifth, the most successful companies start at the top and none of the really successful companies make the mistake of putting a learning initiative in place 'down there' only. The best learning initiatives are where executives lead from the front. This relates strongly to the types of actions involved in the up front principle. Then executives who have been involved in a learning/improvement initiative can ask their staff to follow, as in 'Do as I do, this is great'. The other approach, of 'You need this, but I don't', leads to resistance and frequent failure. (Think of this as waste of all forms.)

Finally, leading companies do not use sledge-hammers to crack a nut. They carefully select and design the learning content and format, being flexible to individual needs, but often ensuring that core learning is common to all. This provides a common language, process and knowledge base around the organization, setting it up to move forward.

SUMMARY

An ideal learning/improvement environment was created at Semco and another in Kodak Australia, in which executives clearly led from the front in both cases.

In Kodak, the CEO set personal improvement goals, a measurement index of performance for himself and his senior colleagues, and then demonstrated how serious he was about learning by driving the processes that he was involved in forward aggressively. Then, and only then, did he ask the same of others in the company, and the cascading process began. The same process occurred in Hewlett Packard, which can be traced back to its origins in HP's Japanese division 30 years ago and was followed in the USA, then taken worldwide by the CEO 'of the 80s', John Young. HP, under the leadership of John Young, achieved a planned, ten-year, ten-fold reduction in quality-related costs, from over 20 percent of sales, to 2 percent of sales. A saving of a massive 18 percent of sales was made and kept up associated with dramatically higher customer satisfaction, higher productivity and much higher company stock values. Did all this happen by itself, or because the CEO gave an inspired speech or even hundreds of such speeches. Did John Young have a magic wand that only a few CEOs had? Clearly not, but rather HP made a very substantial investment in training and education of its staff, a big multi-year investment driven by the learning principle. That major investment set up the human resource capability needed to achieve the ambitious goal set by the CEO.

The learning focus that is common to leading companies is closely connected to the other principles that concern staff. Without the learning however, principles such as alignment, distributed leadership, micro to macro and even the principle of discipline are really difficult to achieve. With a learning ethos in the organization, and actions to match, the sky is the limit.

13

Principle 10
Being disciplined

> *'Tough' doesn't mean beating up on people. It means sticking to the necessary policies and actions no matter how enticing the reasons for easing up.*
>
> Philip Crosby

INTRODUCTION

Best practice firms have not simply empowered their workforces and 'set them free'. This would be a ridiculous notion, ultimately leading to anarchy. Top companies have more form and structure rather than less, lots of standardization and documentation, with a strong systems perspective. By discipline, we do not mean the notion of punishment but we do mean a high degree of 'structuredness' within the workplace and an adherence to doing things consistently in the right manner. We note that what is 'right' will be different for companies that are primarily process-focussed, market-focussed relationship-focussed or customer-focussed. In a process-focussed oil refinery, right means doing it by the book and sticking with protocols and standards precisely in the plant. In a luxury hotel, right means allowing all staff to break the rules, or at least allowing staff to interpret rules much more loosely than in the oil refinery, in responding to customer requirements.

Many organizations seem to have confused empowerment with abandonment. A number of firms have stripped middle levels of management from their organization to facilitate increased speed of decision making, improved communication and elimination of a (perceived) barrier to change. However many of these have failed to put adequate systems in place that address the 'supporting' aspects of middle management job roles. These include activities like developing work procedures and job standards, establishing goals and measures, recording and analyzing equipment performance, setting and managing budgets and assuring quality. These standardization and documentation activities are not bureaucratic but support the development of individuals and teams. Too many firms have failed to differentiate between *coercive* and *enabling* forms of bureaucracy (Adler, 1992).

Consider McDonald's. It is well known that McDonald's provides consistently standard products and services across time and across the globe. The systems and the disciplines of these standards, in order to achieve such consistency, are nothing short of terrific, whether one's personal taste is 'for' or 'against' their Big Macs.

Now consider a wonderfully disciplined automotive company such as Toyota. At Toyota plants we have visited, the shopfloor are working more than 90 percent of their time on value-added tasks, and they are doing so in a highly standardized, carefully designed manner. Without the disciplines of these workplace and if we had really 'set everybody free' from the shackles of the feudal system which was the forerunner of our earlier industrial and human resource policies, we would find that every Big Mac was different and that some Toyotas had three wheels while others had five, and occasionally some would have four wheels. These companies have achieved self-discipline and team disciplines in the workplace as positive influences on getting the job done (see Figure 13.1).

Consider a bank with 1,000 branches offering the same transactional and lending products across its network. In our experience, there is room for improvement in terms of the disciplines of standardization and process management in most of these organizations. We have found banks doing things differently in different branches and certainly in different regions because of the lack of discipline and standardization. As a result of this, these organizations pay a major 'cost of complexity', have high error rates, and are lacking in efficiency compared to best practice 'disciplined' organizations such as Medco, McDonald's and Toyota. There is lots of room for improvement in respect of the application of discipline and process standardization in most organizations but it is particularly acute in the private services sector and in government and never more so than in the professional services sector.

Holden's Engine Company and General Motor's Holden Commodore plant have 'everything in its place' policies. Every tool in the workshop has a set place and even the pot plants within the factory have circles painted on the floor to indicate their correct position! The precision and the standardization at first seem to be 'over the top' in some of these sites, but these symbols set a standard of discipline which everyone is expected to apply in their value-adding work. There is no such thing as a tolerance of error and sloppiness in these organizations. At the Uncle Ben's (Mars Corporation) factory in

Principle 10: Being disciplined

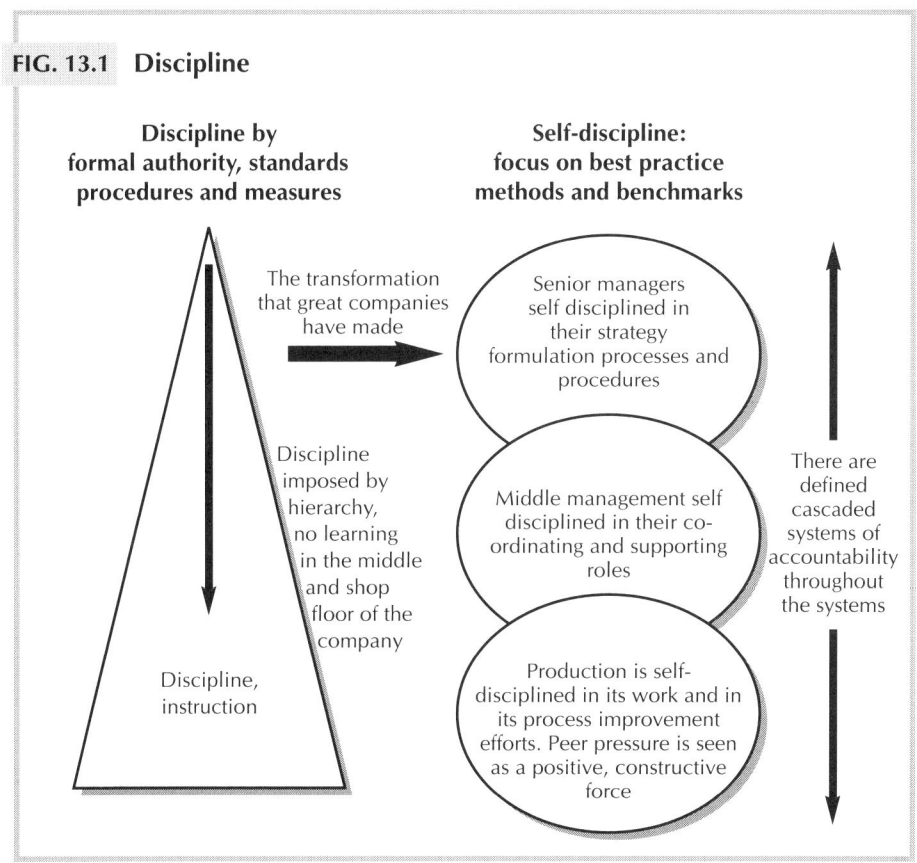

FIG. 13.1 Discipline

Wodonga that produces over 2 million cans of pet food per day, there is a very strong set of disciplines as explained by the relationship between their systems, structure and behaviors. At this site, all employees clock on every day, which sets a standard about punctuality. This includes all job grades including the chief executive. Nobody clocks off. There are rewards paid to employees for continued punctuality and attendance and everyone understands and adheres to the disciplines of these standards and expectations. It pervades the whole company in every process that it engages in.

In virtually every excellent company we have contact with, there is a strong focus on process disciplines and standards. Good airlines and manufacturers have been doing this for decades. Good banks, insurers and hotels are following rapidly in these disciplines.

Is there one best way?

This raises the issue of whether there is 'one best way' to operate a process. Many have criticized the 'one best way' approach of Henry Ford in the Model T Ford assembly line process and blamed 'Taylorism' for our poor industrial systems. What do best practice companies do in the late 1990s and beyond? Was Henry Ford's way and Taylor's way right or wrong? Based on detailed observation of many successful service and manufacturing organizations, we believe the Ford way of the 1910 system may well have been best practice then and is still half right today. There were essentially two major ideas in early models of industrial production. One was that processes should be conducted in the standard 'one best way'. The second idea was that the one best way should be identified and controlled by specialists (e.g. industrial engineers) and managers, and that production workers or salesmen etc. should just do what they were told. This 'military' model of blind obedience leads to deskilling and little or no continuous improvement of processes, because managers and specialists can't know the detail of how to make thousands of small changes to production, administrative and sales processes. So we relied on infrequent, large-step breakthroughs or brilliant innovations.

This was not Taylor's view, rather he was a strong advocate for a democratic process and of more rather than less power to the shop floor. Taylor advocated industrial progress and harmony through co-operation, as a major change from the military model of management. In many ways Taylor was 'ahead of his time' and many of his fundamental ideas of management make a great deal of sense today, some 100-plus years after he started his work.

Then we saw a re-industrialized Japan, which had listened to Deming and others, and had involved workers in process improvement. We tried to borrow the practice of quality circles, which worked well in some places for a while but then fell away. This was because we had failed to make a number of other deeper, more fundamental changes and *because we tried to bring in a new practice without having any of the right principles in place to guide its use*.

Now we can, with the wisdom of hindsight, say that the Henry Ford/Taylor approach of 'one best way' was and still is substantially right because best companies have applied a very high degree of discipline and standardization to their work in order to run their processes in the 'one best way'. The best known example is McDonald's. However we now know that there is more to it than that! Let us describe these best company practices as if *everyone* has two jobs. The first job, we'll call Job 1 is to efficiently run the processes the 'one best way', doing it 'by the book' in a standard, disciplined manner. This presumes there is a 'book' of process maps to conform to, which not all processes and companies yet have. To summarize this best lets call this 'conformance to standard'. But this is not enough.

Job 2 is where each and every member of an organization, especially the frontline workers, have the commitment and skill to constantly strive to improve Job 1. This is not done in an unstructured, ad hoc way in good companies. It is formalized. When a better way is found to run a process, the previous 'best way' is improved, then refrozen to a new standard in its new 'better way'. All this presumes that the organization has made the transformation from treating its frontline staff like 'mindless robots', to recognizing that only frontline staff really know the process problems and therefore can know the improvement opportunities. Best companies have harnessed the brainpower of their whole workforce in doing Job 2 as well as the doing power of Job 1. Companies who are only using their workforce for Job 1 can rarely survive for long if their direct competitors are truly mature at company-wide Job 2. So to summarize this, best workforce management practice must add the Job 2 task of 'process and performance improvement' to Job 1, of 'conformance'. The world's best companies, such as Xerox and Toyota even have standard protocols for doing Job 2 in a standard way!

Job 2 clearly relies on the principles of discipline, learning and distributed leadership.

Definition of discipline

As described earlier, the nature of disciplines observed in industry leaders we have visited or worked with is of an enabling nature, and certainly does not mean coercion or punishment. Rather it is as expressed by one executive in Hewlett Packard as 'Say what you do, and always do what you say'. More than this, the disciplines that are common to 'best in class' companies derive from a formality that they have and a desire to adhere to systems and structures for doing things. In operational terms, on the front line, whether in a hotel, supermarket, bank or factory, this means setting and adhering to work process and product/service standards.

Consider a bank with 20 retail regions and 200 retail branches, in which retail sales staff issue home loans, personal loans and a variety of other products. How many different ways should each of these products ideally be configured? Is it OK to have 200 ways to open a checking account? Does this drive efficiency and effectiveness up or down? Think of the inefficiency in the 'back office' processing area of the bank when they get dozens of differently configured sets of documentation passed to them by the front office for say, business loans. There is tremendous 'to-ing and fro-ing' inside the bank across departments and, even worse, back to the customer 'for more information' due to the lack of standards and discipline in the first instance. The lending decision process takes longer, costs much more and is higher in default risk due to the lack of rigor and standards. Customers may become impatient and

PART 2 • MANAGEMENT BY PRINCIPLES

> ### SYSTEMS OF DISCIPLINE AT MEDCO
>
> Medco dispenses medicines by mail to 50 million patients in North America. As Bob Despina, Vice-President of the New Jersey Pharmacy said, 'We have SOPs (standard operating procedures) for absolutely everything. After all, the products we are distributing are medicines! The industry standard is one non-conformance per 10,000 items and we are better than twice as good as that standard'. It should be noted that a non-conformance might be a single typo on an instruction sheet or prescription. The systems and standardized practiced disciplines are evident as one walks around the New Jersey Pharmacy. The rigors required of this operation are immense when one considers that Medco is mass-producing hundreds of thousands of scripts to each individual customized requirement. The disciplines are reinforced with an intensive set of measures and fast feedback and reporting of those outcome measures. Critical measures include customer service, quality, cost per unit and turnaround time.
>
> At Medco, there is a clear understanding and delineation between what we call 'Job 1' and 'Job 2'. Job 1 is to run the standard operating processes and procedures of the organization, and to do this in a very disciplined way by the book. In other words Job 1 is about conforming to the standard operating procedures and standards and Medco is meticulous in its drive to achieve this. Medco also is strongly engaged in Job 2, where Job 2 is to continuously improve the standards and the operating procedures but in a structured and formalized way. Medco only undertakes about half a dozen improvement projects at once across the organization. It is not involved in a multitude of continuous improvement projects but has used the Pareto principle of focussing on the vital few rather than the trivial many and uses continuous improvement teams (call quality action teams) to drive home the benefits of its major process improvement projects.

leave, to find someone who can get it right the first time, quickly. Employees at all levels are frustrated and dissatisfied with their work.

How would this better organization do it? They have clear product and process standards as well as service standards, and these are specified, communicated and adhered to. This takes a high degree of organizational discipline! Every lending officer in every branch 'in the field' adheres to the process requirement and collects the necessary information such that the loan application file is in specification when it reaches the 'credit assessment

Principle 10: Being disciplined

office'. This saves time, money and relieves an enormous amount of frustration for everyone, including the customer.

The same applies to many pure service situations. Good restaurants have product and process standards that they adhere to. McDonald's is probably the most obvious and globally famous example of adhering to product and service standards, anywhere, anytime. Some would say they have created enormous value from this standardization, to the point where standardization to that level can be considered an 'art-form'. Clearly, we would agree that there is great value to McDonald's customers and therefore to their shareholders in this adherence to standards, but let us also clearly make no mistake about whether this is the result of art or science. Art has nothing to do with it; everything is nailed down and the objective is to create such effective control over all organizational processes that nothing is left to chance. It may not be 'science' in a purely technical sense, but it is as close to 'organizational science' as we can get, in the sense that everything is designed and managed as a set of systems.

> *This rapid growth was built on particularly strong systems that could be taken anywhere and uncompromising disciplines of adherence to these standards.*

The discipline in excellent companies such as McDonald's comes from its systems and published standards plus the accountability and training that enables adherence to these standards. We can easily observe many of the systems and disciplines in the retail outlets of companies like McDonald's. The manufacturing (cooking and packaging) processes have a real precision to them, coming from both technical inputs and operator controls. Behind the systems that the consumer can see are further sets of strict disciplines, of raw material standards, staff training, retail store design and construction, franchising standards, financial disciplines and many others. The result is many billions of products produced efficiently and sold at a profit with enormous repurchase rates and customer loyalty. No matter whether or not any of us personally likes the products, it is impossible not to admire the tremendous organization and management that led this company to revolutionize the fast-food business and create a truly global empire in a very short time. This rapid growth was built on particularly strong systems that could be taken anywhere and uncompromising disciplines of adherence to these standards.

There is no difference in how this principle applies across any industry. Let's move a long way from fast food to oil, gas and petrochemicals or indeed to any processing or manufacturing company.

At one of the world's chemical giants, ICI, in their integrated plastics plants that crack naptha, electrolyze salt and then make a range of plastics such as the polythene (plastic wrap) used in packaging that we consume every day, consider the role of process disciplines. First consider the 'old ICI' where one of us worked as a development engineer two decades ago. The main chemical processes run continuously, 24 hours per day, and the first thing that happened on every change of shift was that the new shift would re-set all the process settings such as operating temperature etc. to their favorite settings, simply because of personal or 'team' preference. The plant ran reasonably well, about the same under both sets of operating conditions. Next morning the day shift would come in and reset the plant yet again. This might be OK except for one critical thing, the product specifications were slightly different, which made life very difficult for customers who bought the raw plastic and had to deal with these variations in their extrusion processes.

This variation was completely unnecessary, and in the 'new ICI' plant standards have been achieved that everyone adheres to and the product variation is essentially eliminated. All it needed was the application of the principle of discipline, as well as measurement and reporting (see Chapter 14) and the distributed leadership (see Chapter 5) that led to successful implementation.

There is another major and obvious benefit from having the disciplines of process focus systems standards that is very powerful. If the process is not 'nailed down' to a consistent standard, it is hard and may be even impossible to engage in systematic improvement. Given the different way that the 'old ICI' allowed its shift teams to operate the plant, improvements to 'the process' were not possible because there was simply not one single process standard to improve. Even new investments in improved technology were much harder because of the unnecessary operational variance they had to contend with and be rebuilt to. In the 'new ICI', process improvement is formalized from one standard to the new improved standard, and follows the sensible 'unfreeze, change, refreeze' approach that can only occur if the discipline principle is in place.

It is the same in services. In a bank where each branch has its own favorite way of conducting a process like opening a new account, how does the organization engage in process improvement? In 200 branches, there are at least 200 versions of the process to improve, and it usually becomes all too hard. The will to improve is there but the means is not because of the lack of discipline, meaning lack of process focus and standards. We would probably all agree that of these 200+ ways of opening an account, some must be substantially more efficient than others, but the inefficiency remains embedded in, due to the lack of process discipline. Back to McDonald's, if an employee in the field or a technician in a quality control laboratory identifies an improvement that is worthwhile implementing, can it be effected? The answer is clearly yes, with speed and positive outcomes, based on disciplines of doing 'Job 1' on which 'Job 2' improvement work can be built.

Many people who work in organizations that do not have a strong set of disciplines often respond negatively to the notion of discipline as a fundamental principle of good management. The common criticism is that 'Discipline comes

Principle 10: Being disciplined

with bureaucracy, which is bad'. This is a critical touchpoint of the discipline principle. It is true that discipline requires systems to replace art, standards to replace variance and chaos and policies to replace whim and capriciousness in the workplace. These systems, policies and standards do require administration, some would say bureaucracy and we accept that, but it is value-adding, not destructive bureaucracy. The bureaucracy of providing standards and measuring to those standards provides the platform through which every hamburger or bank loan or hotel room can reach the specification. This platform can then be adjusted in the spirit of improvement, and even leads to a better platform for continuous improvement, or 'Kaizen'. So in the world's best companies, it is a 'Yes' to a limited amount of bureaucracy, and a rejection of the myth that bureaucracy is necessarily bad. The extent of discipline that is optimal is a function of the type of business being conducted, its industry position and strategy, and the degree of stability in the business environment.

> **Bureaucracy that provides and spreads best practice systems, and supports improvement of practices and processes, is greatly value adding.**

Bureaucracy can be enabling in style, not coercive. Bureaucracy that exists purely to administer central power generally is value destroying, but bureaucracy that provides and spreads best practice systems, and supports improvement of practices and processes, is greatly value adding, and in fact is the ultimate basis for the existence of large organizations.

Why does a globally successful company such as Shell exist on this multinational basis and generally out-compete single site retail petrol outlets? If it is not the systems and process standards that lead to product and service standards, then what is it? Some people might, in playing 'devil's advocate', say it is the strong Shell brand. Let's test that, very simply, by considering what would happen to the brand and its value if the process, product and services standards were relaxed or did not exist. Clearly, the brand is there to signify these standards, and brand value would quickly erode then evaporate if process, product and service standards are relaxed.

What would 'McDonald's' mean without the principle of discipline that drives the standards in everything it does? We think the answer is 'very little'. It is as fundamental as that, and industry leaders such as Shell, McDonald's, Sony, Hewlett Packard and Singapore Airlines have consciously used the principle of discipline to take them 'out front' in their industries.

A second criticism is that discipline stifles creativity and innovation. We agree that coercive discipline surely does drive out creativity, but the principle of discipline as applied by leading companies is enabling, not coercive. The creative aspects of 'Job 2' can be much better implemented in a company that is strongly disciplined in its work, rather than one that is undisciplined. Some companies have even created and achieved success from applying the principle of discipline to their 'Job 2'. The improvement processes and change processes themselves, that is Job 2, are done in standard ways. People are skilled up with standard language, tools and techniques for improvement itself.

One of the very best companies we have worked with in this regard is GE. The discipline of fundamental process is very strong in GE, whether it's widgets or financial services, and GE has very strongly disciplined structures for process change. We were very impressed with the level of statistical skills and formality of analysis with which GE Capital Finance approached business improvement, when we were called in to assist. Further, although GE is a company of a high degree of discipline, with strict standards, having embarked on a global pursuit of 6-sigma quality[1] in all its business process, there is a superb sense of dynamism and energy at grass-roots levels in this company. Clearly GE has achieved much of the enabling discipline without the stifling or coercive aspects, as there is little evidence of the form of bureaucracy that impedes progress. Rather, GE's bureaucracy demands progress and facilitates it through the discipline provided in policies, standard practices and performance requirements.

Let's test the 'stifling creativity' criticism in the extreme of a project-based company such as a management consultancy, or even an advertising agency. The CEO of a large and quite successful advertising agency once challenged our principle of discipline, claiming that she needed 'empowered, free-wheeling, creative artists and artisans'. We understood this reaction, and asked her a series of follow-up questions:

Question How much of your workforce is really engaged in the creation of concepts and how much in 'production', that is bringing concepts to reality?

Answer It would be 5 percent creative effort, 95 percent production and process.

Question Do the creative people and the production folks get on well, and are the work pass-offs between departments smooth and seamless?

Answer No, they always squabble and fight.

Question Does your company do a lot of rework?
Answer Yes, lots.

Question Are your projects often late?
Answer Sometimes, but more often we just get the job done by working all night and all weekend.

Question Do you formally use project management systems to organize the timing, costing and specification of your briefs?

Answer	No, but we generally muddle through OK.
Question	Are your projects and responses to briefs better organized than they were 10 years ago?
Answer	No, not really.
Question	Has your productivity, quality, delivery or flexibility increased in the past 10 years?
Answer	I'm not sure, perhaps not really. We've made some small gains using technology.
Question	How's your productivity and competitiveness going?
Answer	Still OK, but not nearly as good as 10 years ago. We basically rely on some brilliant people and long-standing customers.

Another criticism is that discipline reduces empowerment. People who believe this may be still thinking of the 'other' form of discipline. That is the coercive form of discipline characterized by the well-worn quote 'The beatings will continue until morale improves!'

We believe that in contrast to the negative impact of coercive disciplines, enabling disciplines provide the structure for doing 'Job 1' well so that employees are not forever fighting fires and doing rework. This actually frees up time and other resources to do improvement work. Just add process improvement skills! This produces rather than reduces empowerment, particularly the empowerment to improve work processes and hence competitiveness. If applied well, people can thrive on the structure of a well-disciplined workplace.

Some people criticize the well-structured smooth-running workplace as boring. We return to the phrase 'brilliantly boring operations' that we have heard at companies like ABB and HP. There is nothing boring for the people at these places. It's just that they get their kicks from the challenges of driving improvement (Job 2) of their businesses to even higher levels of value creation, rather than fighting fires within Job 1 that stop the business going forward.

The final criticism we hear is that discipline smacks of 'Taylorism', which is bad. Many people have the perception that Taylorism equates to treating people badly. They also believe that Taylorism was bad because it meant doing things the 'one best way'. We respond that structure and process standards are good for everyone, certainly for customers, shareholders and managers, but also for rank and file staff. The disciplines we have seen in leading companies provide everyone with additional strength of purpose and support the principle of alignment as they become the wherewithal for ensuring that the strategic priorities and corporate intent is carried out.

EVALUATION OF THE PRINCIPLE OF DISCIPLINE

The measurement of discipline can be done as a holistic evaluation, then in parts:

To what extent is your organization a highly disciplined workplace?[2]

                   Low 1 . . . . . . 2 . . . . . . 3 . . . . . . 4 . . . . . . 5 High

To what extent is there a structured set of well-formed processes and process standards in the organization?

                   Low 1 . . . . . . 2 . . . . . . 3 . . . . . . 4 . . . . . . 5 High

To what extent do people at all levels in the organization adhere to process standards?

Executive management	Low 1 . . . . . . 2 . . . . . . 3 . . . . . . 4 . . . . . . 5 High
Middle management	Low 1 . . . . . . 2 . . . . . . 3 . . . . . . 4 . . . . . . 5 High
'Shopfloor'	Low 1 . . . . . . 2 . . . . . . 3 . . . . . . 4 . . . . . . 5 High

Truly, in excellent companies, senior management know that disciplines are not only for front line processes. Companies like GE, Motorola and Kodak practice high levels of process discipline all the way to the top. The discipline principle applies everywhere in the world's best organizations.

BENEFITS OF DISCIPLINE

The benefits of the discipline principle can be summarized as:

- It creates the support needed to get the most out of 'distributed leadership' environments.
- It creates a clear 'peg in the sand' to help employees to drive improvement.
- It improves efficiency through standardization.
- It increases the conversion rate of learning into business improvement.
- It particularly helps process-focussed companies to drive reliability and consistency.
- It builds quality into processes.

IMPROVING AND SUSTAINING DISCIPLINE

The companies that succeed with the discipline principle build it up together with the principles of management and reporting and then distributed leadership. In a very successful Kodak business, the CEO and top management team began by constructing performance indices for themselves, and then when everyone realized they were serious, it spread by osmosis. Pretty soon they had demonstrated that performance improvement is only sustained if it is based on process improvement. They formulated detailed policies, plans and procedures, and made these into 'living' documents. They communicated these intensively and invited all the members of the company to do the same by putting more structure into work processes at all levels. People found that once they had standards, they could observe variations, as undesirable deviations to the goal. People measured these deviations and after a good deal of upskilling began to use improvement techniques to reduce variation and improve quality, cost and delivery responsiveness. The business outcome was that the plant, which is one of Kodak's major film production sites, went from being something of a 'basket case' to being 'best in class'.

A similar story is the infamous GM Fremont (California) plant (Adler, 1992) that was revitalized, principally by Toyota, from being a terrible GM plant, even by *old* GM standards, to a very productive one as a joint venture between GM and Toyota, known as NUMMI. It's a story of transformation from very little discipline, and what there was purely coercive, to a tightly disciplined workplace, lean in the extreme with highly demanding work standards, yet with strong empowerment of enabling discipline.

SUMMARY

In summary, discipline in the workplace is not negotiable for those who want to excel. Whether it is an advertising agency, banking or a brilliantly boring manufacturer, process, structure and formality without the costs of going overboard are the best way to build a platform of excellence. To deny discipline is to accept that a little anarchy – or at least disorganization – is acceptable. Perhaps the final word should be drawn from the quality guru, Philip Crosby, who talks of 'management as ballet'. In professional ballet, everything is 'nailed down' except the dancers' feet! The movement, music, props, lighting are all planned and executed in a highly structured, highly disciplined manner. Crosby compares this to the lack of discipline in an ice hockey game. Even for those who are more attracted as spectators to ice hockey than ballet, the question is about risk, competitiveness and predictability of outcomes. Ice hockey involves a high degree of unpredictability of process, which makes it attractive to spectators, but would we like to run our companies that way?

Finally, if there were two competing organizations, in any industry, and one was managed and conducted in an undisciplined manner, whilst the other had highly structured standards and disciplines, which one would win the competitive battle, and by how much?

Notes

1. 6-sigma quality means error rates in a process of about 3 parts per million items. To achieve this, whatever the process, excellent process controls and quality disciplines must be in place.
2. The nature and exact type of discipline should relate to the strategy and nature of the business.

14

Principle 11
Measurement and reporting

People really like being measured, when the measurement is fair and open.
Philip Crosby

Don't tell me how hard you work. Tell me how much you get done.
James Ling

INTRODUCTION

Best-practice companies measure a range of non-financial parameters as well as financials. They recognize that corporate value potential is similar to an iceberg. The financials represent the 10 percent we can see; the other 90 percent the operational, technological and organizational capital base we cannot directly see in the company accounts and which needs to be measured, evaluated and actively managed. The measures typically used by leading firms relate to business goals, business strategy and positioning, operational goals, organizational goals and external stakeholders.[1] In many leading firms, organizational goals relate to their key set of management principles. For example at Medco, this means measurement against their 'five pillars' of strategy and value creation. Measuring and reporting/publication of operational parameters such as productivity, quality and safety close the loop on the firm's objective setting and planning process, recognizing that 'What gets measured (and reported) gets done' and 'You can't systematically improve it unless you measure it'.

Distributed leadership needs distributed information! In addition, the effective use of measurement and reporting systems is related to the organization's preparedness to act on deficiencies that are identified. Consequently, the degree to which this principle is applied effectively is related to the organization's ability to change (Principle 8).

With reference to Figure 1.3, the operational performance measures need to be fed back in a timely, accurate manner to teams of front line workers, whether we're talking about a factory or a service operation. The critical principle here is that these teams can relate their actions to the critical performance outputs that they influence by their actions. Similarly, managers can relate their actions to the critical set of organizational and team capabilities that they influence by their actions. Effective measurement systems can be useful tools to close the mindset gap between management and the workforce. This is why the feedback needs to be fast and at the right level of aggregation, so that all employees can clearly understand the impact of the actions that they take in areas outside their immediate sphere of responsibility.

It's really just a case of ensuring and driving alignment (Principle 1). If we want people who run a business to do it well, then we need to provide the feedback loop on system outcomes to them, presented in a way that makes sense to their sphere of action and responsibility.

In all of the operations of the best practice companies we have studied, there are attractive information centers with well-designed bulletin boards that graphically depict these performance attributes and trends. Workers congregate during break times and before and after their work shifts in these centers, which are usually well-lit and ergonomically styled, and discuss the *connections* between *what they do* and *how they are performing*. This builds commitment in the workplace, helps everyone understand the causal effect between actions and performance and builds an alignment between workers and their managerial control systems. We have seen the power of this in banks and in factories. Also, these leading firms do not fall prey to the measurement complexity we've seen in many organizations: they consider only a few key measures – typically five or six, never more than eight.

It is critical to our understanding of why this works to state explicitly that measurement alone is not enough. We have observed that it is the closing of the cycle via the appropriate reporting of measures which are at the right degree of detail, back to those who have control over the actions in the operation, that leads to improvement. In many firms, aggregation is not performed, or is performed poorly, resulting in an excessive number of measures and ill-directed organizational improvement effort. The people who should be exercising control over a system or who are operating a process need direct performance data on that system and the simpler, more direct the information, the better. Simply put 'Tell me how we are doing, in terms we can relate to, so that we can get on with doing the work [Job 1] and doing it better [Job 2]'.

Principle 11: Measurement and reporting

The evidence is that publishing comparisons of output measures is a very powerful motivator. Examples abound at both the operational level and at the strategic/executive level. We know of one organization that decided to focus on the improvement of its safety record and did nothing more than start collecting and organizing information on the safety performance of its various departments across its manufacturing sites. Graphs were produced and posted around factories of the various manufacturing departments, with the names of the heads of those departments inside the columns of the graphs. These graphs showed the number of lost-time incidents and serious safety incidents per thousand labor hours, sequenced from best to worst. No other action was taken.

Within a relatively short period, just the action of measuring and reporting this information in a public way around each site led to a substantial improvement in the management of safety issues and in the performance of the organization in terms of safety. Sloppy habits were cleaned up. Clearly, nobody wants to be injured or have their work peers injured, and therefore nobody wants to be at the wrong end of that graph. Consequently, a productive, constructive set of peer pressures was created through no other managerial intervention than the measurement and reporting of safety performance in the right way. The change in behavior was dramatic in a company where speeches, seminars, newsletters and exhortations on safety had been previously ineffective. Those department leaders at the 'poor' end of the safety performance scale changed their approach overnight and those who were at the other end of the scale continued to strive for improvement. Such is the power of measurement and reporting, even when it is enacted without any other principles or levers. Of course, when skills are upgraded, rewards and recognition systems kick in and full alignment and integration are achieved, this power is magnified.

A critical breakthrough for many firms in respect of measurement and reporting is the issue of who owns the measures and who owns the data.

The second phase of this became a training and development phase, however instead of an executive announcing that everybody would be going through a safety training program, the demand for this training came from a series of requests from the shop floor. This demand was genuine and the training was taken very seriously and led to even further improvements. Why hadn't the sloppy habits been fixed for years before they were measured and reported? It really was the case that 'People do what you inspect, rather than what you expect'. So formalizing it, measuring and reporting it, brought the focus that catalyzed the actions that were previously missing.

A critical breakthrough for many firms in respect of measurement and reporting is the issue of who *owns* the measures and who *owns* the data. In this regard, by far the best results have come when the measures have been properly structured and set up such as to reflect actual performance goals of the organization, but done so in such a way as to foster ownership of the data and the measures by the employees who conduct the actions that affect these measures. These employees become empowered and take ownership over these measures. It is in this way that an organization can achieve true alignment of strategy, actions, and performance outcomes with the feedback loops from performance outcomes back to strategy and actions being achieved in a closed loop manner as shown in Figure 1.3. This is one of the critical differentiators of the 'new world' organization as depicted in Figure 1.3, from the bandaid-like company which is unco-ordinated and hardly has a structured improvement process as shown by Figure 1.2. Figure 14.1 shows the major difference between 'Company Old' and 'Company New' in terms of measurement and reporting.

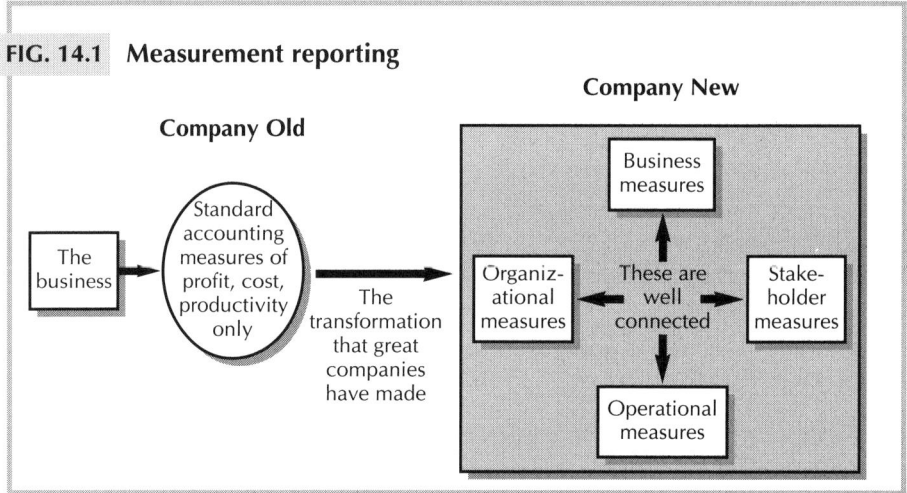

FIG. 14.1 Measurement reporting

A final word for now on measurement and reporting. They go hand in hand with Principle 5, 'Being up front'. Indeed, a good, open performance management system is a major part of how companies can transform themselves towards being up front! We hope these connections and their compelling common sense within this system of principles are now becoming increasingly obvious to the reader.

Leading companies are information rich. Decisions are based on fact and relevant data. This is not just the decision making of executives and managers but since the leadership is distributed throughout these businesses (see Principle 2), everyone must be well informed. The measuring and reporting of a business is critical to 'closing the loop' between strategy, actions and outcomes. Everybody

Principle 11: Measurement and reporting

in such organizations is contributing to informing others of critical information. Let's examine this at two levels, management and workforce.

For managers, it is a fundamental of good organizational practice that they can guide their actions and tactics through being well informed about business strategy. When they are making decisions on the firing line, they must have a strategy template to guide them, but this is not enough. Sure, tactics and individual decisions must be guided by strategy, but Figure 14.2 shows that this is an open loop.

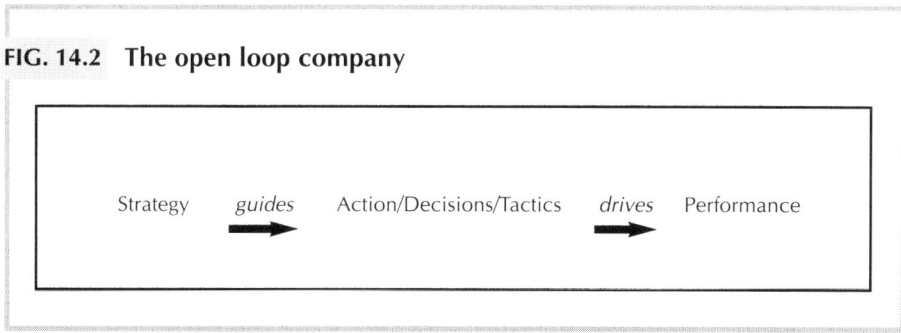

FIG. 14.2 The open loop company

Measurement and reporting is the principle that closes this loop, leading to both learning and accountability. Figure 14.3 shows the closed loop system in which strategy, actions and outcomes are connected.

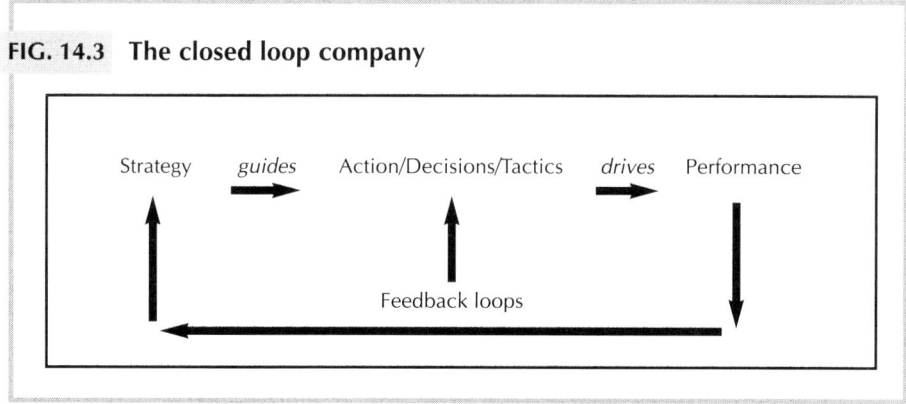

FIG. 14.3 The closed loop company

The poorly measured business is like moving with our eyes closed, and we should remember that these days we must move very fast. In a familiar room, it may be possible to function with our eyes closed as long as the environment does not change much. But what happens if customers, competitors and regulators reshape the room we are in? We need constant feedback on how we are doing so that we can link our actions, the environment and our operational and business performance.

A well-measured company has its eyes wide open, not shut. The same applies to individual managers and executives. A key to this is to make the measures relevant to the controls of the person or team taking the action, and to provide the information quickly so that close control can be achieved over the system being worked on. So for a marketing manager in retail supermarkets, we now see the ultimate in timeliness of information provision, namely live sales data appearing on the computer screen as the sales occur. At Walmart's head office, marketers track live sales by identifying items for any store or set of stores, so that 'steering controls' can be exercised based on timely facts.

Production managers can steer their ships better if they get accurate, recent data on productivity, quality, safety, etc. Live production data or perhaps hourly summaries of production parameters provide the feedback loop to allow for good control and adjustment.

For a CEO, daily, weekly or monthly figures on cash flow, profit, volume and market share allow for adjustment of policy. Without these measures and the high-quality reporting of them, these various levels of functional and executive management would be less effective.

The same principle applies to every direct and indirect staff member 'down the line' in the organization. For plant operators in a refinery or chemical plant, imagine if we asked them to control chemical reactors without giving them live data on temperature and pressure of their chemical processes. So if we want them to contribute to productivity and quality improvement, cost reduction or safety management, we must likewise provide a stream of data on these items so they can effectively practice 'distributed leadership'. For many years, managers in many companies did just the opposite! They worked on the principle that information is power and they kept the power close to their chest. Now that power is distributed so that everyone can use his or her brain to work on business improvement.

Of course it is the same in service jobs and service industries too. Bank tellers can contribute much more effectively to productivity and service quality improvement if they are provided with measures and trends of just how it is going. Information provision has no downside in this regard. It motivates improvement, can be the basis for building accountability and leads to increased job satisfaction when combined with 'distributed leadership' and 'embracing change'. Imagine those bank tellers or their branch being constantly pushed to improve productivity or service quality but being given either poor or no feedback on how they are performing. Why ask people to work in the dark, when it is possible to light their workplace brightly with

Principle 11: Measurement and reporting

high-quality performance data? This is particularly so now that we are asking everybody, bank tellers, factory workers and all staff, to work harder and walk faster and faster. There is no excuse for keeping them in the dark.

Perhaps the best evidence of this comes from call centers and factories. In call centers, software systems can provide live data of number of callers waiting as well as average and longest wait time. Operators can work accordingly, judging when to answer calls before doing other tasks such as 'paperwork' or making outgoing calls. In an operational sense, this live stream of data on their screen or on an overhead electronic board is the ultimate in 'fast feedback'. They can immediately use it to optimize their activity and see the operational outcomes. What would happen in a call center if this information was not supplied? Service would go down and operators would clearly make sub-optimal decisions about when to deal quickly and efficiently with clients, when to cross-sell and when to do other things, including take breaks.

In leading factories, it is a wonderful sight to see teams of workers gathered around information centers that provide relevant, accurate, timely data about the performance of their team, department or site. They look eagerly at statistics and trends in quality, productivity, safely, etc., and can activate their brains on things other than just doing their primary, often repetitive production tasks (Job 1). They talk to each other about why things are happening as the data suggests. In the best of these, information is presented in graphical form so that people can quickly relate to trends. Operators can use the data to develop a perspective of cause and effect between their actions and the real-time plant performance outcomes. They are given the chance to become involved. They can take some real ownership. They can take pride in knowing they contributed to positive trends and can search for answers to the problems that cause negative trends, but only if they can see the data!

> **There are still many people in the workplace who play politics with information**

So it really is the same principle for the bank teller and the bank's CEO. Yes the measures are different, each needing to be right for the context of decisions and actions taken, but in both cases the loop must be closed between intent/purpose, action and outcome if we are to expect superior and increasing performance. This case, for providing full information relevant to all employees, is so compelling that it is really quite amazing to consider that there are still many people in the workplace who play politics with information, keeping it close to their chest. These people are clearly maximizing the wrong item of value, namely their own selfish wishes and short-term power rather than the organization's competitiveness. We would argue for counselling such managers to change these practices or find a business that does not want to achieve forward progress.

The best of measurement and reporting practices is when work teams themselves take ownership over the collection of the data and processing it into performance information. In a manufacturer of household doors, the new factory manager saw that workers were not informed about daily production and error rates, scrap, etc. She set up a notice board in the staff canteen, and asked team leaders to measure and bring in the numbers from the previous days' production as they came in for lunch. Daily production in most departments varied in a 40 percent range. Workers had previously been vaguely aware of this and certainly did not view it as their concern. Some three months later, everyone eagerly awaited 'yesterday's' numbers and spent much of the lunch period discussing the 'why'. Average output had risen 25 percent with no other intervention other than the measurement and reporting. Teams of workers just naturally worked out the cause and effect between what they did and the production outcome. New productions records were set, then reset. And all this for the cost of a large whiteboard and some pens! Later, the measures were redefined, quality indices were developed and some simple computer systems were brought in to 'institutionalize' the measuring and reporting, but the same powerful principle, of measurement and reporting, was not changed or diluted. Pretty soon, teams of workers were challenging themselves to reset records of high production and low scrap. They actually made a game of it, and as soon as it became 'fun', the energy in the workplace soared.

Internal and external benchmarking can be very useful activities in line with the principle of measurement and reporting. Many companies use internal comparisons of performance to highlight strengths and weaknesses of internal business units, then closely examine the process of differences that drives these business and operations performance differences with a view to learning and improvement. Our experiences in this include the following.

- A global tire company that benchmarks the performance of its 20-plus manufacturing sites around the world on over 20 measures of productivity, quality and safety. Local executives are held accountable for performance improvements on these measures, and are 'encouraged' to visit and learn from (that is to process benchmark) other operations and businesses within the group.
- A large bank with some 1,800 branch retail outlets that produces and publishes a league table of branches, rank-ordered by productivity. Again, leaders are encouraged to share their 'best practices' with the lower-ranked branches.
- A residential housing construction company that measures the cost of producing a 'standard' house across its 50 branches, in sufficient detail so that real learning and improvement can occur. No single branch was even near

the top of the table in all aspects of construction cost, so that every single branch was able to benefit from the measurement and reporting exercise. This exercise was so successful the first time it was done that is regularly repeated every six months and has been extended from a construction cost exercise to include all aspects of the business including selling and marketing processes, and customer satisfaction drivers.

From these examples and many others like them, we can see that measurement is a necessary foundation on which improvement can be built. Without measurement it is very difficult to achieve real accountability or even to know whether improvement initiatives are working.

Further, reporting of measures in an open way can be a very powerful motivator of that improvement. In the best of all worlds, comparison between business units can lead to healthy competition and the achievement of improved performance can be set up as a matter of fun, rather than grinding hard work. Even if it is not fun, then it can nearly always be designed such that everybody wins.

EVALUATION OF MEASURING AND REPORTING

Since measuring and reporting can and should be done at a number of levels and in more than one way, it is best evaluated at that level of detail rather than in aggregate.

First are the measures that are needed for managers and executives to 'steer the ship'. Business measures such as those produced by the financial accounting system are clearly important but they are often too aggregate and too late to provide for good steering controls. They measure the past, usually not the present and never the future. Managers need current information on the operational and marketplace pulse that is closely related to the levers that these managers hold, and that are the drivers of the business performance outcomes that eventually are reflected in the accounts. So, for managers there are a number of key types of measures to assess against.

To what extent does the organization measure and track performance of key financial parameters?

Low   1 .... 2 .... 3 .... 4 5   High

To what extent does the organization measure and track performance of key customer parameters?

Low   1 .... 2 .... 3 .... 4 5   High

To what extent does the organization measure and track key operational measures such as productivity, quality and service?

Low 1 .... 2 .... 3 .... 4 .... 5 High

Further, managers need to be given timely information at the right level of aggregation for them, so they cannot but engage in closely connecting cause and effect, that is connect what they do with how they're doing. Measures need to be 'line of sight'.

To what extent is the 'loop closed' connecting managers' levels of control, decisions, etc., with relevant performance outcomes?

Low 1 .... 2 .... 3 .... 4 .... 5 High

Good measurement and reporting can be the basis for managers taking ownership over the work systems and outcomes and achieving real accountability.

To what extent do managers accept accountability for performance?

Low 1 .... 2 .... 3 .... 4 .... 5 High

We contend that in most leading workplaces, where about 10 percent of staff are managers and 90 percent are operational staff, that the exact same principle is applied to the staff as to the managers, but in their narrower domain.

To what extent do workers get and stay involved in understanding operational performance as relevant to their work area?

Low 1 .... 2 .... 3 .... 4 .... 5 High

To what extent do workers accept accountability for performance?

Low 1 .... 2 .... 3 .... 4 .... 5 High

From these diagnostics, it is possible to tell whether the key principle of measurement and reporting is energized in a business, and where improvements are possible. Finally, an overall judgement should be made as a reality test for the whole company. This tests the alignment of the business measures and the operational measures, and the measures that managers work to, versus those that drive work teams. In the world's best companies these measures are in harmony with each other, in that work team operational measures are the things that drive and aggregate to whole business unit operations measures, and further the business unit operational measures drive competitiveness in the marketplace and so produce superior financial returns.

> To what extent does the business have a connected set of team-level and business-level operational and business measures that form a coherent performance management system?
>
> Low 1 .... 2 .... 3 .... 4 .... 5 High

The relevance of these measures to the business strategy is important too. Good companies do not just measure things for the sake of it or because neighboring or competitor firms do it. They derive their measures from what is important to their business strategy. If the company competes primarily on cost, then it must measure and report cost particularly well. If the strategy is differentiated through superior service, it must carefully construct measures and report on service parameters.

> To what extent are the things we measure and report derived from our strategic priorities?
>
> Low 1 .... 2 .... 3 .... 4 .... 5 High

Two special measures

We have observed two special types of measures that most industry leaders do and do well, that most industry 'laggers' don't do well if at all. The first is the measurement of employee satisfaction. Most truly excellent companies are actively engaged in managing employee well-being and to manage it well they realize that they must measure it regularly and systematically. So they conduct employee opinion surveys or in some other way develop a deep understanding of the extent of employee satisfaction, dissatisfaction drivers and the organization's rank and file 'mindset'. The surveys are anonymous and they ask for a range of views from employees at all levels about a range of items, from brand image, to how the boss treats staff, to what employees think of service and quality, to whether employees trust the company, to how employees keep informed about the business, to what they think about pay and conditions, to whether they would leave the company given a chance. There are just so many things that managers should want to measure about employee opinion and the best ones do!

In leading companies, this employee opinion data is rigorously analyzed, then fed back to managers and employees. The next step is for managers and employees to discuss the data in a situation of mutual trust and move forward together in a spirit of improvement. Some companies form indices of employee satisfaction based on these measures and set targets and accountabilities on them. The motivation for measuring and wanting to manage employee opinion comes from the service-profit chain. As articulated by Heskett et al. (1994), the simple and powerful logic is that satisfied employees will provide better quality and service to each other and to paying customers, who in turn will be more satisfied and stay, leading to profits and hence satisfied shareholders.

This brings us to the second 'special' measure, customer satisfaction. Many have written about bringing the 'voice of the customer' into the company and systematic and regular formal measures are one way of doing this in addition to keeping in close touch with key customers.

Although the logic for engaging in these two special measures is compelling, and the measurement tools are quite readily available, many companies have never done formal, systematic measures of both. Those companies can often tell their labor cost variances to the nearest millionth of a cent!

BENEFITS OF MEASUREMENT AND REPORTING

We believe that the benefits of strong measurement and reporting are so powerful and to some extent 'self-apparent' that this section can be brief.

The fundamental contribution of measurement and reporting is the 'closing of the loop': the provision of feedback control to people at all levels in the business.

The benefits of good measuring and reporting are that they make for good alignment and performance improvement. The measures and accountabilities that are given and accepted up and down the business can align workers' and managers' efforts. When this idea is applied across the value chain and the business functions, then what do the measures drive and support if they are well designed? Integration (see Principle 3)! Indeed the measures become the performance management system that are nothing less than the glue of the organization, both vertically and laterally.

IMPROVING THE ORGANIZATION'S MEASUREMENT AND REPORTING

How can managers and others use this principle as a guide to actions? We would advise the following practical actions.

- Link measurement to management. Ensure a cultive of measures, goals and targets is established and maintained.

Principle 11: Measurement and reporting

- Communicate right around the business that measurement is an indispensable part of good business practice – it is not optional.
- Further, anticipate that some people will resent 'measurement', but work consistently to explain the need and position, and overcome the resistance to measurement.
- Demonstrate the value to each employee of a solid measurement and reporting system.
- Make 'top down' meet with 'bottom up' in establishing measures and measuring processes. Top down means deriving the key parameters of performance from the business strategy, marketing priorities and operations focus. Bottom up means 'workshopping' with employees to develop the logic of (and imperative for) measuring key financial and non-financial measures. The same goes for measuring and reporting systems and formats, which should be mostly user-driven.
- Seek the involvement of employees in formulating individual, team and departmental goals and measures
- Start with a small number of key measures in any given area, and build incrementally, rather than with the most complex, high-tech system, which could put people off.
- Give employees a sense of control of the measurement process and the measures, rather than the opposite.
- Communicate intensively about how the measures and reports are for all to see, in the spirit of providing data for driving business improvement, rather than assessment or any other motive.
- Ensure that measures are designed to facilitate improvement.
- Conduct information sessions to explain the meaning of the measures and how to use them.
- Have measures prominently displayed and make them a key discussion item at each work group meeting.
- Conduct regular (quarterly?) review sessions to discuss how the measures interconnect and relate to business outcomes.

SUMMARY

In summary:

- Measurement and reporting of operational and business performance can be a call to action in that it can be a powerful motivator.
- The reporting of quality information in a timely way increases decision quality.

- Employees at all levels will feel 'included' in the organization, when they are seen as important enough to be part of measurement and reporting systems.
- Employee commitment is built up as is contribution to business goals.
- As an integral part of 'closing the loop' between strategy, actions and outcomes, measurement and reporting are closely related to other key principles of alignment, discipline, up front and out front, in a positive reinforcing way.

15

Principle 12
Customer value

There is a lot more to golf than having the equipment and the intent.
Philip Crosby

INTRODUCTION

Customer-value creation means turning the ordinary into the extraordinary as seen by the customer. Leading companies do more than just know their customers' requirements. They drive to maximize customer value through their organizational activities. They articulate 'value propositions' and focus on providing high levels of 'benefits per dollar' to customers (see Figure 15.1). In order to do this they need to clearly understand why customers buy from them rather than from their competitors. They therefore make extraordinary efforts to 'stay close to the customer'. Depending on their business type, whether it be relationship, market, product or process-focussed, this translates to an ability to articulate clearly the customers they do and do not do business with.

CUSTOMER-VALUE CREATION AT MERCK-MEDCO

Medco's New Jersey mail-order pharmacy processes approximately 150,000 prescriptions per week with a 95 percent turnaround within two days (the other 5 percent is because physicians are not available to clarify ambiguities in their prescriptions). Customer service at Medco can be considered at two levels. At the first level, consider the performance of ▶

> Medco's telephone center and prescribing services relative to industry and best practice standards. Whereas the average telephone answering time nationwide for telephone centers is quoted at 42 seconds, Medco's average is 16 seconds and its call abandonment rate is measured at 1.6 percent which is less than a third of the national average. The first call resolution rate at Medco is much higher than the national average, and customer satisfaction is 98 percent.
>
> At a higher level, customer-value creation is based on adding value to the transactional database and prescribing processes. Medco's clients are the 700 plan partners who pay for the cost of having their patients' medicines dispensed. Partnerships are being formed with these clients in order to help the clients understand and better manage the total cost related to health management of their health program. The total cost is the sum of the costs associated with doctors, medicines and drugs, hospitals, work and sick leave and a number of other factors. And Medco is finding ways to help its clients measure and manage this total cost function. In order to do this Medco is moving from just being a very efficient medicine dispensing processor to using its information base to develop policies with its clients in order to optimize the value which can be created for them.
>
> •••••••••••••••••••

Leading firms know what their current and potential customers value and strive to enhance that. That is they focus on continuously enhancing their 'order-winners' to enhance their value to the customer and hence their competitiveness. They do not embark on 'feel good' change programs unless a clear link can be established between the outcome of that program and customer value. These competitive 'order-winners' are prioritized from industry-wide 'qualifiers'. Finally, managers in leading firms tell everyone in the company about their order-winners so that decisions can be made throughout the company based on the same priorities and criteria.

An example of the principle of driving customer value through order-winners and value propositions is the The National, a leader in the banking industry. The National has a group-wide value proposition 'Tailoring banking to your needs', and is developing products, systems and processes to drive this set of benefits. In order to achieve this, flexibility of product design is the key and information systems and staff resources need to be attuned to this order-winner.

In the paper industry, AP's A plant Mill was uncompetitive with imports, but through reorganization and refocussing of its operations and logistics was able to provide service and delivery performance levels which importers could not compete with. AP changed the rules of competition by which

Principle 12: Customer value

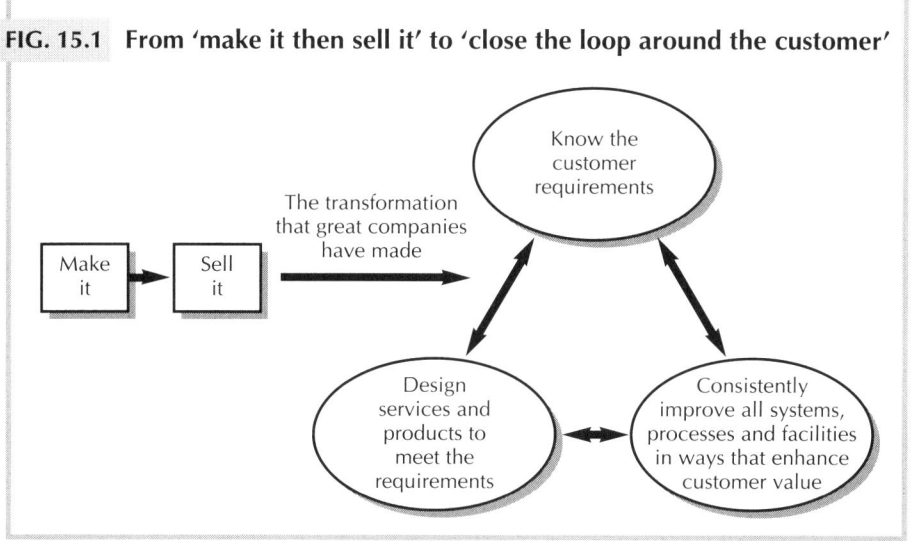

FIG. 15.1 From 'make it then sell it' to 'close the loop around the customer'

industry dynamics in this sector were played out. Of course they changed these rules in order to create a competitive advantage for themselves.

Another great example is IKEA who changed the basis of competition within the retail furniture industry through their intimate knowledge of customer value requirements. IKEA recognized that many market segments were extremely price sensitive and that by introducing disassembled, 'everyday' furniture into the marketplace, their manufacturing, packaging and distribution costs could be reduced substantially, and hence product cost could be reduced significantly as a way of increasing value-creation.

CUSTOMER-VALUE CREATION STRATEGY AT ASEA BROWN BOVERI (ABB)

ABB's strategy in this regard is simple and powerful, as expounded by one of their senior executives in Europe, who stated the following.

- Customer relations can only really be improved through having a platform of operational excellence.
- Only with good customer relations can we jointly plan and execute customer-based strategies and plans.
- Through jointly planning with our customers we can become an insider and not an invader in our customers' organizations.

▶

163

- The best way to do this is to use local people and local resources in local markets combined with world's best practices.

For ABB this means breaking down their very substantial business into small building blocks and giving local managers profit and loss responsibility. This creates local entrepreneurs. An example of customer value creation and partnership behavior from ABB is in its UK Instruments and Controls Division. Product development time has been slashed from three years to what is now usually three months.

Relating customer value creation to resourcing the medium term, the UK Instruments and Control Division of ABB plans jointly with customers on how to service their needs over a three-year time horizon. Then ABB develops the new products, systems and services in order to meet those customers' needs.

A specific example of this is the ICI Chemicals Business that was going to close an uneconomic chemical plant in Europe. ABB studied the plant and proposed a new instrumentation and control system that would upgrade the plant to a viable status such that it could remain open and generate positive cash flow for ICI. As a result of this close customer relationship, ABB achieved $8 million in revenue and the ICI Board approved the upgrade based on payback and value creation, as proposed to them by ABB. From ABB's perspective there was no 'brief' to respond to and ABB were only able to initiate this piece of work through being very close to ICI to seize the win-win opportunity. Like many of the world's great companies ABB strives to 'get into its customers revenue stream'. It is proactive and dynamic in its decision making and policy flexibility.

••••••••••••••••••

Definition of customer value

Leading companies organize themselves primarily around the customer and the satisfaction of customer requirements. They fully realize that it is the appeal of their offerings, products and services to customers, that drives the revenue stream of the organization, that in turn pays for everything, including salaries. This knowledge of the primacy of customer satisfaction is turned into everyday action in leading companies, such that the 'voice of the customer' pervades every activity and process. This is often taken to the point of defining every process in the company formally, in terms of who is its customer, and what the formal requirement is of that customer. From this, standards are set up and measurement and reporting systems (see Chapter 14) of

Principle 12: Customer value

performance against those standards can be conducted. Business plans can include performance targets on those measures. Appraisals of staff can include performance on those measures.

Customers are generally defined as those who use or consume the outputs of any organizational process. Clearly, this does not just mean external customers who 'buy our stuff', but also includes internal customers too. Many processes in organizations serve internal customers, such that the external customer or consumer who pays for the organization's output can be thought of as the tip of the iceberg. What the external consumer may not see are all the internal processes such as:

- the human resources department serving 'the line' with people having the right skills and attitude to do the job;
- the information systems department serving the company with hardware and software management information reports etc., to enable them to be most effective in their work processes;
- the company's senior executive team providing the rest of the company with the vision and policy leadership required;
- the accounting and financial managers providing financial performance data to general managers;
- marketing and sales people providing market intelligence to product/service designers and operations managers on external customer requirements;
- purchasing staff supplying raw materials and consumables as needed throughout the organization;
- throughout the value chain of the company, people who are directly producing goods and services serve those to whom they pass their work, components, reports, etc., 'down the line'.

In a bank, the tellers and customer service officers serve those in the 'back office' and service centers with the output of their 'customer-facing' activities for processing. On an assembly line, each worker and team serves the next worker and team with the output of their work that becomes the input to their 'internal customer'.

In the leading companies we have visited, particularly GE, IKEA, Dun and Bradstreet, and Hewlett Packard, the service ethic can be felt throughout all activities, departments and processes. All members of the organization realize that to work is to contribute 'to serving the customer or to serve someone else who is serving our consumer'.

In one division of Hewlett Packard we visited, this notion even manifested itself down to people's behavior and attitudes when answering the phone.

Most of us answer the phone at work with a 'Hello' and perhaps give our name. In one part of HP we visited, the standard greeting is 'How can I help you?' and when we inquired why this was the standard, the answer was simply that 'People call you for a reason, whether they need to inform you of something, or they need information from you. The telephone facilitates serving customers, internal and external with information, so it's 'How can I help you?'

This may seem trivial, but it is symbolic of what makes these great companies tick.

The value of focus

While customer-value creation in great companies certainly does put the customer first, almost on a pedestal, outstanding companies choose their market segments carefully and do know when to say 'No' to a customer. In a word, they are focussed on being excellent in their offerings in certain ways, certain segments, and they generally do not try and be all things to all possible customers in every segment of the market. Let's consider the examples of industry leaders in banking/financial services, tires, automobiles, fast foods and housing construction.

Financial services companies such as Merryl Lynch, Charles Schwab, or Homeside (a mortgage specialist that is part of The National group) do not take on orders for services outside their defined range of products and expertise. Further, even within their range of services, they know and focus on their particular 'order-winners'. To illustrate this 'order-winner' notion, consider all the possible ways that a business might establish competitive advantage. These include:

- cost leadership
- quality superiority
- product features
- delivery reliability
- delivery precision
- service availability
- responsiveness/flexibility
- innovativeness
- customer relationship/intimacy.

There are many other possible ways to express and define the dimensions of supply competitiveness on which customers choose, but these listed above are a good start. These are some of the things that cause customers to 'buy our stuff' and sustain the revenue stream. We found that leading companies were not generally trying to be all things to all people and segments in the market but are focussed on the specific needs of particular segments.

Mercedes and BMW, Jaguar and Rolls Royce are classic examples of those aiming their products and services at a luxury niche. Toyota began at the other end of the market, producing four-cylinder cars for the masses. When they had achieved a substantial degree of success at this and then attacked the luxury car segment with Lexus, was this a sign of losing their focus? The answer is certainly not, because Toyota set up separate facilities and organization for designing, producing and servicing Lexus, from that of its mass-market products. Separately, distinctly focussed divisions can be separately and distinctly focussed on different segments. Had Toyota mixed its Lexus design, manufacture and servicing with Corolla, what might well have resulted? Corolla may have lost its efficiency and cost leadership in its segment and Lexus may have found its quality and service excellence to be compromised. So customer (segment) value focus means defining specific subsets of the dimensions of competitiveness, such as quality and service for Lexus, value, efficiency and cost leadership for Corolla and trying to excel at this subset of dimensions. We have found that the excellent companies we visit have a strong customer focus, and usually a focus on particular target segments.

What happens to those who try to excel at all the dimensions of competitiveness? Usually they are condemned not to excellence at these dimensions, but rather to mediocrity. So the leaders, then, focus on excelling at a few specific things, being careful not to try to excel on too broad a front, but also being careful to maintain at least minimum standards on those dimensions that are not their specific order winners, which we call 'qualifiers'. Qualifiers are the dimensions that others may excel at, but as they are not order-winners for us, they just need to be pursued up to an acceptable level. Great examples of qualifiers from a company that led its industry in global growth for two decades is McDonald's, which does not try and excel at flexibility and innovativeness. It does excel at providing product consistency, timely service, brand leadership and value for money in its segment.

Goodyear Tire Company uses a focussed factory concept, in which it separately operates factories that pursue long runs of passenger car radial tires, from the factories that are driven by flexibility, which make many different types of more specialized tires. If it mixed these two types of factories together, the passenger tire operation might compromise or lose its cost and quality focus and the specialist tire operation might lose its flexibility focus.

Sometimes, order winners can become relegated to qualifiers. In the photographic film market, in which Kodak and Fuji and others fight the good fight in most of the world's markets, quality of color balance used to be an order-winner, but once all the suppliers could reliably produce film with an excellent color balance quality, it is no longer a potential differentiator and becomes a qualifier.

We have recently been working with an excellent company that makes automobile airconditioners, part of the Denso group of companies that supplies parts and sub-assemblies to the auto industry. It used to command premium prices due to its superior product reliability, but see this order-winner rapidly evaporating as competitors catch up on quality, so it must develop new capabilities such as innovative designs which will drive both cost and product performance to new levels.

To summarize, leading companies are very strongly focussed on their revenue streams and strive to satisfy customers and target segments' specific requirements better than anyone else, by organizing all processes, customer-facing and support processes on specific customer value creation.

In leading companies, the order-winners are not only agreed by managers across marketing and operations, etc., but have been carefully communicated to all employees. Since leading companies also practice distributed leadership (see Chapter 5) all employees make decisions in their own domain and need to be well informed about specifically 'How do we compete?' and 'What do we want to excel at?'

CUSTOMER VALUE CREATION AT IKEA

IKEA is an excellent example of a company that has turned shopping for household goods and furniture from an ordinary experience into a 'different experience'. IKEA makes its inventory system accessible to customers. IKEA provides cafes and child-minding in its store. And yet IKEA is very strongly into cost-focussed competitiveness and is certainly into producing and delivering furniture for the mass market, not the luxury niches. IKEA's value proposition is specific, focussed and unique.

Some companies find that they can be innovative and do more than just respond to customer needs, but lead their customers' needs, even those needs that customers didn't know they had! How many of us knew we wanted a Walkman before Sony launched them onto the market, followed by Discman (CD) and Watchman (TV)? Sony led its customers' needs. Coca Cola rarely tries to do this, as it is not for everyone. Coke has very different order-winners to Sony, and both positions are entirely legitimate and very successful.

The customer focus in leading companies need not involve any rocket science, but rather an organizational discipline of defining down to a micro level

Principle 12: Customer value

which tasks and activities add customer value and which do not. Great companies reduce or preferably eliminate activities that do not either directly or indirectly add value. A great test is to question every task, every process and say 'If our external consumer knew about this, would they be prepared to pay to have us do this?' In great companies, support activities are also organized around customer value creation. Information systems are designed to maximize customer value creation, not for any other purpose.

It almost goes without saying that these customer-focussed leaders try to establish and sustain strong communication links with customers and target market segments. They concentrate on telling customers of the specific focus of their offerings, and in measuring customer needs and customer satisfaction with their offerings. They attempt to waste as little effort as possible on things that customers do not want, or do not want to pay for. Many have found the discipline of value engineering/value management to be a useful tool in formally articulating customer requirements, then organizing to satisfy those requirements (and nothing else) at low cost.

Consider a housing construction company that we have advised that comprised many different builders in many different cities. Each did some things well but none of these branches did all things well. A value engineering exercise led to a shaping of best practice around the company in terms of what customers like in house features, design and selling process, and also allowed for about 12 percent of cost to be taken out of the construction cost total, by focussing on only doing the specific order-winners to a standard of excellence and doing everything else at an industry acceptable standard.

EVALUATION OF THE CUSTOMER-VALUE PRINCIPLE

A company can evaluate the extent of its customer-value creation focus based on the components of:

To what extent do we measure existing customer requirements?

 Low   1 .... 2 .... 3 .... 4 5   High

To what extent do we gain customer satisfaction of our products/services?

 Low   1 .... 2 .... 3 .... 4 5   High

To what extent do we benchmark our products/services against best in class competitors?

 Low   1 .... 2 .... 3 .... 4 5   High

PART 2 • MANAGEMENT BY PRINCIPLES

> To what extent do we have a well-focussed set of order-winners defined in our business?
>
> 1 .... 2 .... 3 .... 4 5
>
> To what extent do marketing and operations work to the same order-winners, consistently over time?
>
> 1 .... 2 .... 3 .... 4 5
>
> To what extent do all employees at all levels understand the imperative of customer-value creation?
>
> 1 .... 2 .... 3 .... 4 5
>
> To what extent do all employees know and relate to the defined order-winners?
>
> 1 .... 2 .... 3 .... 4 5
>
> To what extent does our company anticipate and lead customers' requirements?
>
> 1 .... 2 .... 3 .... 4 5
>
> To what extent are work relationships inside our company, between people and between departments, defined as internal servicing of customers?
>
> 1 .... 2 .... 3 .... 4 5
>
> To what extent is customer-value creation used to differentiate and focus on value creating versus wasteful activity?
>
> 1 .... 2 .... 3 .... 4 5

From the answer to these questions, readers will be able to understand clearly their organization's overall strengths and weaknesses in customer-value creation, as well as specific aspects of it. This can lead to the formulation of action plans (described later in this chapter).

BENEFITS OF CUSTOMER-VALUE CREATION AND FOCUS

The benefits of being great at doing the very things that satisfy and delight customers, and focussing on doing little else, are pretty obvious. To take this even one step further, try measuring a business against the likes of Hewlett Packard, who showed that they don't just consider their customers as central to HP's '*raison d'être*', but focus on their customers' customers. The approach in HP to its customers is 'How can we, with hardware, software and services, provide you, our customer, with a superior ability to create value for your customers?' As pointed out earlier, at HP they call it 'getting into their customers' revenue streams'. The benefits are of adding value, as much as possible, therefore maximizing competitiveness and position in the value chain. This notion of 'customers' revenue streams' clearly does not apply directly to all, such as retailers of consumables like McDonald's, but it is valuable in helping everyone to understand the notion of 'getting inside the customer's head' and knowing better than competitors, specifically what customers value.

For an automobile component manufacturer, this notion should feed into its design and production processes. The question is not just 'How can I satisfy you best as my Ford/GM/Toyota customer?', but rather 'How can I design and build my component best to make your product as competitive as possible in respect of your customers?'

This requires the component supplier to know its customer's order-winners! At McDonald's, suppliers of potatoes and beef are acutely aware of McDonald's customer value proposition and order-winners that flow from that, such that the product and service specifications flow effectively all the way from McDonald's customers right back through the value chain to primary producers and packaging suppliers. The benefits of this external, inter-organizational alignment (see Chapter 3) are a more effective, efficient value chain and less waste of effort.

IMPROVING AND SUSTAINING CUSTOMER VALUE

The first point is that we cannot improve customer-value creation unless we know what customers value, or else at best it would be 'hit and miss'. Why leave it to chance, when it is possible to find out reasonably accurately? So the first improvement area in enacting this customer-value principle is the identification of customer requirements and values. From the assessments made earlier in this chapter, how much room for improvement is there in measuring this and in monitoring ongoing customer satisfaction?

Related to this is the widespread communication to all employees, of customer-value knowledge. If it is not already widely known, then a communication exercise followed by others at regular intervals may well be appropriate. This could be linked to statements about 'our order-winners'.

To summarize this, consider whether it would be worth communicating the following.

- In our industry we have determined that customers generally respond to and will pay for the following elements: service, quality, efficiency, timely delivery, etc.
- In the segments of our industry that we focus on, we wish to excel at the following (order-winners)…
- These order winners should drive our product designs, service orientation and operational decisions, including equipment, scheduling of services and production, and the types of people and skills we need.

Once the customer-value dimensions and/or order-winners are established, then the final set of actions regarding this principle of customer value is to produce a plan of action, for going forward or increasing customer value. The plan will include elements of:

- improving our customer knowledge;
- improving our company-wide communication of this;
- improving our product/service designs accordingly;
- improving our operations to deliver specific customer value, consistently at higher levels.

This drives into connections with the principle of discipline (see Chapter 13) in operations.

SUMMARY

To summarize this customer focus principle, we present the results of a best practices study in which we studied first hand, the customer orientation of 20 leading companies around the world. This is shown in Table 15.1 as a series of 20 common characteristics of excellent 'customer-value focussed' organizations. Table 15.1 also shows our assessment of various of the excellent companies we assessed on some of these characteristics, each scored on a ten-point scale of 1 (poor) to 10 (world class). As an exercise in benchmarking, how does your company stack up? A score of above 150 (out of a possible 200) is truly excellent and below 100 can be interpreted as 'needs work' or alternatively as a major 'opportunity for improvement'. It is important to note that these characteristics are presented as general in nature, and do not in any prescriptive way apply universally. However they can be interpreted, prioritized and customized, based on an organization's business position and strategy.

Principle 12: Customer value

Table 15.1 Characteristics common to customer-value focussed companies

Item	Our company (score out of 10)
1. Strong emphasis on capturing customers' 'like' (customers like IKEA)	
2. Transactional base must be super-efficient relative to industry.	
3. But this (2) is not enough. We must enhance revenue by creating superior value on top of transactions	
4. Strong HR investment. When the company was seen as a transaction factory, 'people as robots' was OK. People as empowered, smart service workers is the future	
5. Finer and finer segmentation is occurring	
6. The 80:20 rule of customers: profit seems universal, so *focus*, *prioritize* on the profitable few	
7. Process standardization/ discipline is confirmed as a central pillar.	
8. Leaders must provide a culture of high energy, excitement *and* bottom line performance	
9. Leaders must be personally in touch with customers and their exact requirements	
10. There is a balance of excellent process discipline with vitality, intuition, common sense	

▶

Table 15.1 Continued

Item	Our company (score out of 10)
11. Customer as partner (win-win)	
12. Speed of service as competitive advantage	
13. Information systems are built around customer needs and customer value creation	
14. The whole organization is driven by excellent, *detailed* marketing information and analysis	
15. Internally, corporate to business unit working relations are based on the principle of 'enlightened self interest'	
16. Leading companies are prepared to move fast to reshape structures, processes, driven by customer choice	
17. We pursue learning and spreading of improvement and best practice around the group	
18. Align personal rewards *for all* to business performance and its drivers (when the company does well so do we all as individuals and vice-versa)	
19. Best companies act locally, structuring as small, in-touch, but using the power of a large organization	
20. People are encouraged to challenge boundaries, and mistakes are OK as long as the batting average is high	

16

Principle 13
Capabilities

The wind and waves are always on the side of the ablest navigators.
Edward Gibbon, *Decline and Fall of the Roman Empire, 1776*

INTRODUCTION

To understand what capabilities are, consider the company that has none. How would it fare?

In order to achieve, sustain and focus on order winners and customer value creation, firms invest in core capabilities. In leading firms, these capabilities are clearly defined, widely communicated, highly valued and 'held sacred'. The principle of 'capabilities creation' directly supports the principle of 'driving customer value', as internal capabilities are the means by which superior order-winners are created to attract and satisfy customers. Put differently, the principle of driving customer value considers the relationship between the organizational boundary and the external environment (the customer): the principle of capabilities creation considers the relationship between the organizational boundary and the internal operating environment.

Definition of capabilities

The experiences of Casio, Southwest Airlines, Caterpillar, Canon, Honda, Walmart and others have propelled the capabilities-based view of the firm to centre stage in the arena of general management. Many leading companies have gained a competitive advantage by developing and leveraging unique organizational capabilities. What are capabilities? A review of the literature will reveal 20 different definitions. Irrespective of the definition used, organizational capabilities are complex phenomena that need to satisfy three criteria (this work was pioneered by Prahalad and Hamel, 1990):

- real benefits to customers
- be difficult for competitors to imitate
- provide access to a variety of markets (the test of durability).

Capabilities involve the interactions of individuals, technologies, processes, systems and structures. Capabilities knowledge can be a key input into critical decision-making activities that include prioritizing R&D projects, establishing skills development priorities, developing strategic alliances, identifying upstream and downstream integration opportunities and selecting information technology platforms and designing organizational structures and business processes. We have found that firms that are true 'capabilities-based' competitors are differentiated as much, if not more, by the processes used to define, refine, exploit, continually retest and gain consensus amongst employees of what constitutes their core capabilities set.

Examples of capabilities include Marriott's ability to design and administer training processes that create a hospitality culture, Walmart's ability to create win-wins through vendor relations, Du Pont's ability to roll out its world class safety culture to improve production quality and cost, Black & Decker's ability to support new product introductions.

Leading firms have effective processes for identifying, developing, transferring and exploiting their core capabilities which are tested and developed in conjunction with key stakeholder and customer groups. Capabilities serve as priority areas for investment and decision making and firms that adopt this principle do not compromise capabilities and capabilities development processes during market downturns, corporate restructuring, departmental restructuring, downsizing, cost-reduction exercises, etc. Capabilities competitors ensure that any actions associated with short-term performance improvements are not inconsistent with those to develop longer term competitive advantage through a differentiated capabilities set. We have also found that within leading firms, capabilities are the link between organizational development activity and the creation of the order-winners through which improved competitiveness is achieved (see Figure 16.1). In some instances, new organizational practices may also drive the development of capabilities which spawn new order winning attributes and therefore new customers.

Tandy is a distributor of consumer electronic equipment and toys. Critical order-winners within this competitive environment include market acuity (the ability to pick the latest trend/fad), time to market (the ability to introduce new high-quality products quickly into the marketplace) and operational flexibility (the ability to manufacture a broad range of boutique products). Tandy has identified the following capabilities as critical to its sustained success: attracting and retaining high-calibre staff, developing and managing strategic alliances with suppliers of high-technology components, maintaining a seamless design/manufacturing operation and extracting maximum market intelligence from customer enquiries. Responsibility for the development and protection of these capabilities has been assigned to key staff who develop action plans, targets and measures to improve them and strategies and processes to raise organizational awareness of their value.

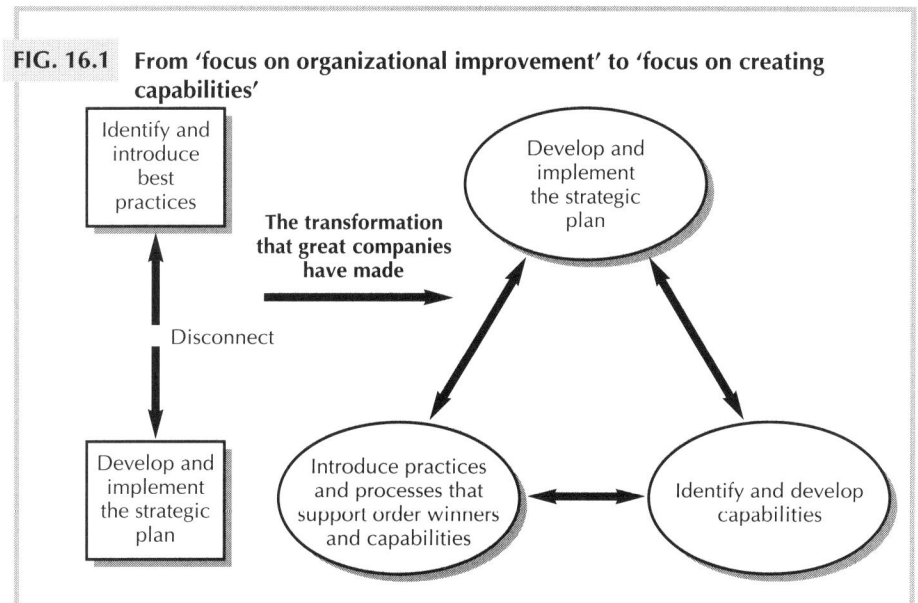

FIG. 16.1 From 'focus on organizational improvement' to 'focus on creating capabilities'

EVALUATION OF CAPABILITIES

How does a company rate as a capabilities competitor? Are capabilities clearly defined and 'lived' in all business and operational activities. Does the business continually test, retest and re-evaluate its capability set? Are capabilities defined to a sufficient level – do they truly support goals and business strategy set – or are they statements of parenthood? Are capabilities an active part of the dialogue of each and every employee in the organization? Are they embodied in each and every decision that people make? From operational decisions about customer and work priorities, engineering decisions about equipment selection and installation through to executive decisions about strategic alliance formation and management, are capabilities a key consideration?

Capabilities competitors are also highly formalized and disciplined in the way they build, transfer and exploit their capabilities and apply 'knowledge management' practices. In leading companies, capabilities are never the responsibility of a select few. Primary accountability for various capability related activities is also clearly defined. Nine capabilities subsystems and practices are provided for evaluation in Table 16.1.

Table 16.1   Evaluating capabilities

	Not at all	To a weak extent	To a moderate extent	To a large extent	To a very large extent
	1	2	3	4	5
1. Capabilities are defined for all areas of business activity.	☐	☐	☐	☐	☐
2. Capabilities are held sacred – a priority area for investment and development.	☐	☐	☐	☐	☐
3. Capabilities can be clearly linked to value propositions and business trategies.	☐	☐	☐	☐	☐
4. Capabilities can be clearly linked to organizational development strategies and practices.	☐	☐	☐	☐	☐
5. We have reached consensus amongst all employees on our core capability set.	☐	☐	☐	☐	☐
6. Our understanding of the relationships between capabilities and business outcomes constitutes a critical area of organizational learning.	☐	☐	☐	☐	☐

Principle 13: Capabilities

	Not at all	To a weak extent	To a moderate extent	To a large extent	To a very large extent
	1	2	3	4	5
7. Strategies and plans exist for capabilities development, transfer and exploitation.	☐	☐	☐	☐	☐
8. Clear accountabilities and plans exist for capabilities development, transfer and exploitation.	☐	☐	☐	☐	☐
9. Capabilities requirements are reflected in the actions and decisions of each and every employee in the business.	☐	☐	☐	☐	☐

BENEFITS OF THE CAPABILITIES PRINCIPLE

What benefits accrue from a company that scores strongly on this principle? First, it ensures that scarce resources are focussed in the areas that yield the greatest business benefits. In too many organizations, talent, money and activity are dispersed in many different areas and we can sense that many of the actions taken are 'long bows' – lots of action that 'feels good' but a low conversion rate to business results. High efficiency … low effectiveness. Second, it helps to ensure consistency of action and direction. Capabilities, if well defined and fully accepted, provide a set of supplementary insights that assist in translating business goals and strategic plans into organizational actions. Too often, strategic objectives and plans fail to create a consistent framework that guides operational activities and decision making where the 'real work' is done. Decisions such as what systems should we buy, what skills should we invest in, and what activities should we outsource? Third, the conversations that are an integral part of the capabilities definition and development process help to develop alignment of views and common understanding between individuals and functions, shape organizational identity and culture and create a common, consolidated course of action and development. Fourth, and very importantly, capabilities help to simplify the business of doing business. As business increasingly becomes a 'war of movement', it is becoming more difficult to establish direction, focus and continuity. Capabilities help to define an internal set of perspectives that assist in these requirements.

IMPROVING CAPABILITIES

How can an organization increase its capabilities strength? What are the actions that a leader can take?

The starting point must come from a set of strategic conversations. The company has to understand its own and its competitors, principal sources of competitive advantage in order to answer the question 'Why do customers choose our products ahead of our customers (or vice versa)?'

With order-winners defined, an organization can then go about the process of identifying what it is about it that creates, (or fails to create), superior customer value in its *current* business environment. Views need to be widely tested and debated and consensus views reached between all stakeholders. The company will frequently need to visit where it's been and how its past actions, successes and failures relate to what it has become and how it has arrived there in order to answer this question.

These capabilities issues need to then be considered in future environments, both probable and possible. Scenarios need to be developed and capabilities tested and/or established and strategic plans revised accordingly.

With the strategic framework defined and confirmed, organizational and capabilities development plans and activities can then be articulated, implemented and reviewed.

SUMMARY

Capabilities creation is fundamental in leading organizations. As the complexities and dynamics of doing business continue to increase, so too does the need to define precisely what is the source of the organization's competitive advantage and to understand it, protect it, build it and use it at all organizational levels. True capabilities competitors consistently delight in using these capabilities in ways that have never been used before to create new markets, services and customers. Capabilities competitors know precisely what organizational characteristics and attributes make the difference to their existing customers and potential new customers.

17

Principle 14
Micro to macro

People don't work for companies: they work for people. All employees want to be proud of everything they are associated with.

Philip Crosby

INTRODUCTION

We all want our work to feel meaningful, connected to the achievement of a result.

In leading firms each member of the workforce understands how his or her individual and team-based work effort connects with, and contributes to, the big picture of business success. Alternatively, each manager has a sound understanding of how his or her individual and team-based work effort connects with, and contributes to, organizational success. That is, a common platform of understanding has been established between the general workforce and management and as a result micro and macro activities are closely interlinked. On an activity level, this connection between micro and macro is reflected in a close connection between the core work processes and critical business processes. Consequently, the activities of management and the broader workforce are aligned and effectively integrated.

Most readers would see the synergies of alignment, integration, distributed leadership, and micro to macro and also see that they are not the same. Each needs separate identification and attention. For example, a firm may demonstrate the principles of alignment and integration but not micro to macro. We have seen many firms where the general workforce share the vision for the organization, understand its business's context of operation and identify with its values yet fail to understand how their specific activities and tasks impact on these goals. Employees are frequently diligently developing and implementing suites of improvements that, although they may have a significant positive impact on their specific work area, only have a relatively minor impact, if any, on business performance. People see and understand the big picture but cannot connect it to what they do on a day-to-day basis.

We have also seen an equally large number of firms where managers regularly take actions that protect short-term business interests but that are unknowingly inconsistent with other organizational improvement activities or workforce efforts to build long-term competitiveness. This can, and does, albeit inadvertently, lead to friction and mistrust and in some instances alienate large sections of the workforce. A classic example of this has occurred on a large scale in many petrochemical industries where large 'chunks' of technical activity, engineering and maintenance, have been outsourced to improve short-term business performance without recognizing the value of these activities in respect of developing the capabilities that build long-term competitiveness. In some instances, key capabilities that took decades to develop have been lost overnight.

We believe that the extent of these disconnects exists, to a large extent, because of the widespread purge of middle managers in recent years and the failure of organizations to recognize their role in making the micro to macro connection. We have observed that many leading firms do recognize this role and as a consequence do not regard middle management as 'corporate carcinogens' – a legacy from a past management era. Rather, these firms view middle managers as an indispensable ingredient for the effective management of the micro to macro connection. Moreover, these firms do not generally view themselves as 'top-down' or 'bottom-up' organizations. In fact they do not have tops or bottoms. They have outer people, inner people and middle people (Mintzberg, 1996). The outer people, the general workforce, sit on the circumference and are effectively connected to the 'real' world and are constantly looking outside the perimeter of the circle for improvement opportunities. These people are engaged in micro activity – they have intimate knowledge of their specific operations (but only a limited knowledge of the overall operation) and do the direct value adding. Inner people sit near the center and are constantly looking around the circle but are effectively disconnected from the 'real' world because they are distant from it. These people are engaged in macro activity – they have a sound general knowledge of the business, its operations and its strategies and goals.

The trick therefore is to have middle managers who connect the micro to the macro – people who can see the outer edge of the circle and then swing back around and talk about it to those at the centre. Figure 17.1 articulates the behavior of firms who have effectively made these connections.

FIG. 17.1 Connection between micro and macro

	Management mindset	Workforce mindset			Management mindset	Workforce mindset
Macro	Sound understanding of business issues. Some customer awareness	Limited understanding of how assigned work effects the bottom line	→ The transformation that great companies have made →	Macro	Good understanding of business, supplier and customer issues	Good understanding of business, supplier and customer issues
Micro	Limited understanding of organizational or operational issues	Sound understanding of requirements necessary to complete assigned tasks		Micro	Good understanding of operational and capability issues across the organization	Good understanding of operational and capability issues within the team

Definitions of micro to macro

'Micro to macro' relates to the personal and team connection of people up and down the organization. Are people generally 'folded in' or 'dealt out' of the company's purpose, goals and performance? In a company that has a strong implementation of the micro-to-macro principle, people at all levels feel ownership and accountability for their own performance, their team performance and the whole organization's performance outcomes. Even more to the point, they understand the connections between performance at these various levels. They buy into connections between micro and macro because of three major connections that they have to the overall company's performance. These connections are described below.

The undeniable logic of it all

No matter whether one uses DuPont charts or anything else, it is clear to all well-informed managers that the bottom line that drives return on shareholders funds comes from revenue drivers and cost drivers. In a factory or service operation, productivity, cost efficiency and waste reduction relate directly to this. Production workers who process materials and operate equipment set processes in place that determine cost outcomes. So do procurement, logistics, product/service design functions and many others.

The connection with revenue drivers is sometimes less tangible and harder to measure concretely, but no less powerful. The check-out cashier, motor mechanic, hotel lobby clerk, salesperson and bank customer-service officer can, by their attitude and actions, determine the extent of repeat business that drives revenue. So it is important that everyone knows the logic of how everyday actions translate and aggregate into total performance for the organization. Built into this are the connections between internal efficiency and effectiveness, marketplace competitiveness and shareholder returns (see Figure 17.2).

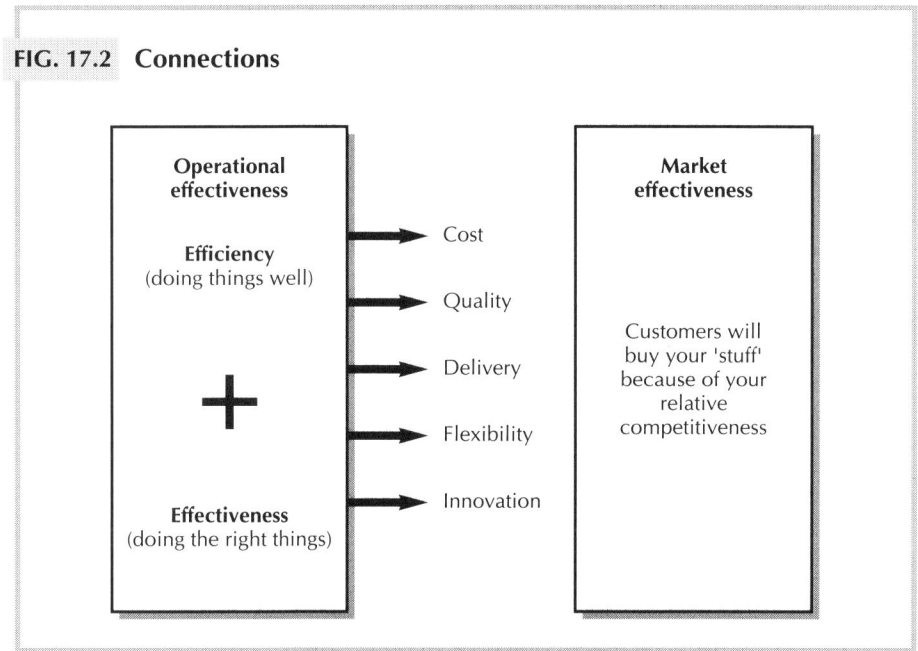

FIG. 17.2 Connections

Since most people in most organizations are immersed in service and product supply and delivery, they need to be taught about the connections between their own operational effectiveness, aggregate operational effectiveness, and business performance outcomes. If we want them to sign on and commit to business excellence, we must provide detailed knowledge of the connections between local operating conditions and the profit and loss statement.

Appeal to the heart

We have found that over 90 percent of people will jump at the chance of achieving satisfaction of doing or contributing to doing a good job. It is true that some people have been given so little of a chance and indeed have been 'beaten up' so often that they seem intractably disinterested in the business welfare of the very company that employs and pays them. Incredible as this is, we ought to face into it and ask why is it so. It is usually because they have been treated as robots without brains or feelings for long enough that they have actually turned their brains and feelings off as they arrive at the workplace. Most people would like to work everyday to do a good job, if only the company's systems, style, culture and managers would let them! To believe otherwise is to deny the very basis of human spirit and existence.

Imagine the perfect business (that does not exist!) in which 100 percent of people come to work 100 percent committed to doing a great job, 100 percent of the time. How much more productive would this business be than the industry average, with other things such as technology being equal? Passion, motivation, commitment, competitive spirit make a huge difference to performance. So we want to engage both our people's logic and their passion.

Take their wallets there

When we asked people in high-performance workplaces why they work so urgently and fervently, there is a third reason too, apart from logic and passion. The third lever of motivation employed more and more by leading companies is rewards and recognition. Recognition is cheap and has no real downsides, so it needs little discussion, except to say that most managers do not use 'positive strokes' nearly enough. Variable rewards are a little trickier because rewards do powerfully drive behavior, and the wrong variable rewards system can drive behavior that is dysfunctional.

At Mars Corporation, variable rewards based on return on total assets and sales growth indices are powerful incentives for all members of the Mars businesses to strive for performance improvement. In the Medco mail-order pharmacy division of Merck, various metrics of operational performance such as turnaround time, productivity and quality drive the variable pay scheme. When we asked a group of technicians in Medco's New Jersey pharmacy why they worked so feverishly, the answer was to tap their wallets and say 'When the company does well, so do we!'

So in summary, getting people to connect their micro-activities to the big picture can be done, meaning motivation in three ways, minds (logic), hearts (passion) and wallets (rewards). Rather than debate which one of these works best, why not ask how best to use a combination of all three, just like Mars and Medco?

The principle of micro to macro requires education to achieve the buy-in being sought. Let's examine an automobile manufacturer we visited some years ago that trained its new production operators basically by getting them in to their workstation and saying something like: 'Copy him'. There was no explanation of company purpose, products, no specific job task training, no safety training, etc. This is *not* being proposed as best practice. There was no micro-to-macro connection in that company. The plant is now closed due to lack of competitiveness. Workers were not allowed to buy into the company's purpose even if they were predisposed to do so. Compare this to Medco's training of call center operators, comprising some six full-time weeks of everything from Medco's mission, performance measurement system, competitive position, as well as the specifics of the job, the IT system, etc. No wonder Medco's call center outperforms call-center averages by so much in terms of customer satisfaction and the drivers of it.

The principles of measurement and reporting and of discipline link strongly to that of micro-macro. The connectedness that we want all our people to feel to the big picture needs to be facilitated by middle-management, whose role is to make these connections through cascading measures and requiring discipline and accountability to them. Then all we need to ensure is that the operational measures, such as productivity, service standards, quality and turnaround time, are derived from strategic or business measures, such as cash flows, market share and customer satisfaction. The principle of distributed leadership is relevant also to micro-macro, since it is through distributing leadership that the responsibility and accountability are offered and accepted 'down the line'.

In summary, strong levels of micro-to-macro buy-in don't happen by luck or through some feel-good initiative. There is no doubt that one of the levers for it is engaging people's passion and giving them the opportunity to contribute so that they feel connected to the company's big picture, through providing job satisfaction. However we can also help this by educating them as to the compelling logic of striving to contribute to competitive outcomes, and through a cascaded system of performance measures we can align the employees' wallets to the shareholders'. The infrastructure is the measurement system, the facilitation by middle managers and the training effort.

EVALUATION OF MICRO TO MACRO

The extent to which an organization has a connection between what all its people strive to achieve and the big picture can be measured in aggregate, and in terms of its components and inputs.

In aggregate:
To what extent do our employees know how their activities connect with and contribute to the big picture of business success?

  Low 1 .... 2 .... 3 .... 4 .... 5 High

Now lets consider the components:
To what extent are business strategies and goals effectively cascaded into personal and team strategies and goals?

  Low 1 .... 2 .... 3 .... 4 .... 5 High

To what extent business performance measures effectively reflected in individual and team performance measures?

  Low 1 .... 2 .... 3 .... 4 .... 5 High

PART 2 • MANAGEMENT BY PRINCIPLES

> To what extent do assigned roles and responsibilities make the micro-to-macro connection rather than leave blind spots?
>
> Low 1 .... 2 .... 3 .... 4 .... 5 High
>
> To what extent are the actions of managers and employees consistent across the organization?
>
> Low 1 .... 2 .... 3 .... 4 .... 5 High
>
> What is the general extent of employee commitment 'to do a great job for the organization'?
>
> Low 1 .... 2 .... 3 .... 4 .... 5 High

BENEFITS OF MICRO TO MACRO

The major benefits of having strength in the micro-to-macro principle relate to the following.

- Unity of purpose up, down and across the organization. With everyone pulling in the same direction, as against pulling in different directions, or not pullling at all, real progress is possible. There is a clear and strong connection between the principles of micro to macro and alignment.
- Consistency and co-ordination of effort. Through understanding and being connected to the big picture, workers in different functions, departments and sites will produce more consistent outcomes that pursue the same goals and competitive position advantages.

IMPROVING MICRO TO MACRO

Perhaps the single most important driver of improved micro-to-macro connection is internal communication. Many channels can be used – person-to-person, newsletters, middle management, performance data on notice boards, broadcast videos, CEO roadshows, letters of strategic direction, regular lunches with staff, management by walking around, and many others. Some of these are more formal than others, and most companies need a mix of channels.

Micro to macro can also be strengthened through having a strong and well-structured performance management system, that connects aggregate business performance to its building blocks and that people at all levels can relate to. In our view, as assumed earlier, this is also best reinforced by activating all three important parts of employee's anatomies, their minds, hearts and wallets! For most companies, this job is never fully completed and these connections need to be revisited, reinforced and regularly refined. Employees in strong micro-to-macro organizations are information-rich, and believe in their contribution. The improvement can be seen in productivity and service/quality that comes from care. As one executive put it at a Kellogg's factory we visited 'We strive to have all our people care for Kellogg's assets, facilities and outcomes as much as they do with their own, at home. That's our benchmark and when we see that, we know we have got it right.'

Figure 17.3 shows the transformation that leading companies have made.

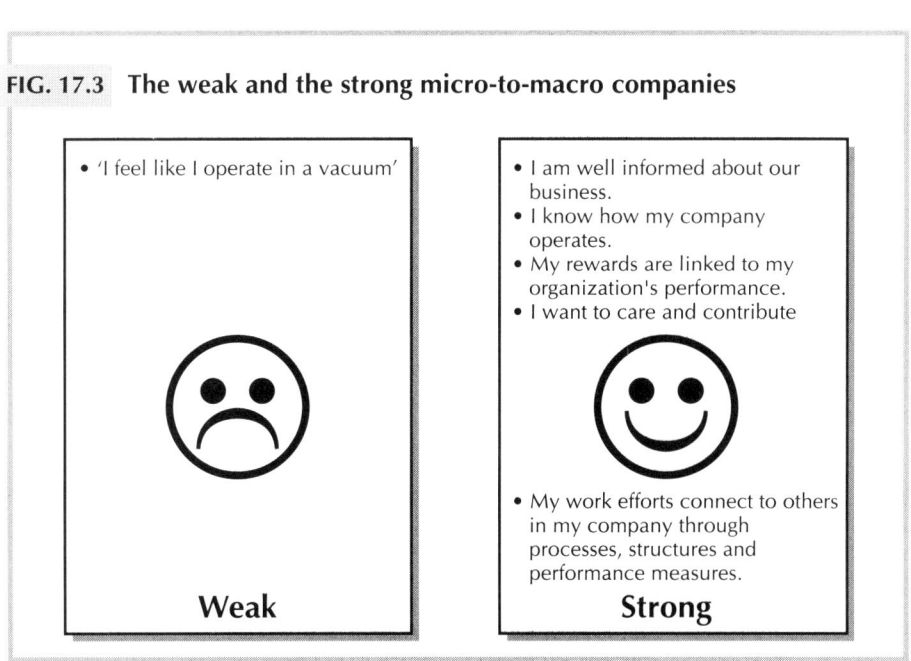

FIG. 17.3 The weak and the strong micro-to-macro companies

SUMMARY

Leading companies don't just know their order-winners. They create customer needs that never existed before. They predict changes in customer needs before they happen. They identify customer needs that even the customers can't identify for themselves. They relentlessly pursue previously unserved customers, etc. A central plank in the achievement of customer value added excellence is the ability to build and maintain a strong customer service work ethic that is reflected in the activities, actions, work processes and decisions of each and every employee, work group, function and department.

In Part 3 we develop a taxonomy for describing customer value that may be used to assist in the achievement of focus and priorization of principal development requirements.

Part 3
IMPLEMENTATION

In Part 3, an implementation process is developed and described. This is done in two main parts. First, in Chapter 18 we describe an implementation path as a set of steps in terms of moving from the ad hoc approach (depicted in Figure 1.2) towards the systematic approach of Figure 1.3, making use of and sense of the principles as detailed above in Part 2.

Chapter 19 presents a set of key success factors that we have observed are common to those companies that have been successful in making the transition from *management by fad* to *management by system*. These factors can be considered as implementation hints or guidelines in terms of 'what works'. For organizations wishing to break out of the fad-based approach to business improvement, to achieve a much sounder systematic approach to management and business improvement, these success factors will be valuable as checking points on their state of readiness to move on implementation.

18

Implementation steps

The test of any man lies in action.
Pindar, *Odes*, c. 500 BC

INTRODUCTION

Having described the management principles and management processes found in leading organizations and demonstrated their value, the critical issue is implementation. How does an organization go about the implementation of the principles described in this book? How does an organization subscribing to the ad hoc model of change (Figure 1.2) move to the integrated, systematic model of management (Figure 1.3)?[1] More specifically, how can principles be prioritized? How does an organization's business and competitive context relate to its principles development needs? Further, how do industry type, business context, strategy and organizational culture (to name just a few important elements) impact on the practices that underpin each principle?

We do not contend that the development, application and exploitation of the management principles detailed in Part 2 is easy. If it were, we would all have done it and there would be little source of competitive advantage. Translating these principles into an enduring set of practices and organizational attributes that drive business performance is a substantial task.

In this chapter, we present a structure for principles development that extends their use beyond that of a cognitive map, similar to the McKinsey 7S framework with which directions for organizational development (visioning), and assessments of organizational performance (diagnosis) can be made. The structure presented provides a framework to help guide managerial thinking.[2] There clearly are no cookbook solutions. Consequently, the models presented should be regarded as a starting point to help to understand, stimulate discussion and assist in clarifying thoughts and simplifying actions. Used effectively, the approaches outlined here enable an organization to formulate systematically and confidently its future directions in accordance with the integrated model (Fig 1.3) described in Chapter 1. This model shows how the principles may be used to guide the development of a single integrated improvement initiative that combines both business systems and organizational systems.

We will further develop this concept in this section and explore how the linkages depicted in Figure 18.1 may be developed. This figure reflects the pivotal role that principles play in forming an integrated business and organizational system. Most organizations have invested considerable time, money and resources evolving their business and strategy system over the last decade. However, we need to be able to articulate more clearly the *nature* of competitive advantage in order to be able to target, in specific terms, the attributes that underpin it.

FIG. 18.1 Using the 14 principles to help link business and organizational systems

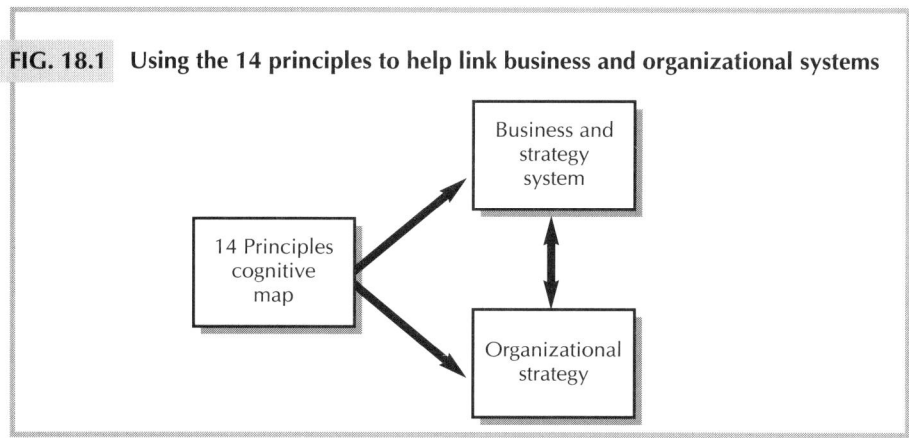

Increasingly significant changes in the marketplace – globalization, increased competition, industry deregulation – are resulting in a lack of fit between the existing organizational culture and new competitive environment. For Shell, the mismatch was triggered by new entrants into the petroleum business and the resultant oversupply of petroleum products. For Xerox, it was the entry of Japanese competitors. For Citicorp, it was a combination of deregulation of the banking industry, globalization strategies of foreign banks and competition from non-bank financial institutions. How these companies responded to this mismatch and the extent to which that response was successful depended very much on cultural norms. For example Shell's culture was very 'technocentric' and geographically and functionally based.

Its highly successful rejuvenation strategy was built around four key pillars:

- increased emphasis on shareholder returns
- more value placed on customer needs and expectations
- valuing leadership more than managerial status
- the socialization of its technology core to the business.

Further, in respect of organizational systems, we not only see problems with the means employed but also the end goals sought. Ideally what we need is to create *the* set of organizational characteristics that best support and/or drive the specific business system using a clearly targeted and small number of interventions. What we find is organizations attempting to create a generic shopping list of 'feel-good' practices such as self-managed teams, empowerment, consultation, continuous improvement, customer focus, process management, etc., that have loose connections (at best) to the business system using a plethora of interventions. Essentially, we want targeted end points and a small number of actions. We've got generic endpoints and an excessive number of actions. Consequently, the inverse ratio prevails – the rate of return on management effort is inversely proportional to the number of actions taken. The implementation framework that we develop in this section addresses this issue head on – that is the need to describe more clearly the nature of competitive advantage and the organizational attributes and practices that underpin it and target actions accordingly.

When the 14 principles are combined with the experience and intellect of key personnel and a well-facilitated process, their application can result in some powerful insights and clarity of thought that can be lacking otherwise. The clarity evolves from understanding and challenging the basis for the current business and organizational direction and more succinctly defining the future direction. It is worth noting that lack of clarity is generally a combination of issues that are both fact and fiction. First, consider the factual basis. Consider these two approaches which are fundamentally inconsistent in kind but often found to co-exist in practice – the broad application of consensus-based approaches and the development of environments that foster individual accountability. Another is an emphasis on building critical relationships and an emphasis on getting things done fast.

Second, consider the fictional basis. Consider simultaneous capital investment programs and cost-cutting activities – consider the achievement of both high quality and low cost. In the fictional case, the perspectives are not exclusive and are, to some extent, consistent. However, they are perceived by many as inconsistent because of inadequate understanding, individual positions or vested interests and organizational predispositions to exclusive (either/or) thinking.[3] We need processes that seek to clarify directions for action and that rigorously test and challenge the norms and principles that underpin it.

In the sections that follow we develop these concepts further in the form of an implementation framework, providing models to test and guide thinking and some practical examples to illustrate their application.

Implementation process steps

The adoption of the 14 management principles can be accomplished by a systematic approach that:

- progressively builds understanding of the approach
- provides consensus and clarity about business directions, business drivers and key strategic issues
- develops understanding of the connections between the business and strategy systems and the organizational and cultural systems
- helps to identify priority management principles for development and the practices that typically underpin them
- analyzes and assesses an organization's principles development requirements
- assists in identifying and driving the set of interventions necessary to close the gap and achieve the necessary changes.

As every company is unique, every change path will be different and hence each company will need to develop an approach that best fits its particular requirements. We present below a generic approach from which this customization can be accomplished. Essentially, there are six steps.

Step 1: Building awareness and executive buy-in
Step 2: Strategic focussing – clarifying business and organizational directions
Step 3: Performance assessment – business and organizational
Step 4: Diagnosis and development of the change case
Step 5: Project planning
Step 6: Implementation and review.

We will briefly describe each step in the sections that follow. Step 2 has been outlined in somewhat greater detail than the others, because of the widespread need continually to refine and sharpen strategic thinking and effectively link business requirements to management principles and the practices that underpin them. Here the models for sharpening business thinking and making the connections between business and organizational systems are developed.

STEP 1: BUILDING AWARENESS AND EXECUTIVE BUY-IN

Step 1 identifies the potential value and the appropriateness of a principles-based management approach within the executive team. The key outcomes from this step are a health check on the existing status of the business and organizational systems, a thorough understanding of the principles of management and a review of the appropriateness and value of a principles-based management approach. Key areas of activity considered include the following.

- *Business performance review* – a brief assessment of business objectives and performance and a brief review of critical business issues.
- *Strategic plan review* – a brief assessment of the extent to which business plans are delivering on objectives, and the factors and issues that impact on the organization's ability to implement its planned actions.
- *Change status review* – a brief review of the organization's change history, capability and effectiveness, which also covers exploring change myths. This typically includes an assessment of the linkages between organizational change activity and business imperatives and the extent to which the process is delivering.
- *Principles status review* – this involves assessing and interpreting the organization's management principles and management system strengths and weaknesses.

STEP 2: STRATEGIC FOCUSSING – BUSINESS/ORGANIZATIONAL DIRECTION

This step, typically involving a series of workshops, is primarily a visioning activity, although it builds on some of the issues identified and change themes developed in Step 1. In particular, it explores the connections between the business system (strategic preferences and strategy set) and the organizational system (principles and practices). The outcomes of this step are clarity and shared understanding about customer requirements, business directions and the organizational characteristics (principles) that support them. Step 2 uses a process described pictorially in Figure 18.2.

The process develops a detailed strategic, principles and practices vision for a defined area of business activity. Success is a function of team effectiveness, participant skills, intellect and breadth of knowledge, preparedness to test and challenge 'the way things are done around here and the directions we are taking', the extent to which example material catalyzes discussion and debate and the quality of process facilitation available. As indicated earlier,

PART 3 • IMPLEMENTATION

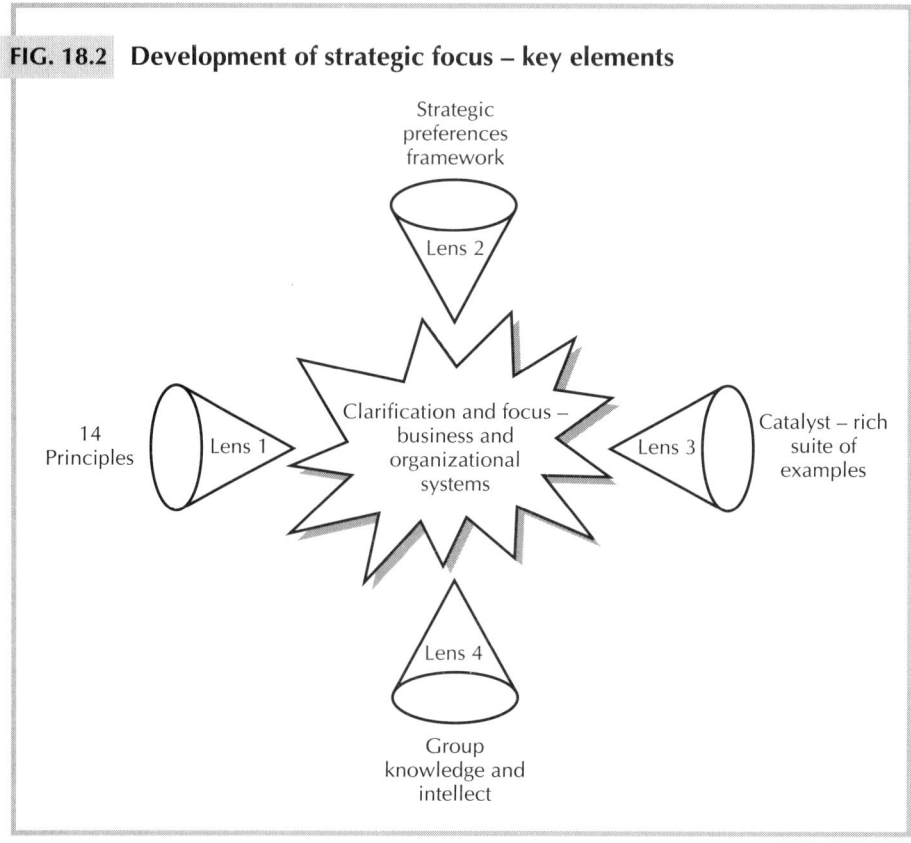

FIG. 18.2 Development of strategic focus – key elements

models and frameworks are used as a starting point for discussion. The 'answers' lie in the hearts and minds of the participants, not the tools used.

We have found the strategic preferences framework to be a valuable tool to test, focus and more clearly define customer requirements and business needs. In today's marketplace customer value expectations are forever rising and at an accelerating rate. The consequences for organizations that fail to adjust their offerings in response to these changing demands are catastrophic.

Organizations need to be very clear about the characteristics of their business environments in which they choose to compete today, tomorrow and three to five years on, and the strategic choices that best fit with it. It is no longer good enough to describe this in general terms. As organizations have become increasingly customer-focussed, so too have customers become more sophisticated in their needs and expectations and more discerning and unforgiving in their actions. Strategic preferences are a way of characterizing the principle of customer-value creation. Strategic preferences (there may be more than one) need to be energized by an appropriate set of organizational capabilities, attributes, characteristics and routines that are supported by an appropriate management style. We have identified four key strategic preferences[4] that may be used to help to refocus an organization's future direction and subsequently diagnose, evaluate and direct its principles development. The four preferences are described below.

1. *Process focus* – consistent provision of commodity products (e.g. McDonald's). These companies deliver a combination of quality, price, 'value for money', reliability of delivery and ease of purchase that is unsurpassed. Their success is underpinned by their ability to execute their core work and operational processes extraordinarily well.
2. *Product focus* – regularly introduce new products with highly desirable benefits (e.g. Sony). These companies are the innovators: highly creative organizations that continually create new markets and products. They are able effectively to translate creative talent into something of commercial value. These are the organizations that create cultures where their employees are prepared to search relentlessly for new opportunities. Their success is underpinned by their ability to develop a stream of new products (and services) that satisfy previously unserviced needs and the reputation and recognition that this brings.
3. *Relationship focus* – capable of developing and maintaining extremely close relationships that create mutually beneficial opportunities (e.g. ABB Technical Consulting). These organizations make it their business to keep close to their customers, know what they really need (as distinct from what they think they need) and tailor their products and services to best suit their customer's specific requirements. Their relationship management knowledge enables them to explore new opportunities with existing customers and to leverage these relationships to create new opportunities with new customers. They are extremely proficient at delivering solutions that satisfy customer needs better than anyone else. Their success is underpinned by their ability to cultivate and leverage a set of intimate relationships.
4. *Market focus* – capable of picking and responding to shifts and opportunities within the marketplace (e.g. Benetton). These companies are very adept at being able to pick the patterns in the marketplace and responding quickly with new and improved products and services. Demand is customer (or needs) led and there is a strong sense of urgency to respond to the opportunity and minimize response time to market. Their success is underpinned by their access to key customer and market information and their ability to interpret this information ('pick winners') and act quickly.

> ### RELATIONSHIP FOCUS – MASS CUSTOMIZATION AT DELL COMPUTERS FOR FORD
>
> A relationship focus can also be developed in the form of mass customization which is typically facilitated through the use of some form of information technology. Consider Dell's relationship with Ford. Dell supplies different PC and software configurations to different individuals within different departments of Ford. When Dell receives an order via the Ford intranet, it knows the full details of the person making the order and the type of computer they need. Dell then assembles and despatches the PC, with the software preloaded, some of which is proprietary Ford software. This relationship focus is personalized through the development of a handful of close relationships between key individuals in the two organizations. The sophistication of Dell's logistics software enables it to perform the customization easily and inexpensively. Even so, Ford does pay a premium for this service, but as it saves time and errors, the premium is considered worth paying.

These strategic preferences should be considered as perspectives, not positions. The demands of an organization's business environment frequently dictate that superior abilities be developed in more than one area. However, an organization can rarely develop and sustain a leadership position in the longer term, in more than two areas. Further, the preferences described above are not static. Today's preference requirements are not necessarily consistent with those of tomorrow. As markets evolve and fragment, products mature and competitor offerings change, so too may the nature of the customers' needs and therefore the nature of a company's offerings. The model provides a useful way of categorizing these changes and their impacts on the organizational forms that underpin them.

Table 18.1 further explores typical organizational characteristics and key principles that support these strategic preference orientations. For an organization to excel in the area of process focus, it must continuously reinvent, renew and improve its core processes and forever scrutinize the real value that support activities and functions add. It needs to be capable of engaging each and every employee in the business of improving and consolidating efficiency gains along each and every step of the major value chains in the business. Only then is it capable of offering reliability of service and 'best in class' value for money. Teams and work group excellence are the cornerstone of its success. Operating disciplines are clearly articulated and roles and responsi-

Table 18.1 Strategic preferences, organizational characteristics and typical key principles

Strategic preference	Organizational characteristics	Typical key principles for development and review[5,6]
Process focus	• Standardization • Strong financial control and production control orientation • Emphasis on process, equipment, plant, stability, rigorous analysis and information • Managerial effort focussed on teamwork, order and attention to detail	• Discipline • Alignment (internal values) • Integration (internal) • Distributed leadership • Micro to macro
Product force	• Emphasis on individuals, innovation and learning • Strong R&D and production orientation. Considerable emphasis on OD activity: hiring and motivating • Managerial effort focussed on leading, inspiring, living the vision	• Capabilities • Alignment (strategic intent) • Skills and learning
Relationship focus	• Emphasis on people, relationships, teamwork and solution development • Strong OD orientation – people recruitment, development, recognition, rewards, management, etc. • Managerial effort focussed on internal climate creation, living core values and demonstrating 'the relationship comes above all else'	• Alignment (customer and internal value sets) • Customer value creation • Integration (external) • Distributed leadership
Market focus	• Strong marketing orientation • Emphasis on action, goals and problem solving • Managerial effort focussed on commercial sensitivity, planning and speech – 'making things happen'	• Time based • Bias for action • Customer value creation • Alignment (strategic intent and values)

bilities are well defined. Process upsets and variations are exhaustively investigated. Success is reflected in the plethora of improvements introduced and level of engagement of employees in improvement activity.

> ### PROCESS FOCUS EXAMPLE – SOUTH WEST AIRLINES (SWA)
>
> The SWA success formula is underpinned by the organization's ability to consistently market low fares, provide reliable services that 'get the customer where they want to go each time and every time' and the ability to make ticketing easy and hassle free. This strategic perspective is supported by its operations strategies and disciplines. For example, it flies into secondary and smaller airports wherever possible to improve customer service and increase operating efficiency. Airports like Dallas's Love Field and Houston Hobby are closer to downtown, and therefore more convenient to travellers and less congested, which helps to assure on-time performance, and by keeping planes in the air, keep costs down. As another example, by adopting a routing strategy of flying point-to-point rather than central hub, planes can turn around in 15 minutes of arrival, a time substantially lower than the industry norm. The airline's entire fleet comprises Boeing 737s which simplifies training and inventory and helps to keep costs down.
>
> SWA's success has also been largely attributed to it's 'cult like' values. SWA personnel operate within a casual, fun-loving corporate culture that comes from the top ranks. It is reflected on the front lines where agents and flight attendants often wear shorts and T-shirts and crack jokes with passengers. Employees know the culture and expect others to live up to it. It has become a reputation and brand image both within and outside the company. In conjunction with its recruitment emphasis on values, this reputation helps to attract new employees who want to fit in that environment. SWA makes it absolutely clear who comes first – its employees. SWA believes that by ensuring its employees are satisfied, and dedicated they will be motivated to ensure the highest standards of customer care leading to repeat business and improved shareholder returns. Because SWA is an airline, it can offer one particularly attractive incentive – discounted or free travel. For example, those employees with no absences or late arrivals over a three-month period receive two free, space available, airline tickets within the company. They can use these tickets any way they wish, including giving them away to a friend. To an employee this is viewed as a valuable incentive while it costs nothing to the airline because the seats are space available.

Product-focussed firms regularly introduce new products and services and new product and service families with highly desirable benefits. These are the innovators – highly creative organizations that create new market opportunities for themselves that never existed in the past. These organizations create their own destiny, they are not controlled by those around them. These are ideas generation and ideas management businesses with highly talented and experienced individuals, often mavericks with an ability to consistently overcome immense hurdles to create something from nothing, thereby regularly and proactively setting 'the standard' within their particular business sector. Their enemy is not the competition but complacency. These organizations are very clear about their core purpose, the capabilities they need (and those they do not need) and are able to create an environment that inspires entrepreneurship and innovation. The inherent conflicts associated with managing creativity and commercial realities are acknowledged and managed as constructive tension.

PRODUCT FOCUS EXAMPLE – ERICSSON

Ericsson principally designs, manufacturers and installs telecommunications equipment. Ericsson is a global, decentralized and flexible organization operating in a rapidly changing marketplace and utilizing a technological base that is changing equally as rapidly. Ericsson believes that its ability to succeed in this environment is a function of:

- the ability to define and articulate a clear direction for the company against which development opportunities can be evaluated and progress can be measured;
- creating and sustaining a work environment that is conducive to attracting and retaining people of the highest caliber. Values that Ericsson consider important include: having the freedom and preparedness to act on ideas, a sense of personal contribution, a preparedness to resolve problems that arise in the pursuit of objectives (perseverance), recognition of an individual's value, participation and teamwork, and showing concern and respect for others.

Due to the speed of change in the marketplace and the technologies used, formal organizational arrangements are becoming less important, whereas informal networks, projects and competence centers are gaining increasing significance. A strong emphasis exists on streamlining and simplifying decision-making processes but ensuring essential safeguards are maintained.

PART 3 • IMPLEMENTATION

> All managers have been given very explicit leadership responsibilities that include:
>
> - inspiring initiative
> - championing delegation of responsibility to the individual at the lowest possible level
> - motivating teams and holding them accountable to deliver on commitments made
> - clear and consistent communication of the vision
> - demonstrating commitment to the vision through actions, words and behaviors
> - supporting and defending values
> - championing the professional development of all individuals.
>
> Ericsson invests heavily in the brains of its employees. These investments take the form of a commitment to ongoing education, expansion of responsibilities and rotational assignments. Further, Ericsson has developed extensive knowledge management systems to capture, develop and transfer key competencies, experiences and project learnings.
>
> •

Organizations that compete on the basis of relationships compete on the basis of values, feelings and interdependency. They do not deliver what the market wants but what the customer wants. These companies make it their business to keep extremely close to their customers and to know what they really need and to be sufficiently flexible and adaptable to tailor their products and services to suit their customer's specific requirements. However, relationship-focussed companies do not merely react to customer opportunities, they also initiate them by alerting their customers to potential opportunities and threats. These organizations are very clear about what they stand for and very clear about the characteristics of organizations that they serve and do not serve. They do not work with companies with minimal relationship requirements and/or whose values and styles are incompatible. Through each activity with their customers, they become increasingly proficient at understanding their customers' business and therefore increasingly differentiated from the com-

Organizations that compete on the basis of relationships compete on the basis of values, feelings and interdependency.

petition. They spend enormous amounts of time developing employees who are extremely knowledgeable about customer operations, highly skilled at managing customer relationships, developing solutions to customer's problems, and they integrate their strategies, plans and activities with those of their customers. These are the 'people businesses' and people who have a natural 'helping' and customer-service work ethic are the cornerstone of their success. They position themselves as essential partners in the realization of the customer's vision. Interaction with key customer contacts is tightly gatekept through a well-understood and carefully managed set of protocols.

RELATIONSHIP FOCUS EXAMPLE – COATED PAPER CORPORATION

Coated Paper manufacturers a range of specialty coated papers for use in glossy magazines and advertising materials. In this market, customers view quality, reliability and cost as qualifiers for doing business. The key and enduring sources of competitive advantage in this environment are:

- the ability to tailor paper properties and production runs to meet specific customer requirements;
- the ability to work closely and collaboratively with a select group of customers and others to develop effective solutions to downstream coated paper processing problems.

Consequently, Coated Paper has developed marketing strategies and production plans around a select customer group. Strong emphasis is given to ensuring customer relationships are carefully managed, and in particular, issues are understood, acknowledged and a prompt response is made. Customer relationship protocols have been developed and key customer contacts are carefully managed to ensure relationships and goodwill are maintained 'above all else'. For example, a major customer was recently in danger of losing one of its major customers due to a series of recurrent paper-processing problems. Coated Paper convened a problem-solving session involving the customer and the customer's customer to increase understanding of the problem, brainstorm ideas and develop solutions. The outcome not only resulted in a change to paper properties that addressed the end customer's problem but also simplified delivery arrangements, reducing transportation costs and plant set up times.

Customer personnel are empowered and possess the necessary blend of commercial, technical and interpersonal skills to ensure that they can quickly

> and competently respond to a range of customer needs. Key relationships have also been established at an operational level through mechanisms including visitations, problem-solving sessions, personnel interchange etc., to promote understanding between mill production operators and customer operators of each other's operation. This helps to ensure that problems and issues can be anticipated, effective action can be taken if a particular paper grade is suspect and problem-solving teams can be quickly commissioned when needed. Comprehensive online data monitoring and interchange between Coated Paper and its customers helps to build trust and understanding and reduce the possibility of 'Friday afternoon' panic attacks.
>
> ●

The strategic preference of market focus is underpinned by the ability to pick the shifts in the market place early and quickly marshal organizational resources to respond to the emergent commercial opportunities. The organizations typically make extensive use of market intelligence gathering and analysis systems/networks to clearly and quickly understand the nature of the opportunity. Demand is customer led and there is a strong sense of urgency to get things done. These organizations can identify very specifically the characteristics of the major market segments in which they compete. There is typically a very high level of activity and strong emphasis on getting things done, developing plans and milestones, complying with schedules and managing time effectively. Deviations to plans and schedules are tightly controlled. These organizations know precisely the time taken to perform each major activity and go to great lengths to analyze and learn from schedule creep. The organizational culture has a strong commercial orientation and the marketplace is typically highly competitive.

> ### MARKET FOCUS EXAMPLE – AXA INSURANCE GROUP
> ●
>
> Axa is the world's second largest insurance group and second largest asset manager. Its sustained success in the marketplace has been underpinned by its ability to quickly detect changing client and intermediary demands, its ability to quickly respond to these changing demands and its ability to leverage its core capabilities into new ventures and growth opportunities. Its workplace model is characterized by :

- an ability to capitalize on limited windows of opportunity
- acquisition of cross-functional skills and knowledge
- making teamwork succeed in an ambiguous, task-focussed environment
- pushing decision making to the lowest possible level
- getting people to take initiative
- pioneering new ways of doing things
- continually evolving the efficiency and effectiveness of its business processes.

These attributes are pursued through a range of personal development, team development and process review activities.

●●●●●●●●●●●●●●●●●●●

It is worth noting that growth strategies may substantially affect leadership demands as they may significantly change strategic preferences. Consider companies competing on the basis of the strategic preference of process focus. Once the business has streamlined its operations and developed unit cost structures that are world class, further improvements in business performance could be achieved by strategies involving the raising of unit costs and/or the reducing of labor costs. However, both of these tactics run counter to the fundamental basis of competitive advantage (value leadership and a committed and engaged team-based workforce). These companies may alternatively opt to improve business performance by revenue (and employment) growth through the application of strategies to enhance asset utilization, shift to higher value-added products, integrate with other operations upstream/downstream in the value chain, etc. In this way they may grow the existing business or opt for growth through the development of new businesses, e.g. exploiting aspects of their formula for success in other locations and other markets. These 'break out' strategies will require the creation of new purposes, new directions and new values. Leaders will need to engage and energize people in new directions and de-socialize them to the very strong operational disciplines and values that they frequently created and reinforced. This dislocation in directions, purpose and behaviors clearly requires a very different form of leadership style than that which the organization has historically needed and nurtured.

Strategic preference categorizations

To understand preferences and their differences, they have been categorized in the matrix shown in Table 18.2. Companies that compete on the basis of process and relationship focus tend to pursue stability, order and predictability. Process-focussed firms strive to stabilize the core work and production processes, both in terms of internal disturbances (eliminate variances and problems and consolidate new improvements) and external disturbances (changes in customer needs and demands). They also strive to develop work teams that are stable in terms of responsibility ('we are all very clear about our team boundaries and responsibilities') and the people who work in them ('we have all worked together for a long time and know each other well').

> **Relationship-focussed organizations compete on the basis of people – intimate customer knowledge and customer contacts.**

Alternatively, relationship-focussed organizations compete on the basis of people – intimate customer knowledge and customer contacts. They strive to ensure that the customer relationship is fostered by long-term associations between key people and an extensive and successful history of mutually beneficial associations. Ensuring consistency and mutuality of strategic plans and directions also helps to create a 'no surprises' customer culture.

Alternatively, product and market-focussed companies organize for ambiguity and change. Product-focussed companies are continually searching for new ways to add value and differentiate products; market-focussed companies are continually looking for new niches in the marketplace. As a consequence, both typically utilize fluid organizational structures, temporary taskforces and SWAT teams.

Companies that compete on the basis of process and product focus tend to manage from the 'inside out' – the energy and momentum for change comes from relentlessly trying to better themselves (process and product focus) or relentlessly pursue the creation of *their* vision (product focus). Conversely, relationship and market-focussed organizations tend to manage from the 'outside in' – the energy and momentum for change comes from responding to new marketplace opportunities (market focus) or from opportunities either presenting or possible, within customers' organizations (relationship focus).

Table 18.2 Strategic preference categorization matrix

	Predictability/stability ◄──► Ambiguity/dynamics	
Driving force – internal	Process focus	Product focus
Driving force – external	Relationship focus	Market focus

Linking principles to practices

Having described each strategic preference, provided an overview of the typical organizational characteristics needed to support it and identified (typical) priority principles for review and development, it is also very important to be able to understand and describe the different practices that reflect each principle in the different strategic preference environments.

To illustrate how strategic preferences impact on the practices that underpin each principle, consider the examples of the principles of integration and distributed leadership, which are developed in Tables 18.3 and 18.4. Here it can clearly be seen that strategic preferences significantly affect the nature of the practices underpinning each principle. Consider integration. Organizations competing on the basis of process focus typically achieve integration through the design of their work processes and work group structures, their use of co-ordination roles to manage group boundaries and by tying the structure together using common values. In contrast, organizations competing on the basis of product focus typically utilize meeting forums, gating mechanisms and agreed decision-making protocols to achieve integration and tie the work system together using a common vision.

Consider distributed leadership. The unit of analysis for market-focussed organizations is ad hoc, or SWAT, project teams. Alternatively, for product-focussed teams the unit of distributed leadership is the individual, since the organization's success is directly related to its ability to unleash and harness the ideas, creativity and intellect of each and every employee. Individuals work together in teams and team outcomes, processes and roles are often loosely defined, as the process is basically divergent. Hence goals are frequently reformulated and roles changed as concepts and ideas develop. Alternatively, in the market-focussed case, the end goal and timeframe is generally very clearly defined and distributed leadership is very much about supporting the achievement of goals, rather than their continuous testing, evolution and reformulation.

As discussed earlier, this material is used as a tool to stimulate group discussion and reaction and the content is not necessarily appropriate to each and every organization. It should also be tested and validated with a broad group of employees and other stakeholders to build a rich platform of ideas, understanding and commitment to change.

Table 18.3 Typical integration practices

Process perspective
Integration focus – internal
Typical integration elements:

- alignment (values)
- chunking work grouping
- co-ordination roles
- work process design
- systems.

Organizations are designed to eliminate functional silos and broaden people's responsibility set and/or work. Co-ordination roles confront and explore differences between work groups. Work processes are designed to eliminate handoffs and clarify work-group boundaries. Systems are utilized to integrate activities. Tie together with a strong team-based work ethic.

Product perspective
Integration focus – internal
Typical integration elements:

- alignment (vision)
- forums and gating mechanisms
- accountabilities
- seamless manufacturing interface
- decision making protocols.

Organizational structure/roles are fluid. Teams are kept small to enhance communication and commitment. Focus on understanding and buy in to the vision to provide a common 'beacon on the hill'. Product development gating points are clearly defined. Decision-making forums and protocols are clearly established around each gating point to 'tie' activities together. Accountabilities are clearly defined.

Relationship perspective
Integration focus – external and internal
Typical integration elements:

- alignment (values and literacy)
- strategy – customer partnerships
- clear customer relationship accountability.

Customer relationships are arranged in a partnership-like form (strategies, commercials and ongoing management). Customer relationships are carefully gatekept. Common company/customer values and mutual benefits underpin relationship effectiveness. Internal integration is facilitated by a clear and common understanding of the customer's business/drivers of success and values that ensure the customer relationship stands above all else, flexibility and adaptability.

Market perspective
Integration focus – external and internal
Typical integration elements:

- alignment (values)
- goals
- forums and gating mechanisms
- information management.

External integration achieved through provision of global, accurate, complete and timely information backed up by effective systems to identify and analyze opportunities. Internal integration achieved through the establishment of clearly defined project-team goals and accountabilities and effective gating mechanisms and decision-making protocols. Values reinforce strong end goal and commercial work ethic.

Table 18.4 Typical distributed leadership practices

Process perspective Distributed leadership perspective: stable work teams ● team operating processes and protocols ● standardization of work routines ● key roles assigned within work team ● enabling learning bureacracies ● rewards based on team performance. Each and every work team is empowered to undertake a range of business, technical and interpersonal responsibilities. Individual roles are defined within broad team concepts. Individuals view their needs as secondary to those of the team. Team activities and improvement capability is underpinned by an enabling learning bureaucracy.	**Product perspective** Distributed leadership perspective: the individual ● broad policies and guidelines ● alignment (vision) ● opportunities for personal development ● rewards based on idea's success in the marketplace. The focus is on maximizing the business value of individual skills and knowledge. Creativity, entrepreneurship and the need to achieve are highly valued. Individuals are empowered to perform a range of tasks within broad guidelines. Managers help facilitate distributed leadership by creating the direction, removing the barriers and developing an environment that manages creativity as a positive tension.
Relationship perspective Distributed leadership perspective: customer interface personnel/ internal resources ● alignment (values) ● interface personnel empowered to 'do deals' with customers ● responding to customer needs in ways that maintain employee commitment/loyalty ● rewards linked to customer retention and business growth. Customer interface personnel build customer confidence by 'doing deals', often in new areas and in new ways. These personnel are empowered to change internal organizational priorities and negotiate resourcing requirements in order to be able to respond accordingly. This response capability is supported by the organization's loose structure and tight values set.	**Market perspective** Distributed leadership perspective: SWAT teams ● ability to rapidly form and disestablish temporary teams ● team goals are absolute ● time critical – test and challenge the rules ● strong set of financial motivators. Teams are fluidly established and disestablished in accordance with emerging market needs/opportunities and competitor actions. Individuals are typically engaged in a range of different assignments within different teams and are able quickly to join teams and develop effective work relationships with others. As achievement is highly valued, individuals often 'bend' the rules to ensure that the 'job gets done'.

STEP 3: PERFORMANCE ASSESSMENT – BUSINESS/ORGANIZATIONAL

The models and frameworks used in Step 2 can then be applied to the current business and organizational systems to both assess performance and gain a detailed understanding of the organization's change history and change context, in particular what worked, what didn't work and why. This is a particularly useful and insightful process that often helps to demystify experiences from the past and attitudes toward the present.

Consider the example of a manufacturer of standard sheet-steel products where this process was applied. This business clearly competed on the basis of process focus – manufacturing and distributing steel cheaper, easier and more reliably than its competitors. A review of its operations with key staff found over 30 key strategic and operational issues warranting attention. Using the strategic priorities and 14 principles framework discussed in Step 2, cause and effect relationships were established and some initial actions formulated. The final list reduced to the five issues discussed below.

Product quality problems

Inconsistent quality had resulted in the operation losing a number of large customers. As a consequence, in order to fill production quotas, the operation was now serving 22 small customers, many of whom had specialist needs and requirements. The operation was clearly not equipped for job shopping – specialist production runs. Moreover specialist-run customers were more demanding and sophisticated in their requirements. Compared to the competitors in these areas, the operation was ill-equipped to fulfill these requirements (no knowledge of their operations, no local infrastructure and poor response capability). Relationships with specialist customers/short-run operations were subsequently ceased.

Lack of micro-to-macro connection

The organization was generally unable to convert its improvement efforts into unit cost reduction. Moreover, where this did occur, the reductions were not passed on to customers, due to poor divisional returns on investment. The organization was found to be working on too many 'long bow' projects or projects with loose connections to its business goals. The operation was also found to lack the necessary systems, discipline and formality to institutionalize the improvements made. Moreover corporate relationships could, at best, be described at arms length and there was a lack of common understanding and commitment to act. There was an urgent need to convene forums to develop understanding and air, discuss and resolve issues of common interest.

Minimal operating discipline

The principal organizational improvement thrust was 'culture change' through a range of activities including work design, business education, team development and leadership development. These processes were emphasizing social aspects, and in some instances technical aspects associated with the operation and work but de-emphasizing business requirements. As a result, teams were found to be operating as 'entities unto their own' and opposing the introduction of what were basically essential operating disciplines. These disciplines were viewed as disempowering and a return to the 'old way of working'. Team attitudes toward enabling disciplines were unlocked by a series of visits to other sites where the advantages of enabling discipline in terms of performance management, learning and continuous improvement were observed, discussed and debated.

Ineffective systems discipline

Information systems were poor in terms of both functionality and information quality. As a result, information was duplicated in manual form and there was a lack of credible information to assist in critical areas of decision making. A thorough needs analysis was subsequently undertaken and a new information system platform introduced. This also significantly improved team co-ordination and overall activity integration across the operation.

Poor integration

Each work group was also operating as a separate entity, that is, co-ordination and co-operation between work areas and shifts was virtually non-existent. Two middle levels of supervision had been removed and there was a need to reintroduce support in certain areas. The introduction of this support was delayed until team operating effectiveness had developed to a point where further improvement and learning opportunities necessitated work group interface management.

STEP 4: DIAGNOSIS AND DEVELOPMENT OF THE CHANGE CASE (GAP ANALYSIS)

As each end point is different and each start point is different, every change path will be different. These differences are in terms of business drivers, change attractors, the magnitude of the performance gap, organizational culture, scars from previous fad burns,[7] leadership capability, individual attitudes and values, executive team personalities and dynamics, maturity of systems, time available, financial strength and a host of other factors. This step analyses the gap between the desired and existing state and identifies the major themes for change and the principal actions to achieve the necessary changes.

STEP 5: PROJECT PLANNING

This step is concerned with consolidating all the information from Steps 1–4 into a case for change. The project plan includes a broad range of perspectives including the outcomes sought, the benefits and risks, the measures of success, the timeframe, the boundaries, commitment-building strategies, communication strategies, the detail of the interventions proposed, the development of change agents, the implications for current change activities, co-ordination issues, project management and resourcing issues and the factors that will support (and impede) success. It also typically involves sharing, testing and validating the change plan with the broader workforce and other stakeholders.

STEP 6: IMPLEMENTATION AND REVIEW

Step 6 is concerned with the delivery of actual change initiatives, converting outcomes into organizational attributes and consolidating gains made. It is also concerned with monitoring and reviewing change-program outcomes, problems arising, evaluating key learnings (organizational change, management principles, business performance) and assessing 'where to from here'.

SUMMARY

In summarizing this process, many of the steps contain little more than good old common sense, hence we have not emphasized them here, as they have been discussed many times before in standard management texts, and both executives and consultants are very familiar with some of these implementation steps. We focussed primarily on Step 2, since it involves understanding yesterday's, today's and tomorrow's strategic preferences and choosing which principles to focus on, based on that strategic preference positioning. This step also illustrates how a particular principle may be reflected in different practices that support different strategic orientations.

Ultimately, what is different about this approach from well-known change management methodologies? The main differential is the systematic use of the principles and their fit to the strategic preference as outlined in Step 2 above. This step provides the focus and connections that make the difference between a poorly focussed change initiative and one that is well focussed.

Notes

1. The reader may recall that the difference between these approaches is of kind, not degree. Figure 1.2, the ad hoc approach of Management by Slogan, is characterized by a large percentage of activity being, in effect, value leaching rather than value adding.
2. In many organizations, talented and experienced leaders perform much of this work intuitively. However, many of us are not as gifted, have doubts and/or require clarification.
3. Collins and Porras (1994).
4. The reader will find similarities between three of these preferences and the three value propositions articulated earlier by Treacy and Wiesma (1995).
5. This list should only be considered as a starting point to stimulate discussion and development. It is not a definitive list.
6. Alignment is a key bedrock principle that supports all strategic preferences although the emphasis shifts between perspectives as indicated. Up front is also a critical bedrock principle that underpins each perspective.
7. What are fad burns? Fad burns are a result of having tried to manage by grabbing at fads and being burned. They leave burn scars. How many burn scars can you count in your company? Don't be surprised if there are about 10, which is the average.

19

Key Success Factors – the system of management

....

Good management consists in showing average people how to do the work of superior people.

John D. Rockefeller, 1913

INTRODUCTION
....

We have identified ten Key Success Factors (KSFs) to progress to a principles-based system of management, that is, to achieve Figure 1.3. These conditions, and their implications in terms of the principles described in Part 2, are listed in Table 19.1 and discussed in detail in the sections that follow.

These KSFs can be considered as a readiness assessment test of an organization's ability to move up the curve of 'management by principles'. Just as the principles can be considered as the foundation stones of building a great organization, the KSFs can be thought of as the ingredients needed to make the jump from Figure 1.2 to Figure 1.3 as the management model of the organization.

Table 19.1 Ten Key Success Factors to develop Figure 1.3

KSF No	Description	Principles implication
1	Understanding the changing nature of business strategy due to the increased complexity, uncertainty and dynamics of doing business and the failure of conventional planning approaches.	The paradigm shift from implementing planned strategies to recognizing and acting on emergent patterns. Increased importance of alignment, external (business environment) sensitivity, identity and relationships over structural integrity and fit.
2	Assuring business and organizational systems are continuously readjusted to mutually reinforce and support one another.	The need to allocate sufficient resources to co-ordinate this alignment effort and the need to ensure adjustments are supported by clear logic and are effectively communicated throughout the organization.
3	Understanding the magnitude of the performance gap and knowing how long we have to make the necessary changes.	Ensuring the fundamental thrust of organizational activity is consistent with prevailing business needs and cultural realities. Not commencing a principles-based rebuilding approach where restructuring is needed.
4	Knowing the limits of restructuring and the growth breakpoint.	Using principles that drive cost reduction as opportunities for business growth.
5	Developing an exceptional sense of reality.	Garbage in ... garbage out. The value of the 14 principles framework is directly related to the quality of the information used and degree of objectivity of those using it.
6	Avoiding fad-surfing.	Unless the organization understands and learns from its change history it may fail to recognize the fallacies of fad-surfing/cookbook management. Consequently, neither the critical mass of support for change nor the discipline/focus will evolve.
7	Keeping it relevant and keeping it simple.	Accepting that the change plan will not provide the answers. Understanding the value of 'the process' and adopting a

Table 19.1 Continued

		'snowball' roll-out approach to build understanding and commitment. Doing less change rather than more – prioritizing principles for development and pursuing their development through a relatively small number of interventions.
8	Getting into specifics – managing the detail not the concept.	Intellectually engaging in discussions about the principles is easy. Translating them into an enduring set of behaviors and practices that take hold requires effective management of the detail. These discussions are key to escaping the 'one shoe fits all' management mindset.
9	Leadership of change – top management support and buy-in.	The organization needs an effective 'guiding coalition' to manage and co-ordinate the change effort and exceptional change agents to deliver and consolidate real change on the ground. Leadership needs and style are contingent on a range of factors including customer style, business type, performance drivers, culture, change activities, timeframe, etc. But always strong firm leadership is a prerequisite.
10	Stakeholder engagement.	The needs and aspirations of key internal and external demand groups who have power and influence over business performance need to be built into the review process.

KSF 1 – UNDERSTANDING THE CHANGING NATURE OF BUSINESS STRATEGY: FROM PLAN TO PROCESS

Summary

Business is becoming a war of movement. As a consequence of unpredictability, complexity, uncertainty and discontinuity, strategies are increasingly developed through reactive and evolutionary (rather than purely defined and planned) means. To be proficient in an emergent strategy environment requires a strong sense of purpose and identity (know what to look for), extensive relationship networks (ability to look for it), high-quality information (timely, complete and accurate) and adaptability (the ability to respond). In short, organizations need to be full of business thinkers where everyone is engaged in the process of strategy development and contributing to the process of strategy realization. In these environments we do not want organizations developed around a *fit* model but an *alignment* model. This alignment activity becomes the new business mission. This implies that understanding the processes by which strategies develop and are effectively implemented is becoming more important than building an organization around the actual content of the strategy set per se.

Just how does the business environment affect an organization's principles development needs? Today virtually all organizations are exposed to increasingly turbulent and complex business environments. This is not to say that this was not generally the case in the past, but what is different today is the *level* of turbulence. During the last 20 years, the level of turbulence has progressively escalated in most industries. For those few organizations that continue to operate in 'stable' environments the structural benefits that they have enjoyed in the past are less prevalent and less relevant. Factors such as industry type, facilities location, customer base, product lines, markets, market share, demographics, technology, etc., simply do not provide the same magnitude of benefit that they did in the past. In fact some managers would argue that yesterday's benefits have become today's 'liabilities of inertia' – the organization is paradigm-bound and people are living in the past, not the present.

How do most organizations connect their activities with their business environment? They analyze their respective competitive situation and develop missions, visions, plans and strategies to best respond to it, capitalize on it, preempt it or, in some instances, change it to best suit them. Historically, strategic positioning processes have been used as the centrepiece around which to develop and configure the organization and its resources to energize the chosen direction, focus organization activities and maximize the business value of scarce resources. Has this process worked? Put differently, just how many of the future plans that a company makes are successfully implemented? By successful implementation we mean they are actioned and the outcomes deliver on the objectives. Consider and contrast the association between today's business strategy set and yesterday's business plan. Pick a two to three year time horizon. The associations are typically weak and for most firms, only about 10 percent of what they plan to do is achieved.

What have we done about failures of strategy? Actually a great deal. In fact, we could be accused of studying it to death. We have dissected and analyzed it from every angle. We have held countless seminars about it and written numerous books about it. We've advocated recipes to address it. We've formed business schools around it. We've identified and applied the learnings in subsequent attempts – but our overall batting average has not improved much. Are we addressing the right question? What if our strategy failures are not failures of implementation but failures of design? What if the very nature of doing business is such that for most businesses we simply cannot develop definitive plans more than 12 months out?[1] Further, what if our predisposition toward planning, predetermination, predictability and proactivity and our predisposition to regard reactive management as 'poor' management is part of the problem? If we often cannot predict discontinuities, avoid crises and influence our business environment, then our ability to react to it quickly and effectively should be regarded as legitimate management work. In fact we have found that crises often provide a unique opportunity for change and can constitute a positive event.

Returning to the planning issue, why then do we plan and what is the future 'role' of planning? Many planning participants argue that the value of the planning process has less to do with the plans produced, which are often considered superficial and/or academic, and more to do with the understandings, relationships and collective common purpose that evolves. These experiences are consistent with the views of some contemporary business strategy theorists and practitioners. Mintzberg (1994), argues that business strategies develop through two different streams. First, they materialize out of future plans and aspirations, the low-hit 'intended' path, and second, they evolve out of past patterns of behavior, the 'emergent' path. Few strategies are purely one stream or the other, as one suggests no learning and the other no control. Effective strategies mix these characteristics in ways that reflect the conditions at hand, notably the ability to predict as well as the need to react to unexpected events (Mintzberg, p.25). However, the level of turbulence, unpredictability and complexity that exists in most business environments implies that adaptability is often the dominant factor. The trends of increasing levels of business environment dynamism and complexity imply that this dominance of emergent strategy over realized strategy will continue into the future. Strategic targets can be expected to shift and continue to fragment into a multiplicity of smaller targets and ever faster and faster speeds.

What does it take to be an organization that is proficient at emergent strategy formulation and execution? Business environment sensitivity, clear organizational purpose, high levels of employee engagement and individual adaptability are clearly elevated to center stage. In increasingly turbulent environments, relationships, purpose, identity, information and adaptability become more important than structural fit which continues to be the goal of many organizations (consider McKinsey's 7S model). In *unstable environments*, we do not want structural fit as it frequently works against the very attributes we seek to develop. The concept of structural fit is increasingly replaced by one of alignment. The focus on structural advantages (what we've got) is increasingly replaced with concept of capabilities (process attributes that reflect how good we are). It should not be implied that an organization will always seek alignment today to produce alignment tomorrow. For example, if the business environment is expected to change significantly, then the organization might begin to change its leadership style in a way that facilitates different strategic thinking and prepares the organization for the anticipated changed marketplace conditions.

> **The concept of structural fit is increasingly replaced by one of alignment.**

Hence, the dominant strategy paradigm shifts from top-down rational deduction to bottom-up intuitive synthesis. We need a business full of business thinkers where everyone is engaged in the process of strategy development and contributing to the process of strategy realization. As a consequence, an organization's ability to define and agree its purpose, develop shared understanding, broaden employee perspectives, forge critical external relationships, source key information, pick the patterns early, accept reactive management as a way of life, work with ambiguity, risk and uncertainty will become increasingly crucial.

In respect of the achievement of external environmental sensitivity, consider the role of information technology. Many organizations are becoming more sensitized to their external environment through the extensive use of various forms of information technology. Global information capturing, information building, information analysis and information-utilization technologies in addition to other information technologies (e.g. e-mail) are clearly useful tools to assist with this requirement. However, that is all they are – tools. Unfortunately in some organizations the use of information technology tools has come at a price – the maintenance and development of effective internal and external relationships. When overused and overextended, information management tools clearly hinder effective relationship management. Our experience over the last half century also suggests that the more time people spend interacting with technology, the less time they are inclined to spend interacting with one another. In fact in some organizations technology has become a substitute, rather than a complement, for personal interaction. Used as a major socialization agent, this benign medium can undermine alignment and integration and produce an extremely unhealthy culture.

KSF 2 – INTEGRATED MANAGEMENT OF BUSINESS STRATEGY AND ORGANIZATIONAL DEVELOPMENT SYSTEMS

Summary

Today, most organizations have a relatively low level of connectedness between their business and organizational systems. In particular, the connections between business systems and organizational systems, the what and how elements of Figure 1.1, are underdeveloped. In leading companies, this work has become the new strategic agenda for the CEO. One key activity area involves a variety of forums, processes and conversations to increase understanding and partnering between business strategists, organizational development professionals and employees at all levels.

What are the implications of this changing strategic agenda on organizational development activity and those who provide it? Consider Figure 19.1. We have previously argued the looseness of the planned-to-realized business strategy link and the extent to which business strategies are increasingly formulated by the emergent path. Consequently, the extent to which planned organizational strategies, if fully implemented, support realized business strategies is extremely tenuous. This problem is further aggravated by the contaminants to planned organizational strategy. The plethora of new managerial paradigms, tools and techniques that consistently bombard an organization, the decentralization of many organizational development activities, in addition to changing societal and employee norms, frequently results in realized organizational strategies bearing little, if any, resemblance to those planned, irrespective of changes within the business context and strategy.

This lack of strategic connectedness has significantly contributed to the decline in the status and the effectiveness of the organizational development practitioner in recent years.

Leading companies have developed the ability to recognize this relationship deficiency and work on more closely coupling the processes of business strategy formation and organizational/people development. This work is initiated and championed by the CEO. Jack Welch of GE is a leading example of a successful CEO with this focus. These leading organizations have formed one integrated improvement initiative (see Figure 1.3).

Consider strategy conversations. Executives often struggle to agree on a common purpose and direction. Alternatively, they may agree on the general direction but fail to reach agreement on the specific short-term actions to take (this is explored further in KSF 8). What do they typically do? Bring in more information, more experience and sometimes more people to shore up their positions. However, the basic problem often does not relate to the information, per se, but to individual participant values, biases, prejudices and pre-

Key Success Factors – the system of management

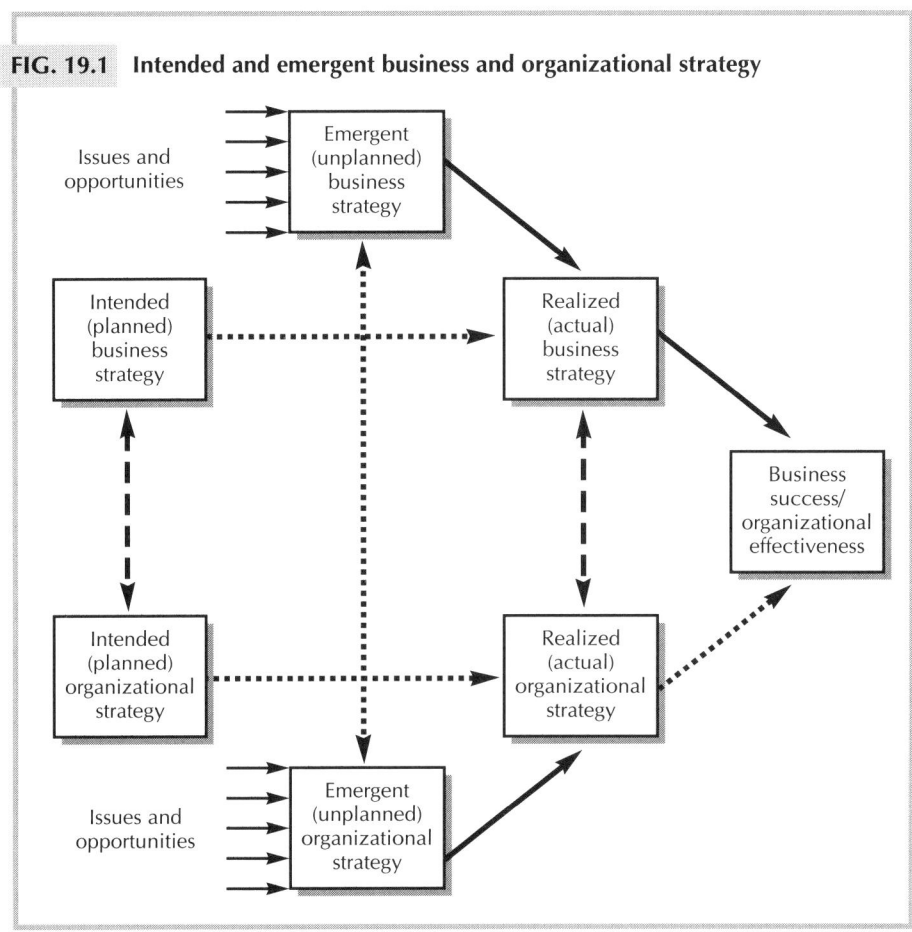

FIG. 19.1 Intended and emergent business and organizational strategy

dispositions. Different people perceive, interpret and react to the same information differently and have differing sets of motivations to do so. These differences need to be acknowledged and understood and the group 'unlocked' and the process 'depoliticized' if a true common purpose is to be developed.

CEOs are uniquely placed to discuss how the company should be organized to carry out its strategy, how it can engage others in the process, how it can create the necessary conditions for change. Business-literate organizational development professionals may also have a key role to play in this activity, in addition to helping to ensure that 'the right' people are attracted and retained, that strategy evolves with culture, that employees are involved and engaged in the strategy conversation, that new capabilities are developed and that the capacity to change continues to develop.[2]

KSF 3 – KNOW THE MAGNITUDE OF THE GAP, KNOW HOW LONG THERE IS AND KNOW THE CULTURE

Summary

Some organizations have failed adequately to assess whether they are in the rebuilding business or the restructuring business, or alternatively, failed to review and re-renew their position in the light of emerging events and actions. Many organizations are in the rebuilding business when they should be in the restructuring business and vice versa. The difference between these two approaches is one of kind, not degree. Working both processes in parallel frequently produces limited short-term gains only, as the fundamental inconsistencies between the two result in each approach undermining the other.

A principles-based management approach creates a framework with which to review organizational effectiveness, envision the desired future organizational state and direct organizational development. However, its use needs to be considered in the context of the firm's predisposition toward change, the magnitude of the performance gaps and the length of time available to make the necessary improvements. Consider the two extreme states of firm behavior: firms with a strong *predisposition toward change*[3] and firms with a strong *predisposition toward opposing change* – preserving the status quo. This predisposition and opposition toward change can be associated with many issues: change drivers and actuators, business environment, change strategy, business strategy, prevailing culture and norms, individual attitudes and values, individual agendas and interests, management style, organizational structure, work processes, systems, technology, etc. Clearly most firms are somewhere between these two extremes which we depict in Figure 19.2 as Firm A (predisposition toward opposing change) and Firm B (predisposition toward change).

Firm A typically exhibits some of the following characteristics.

- Insufficient pressure for real change – industry/firm performance in decline but the business is still profitable.
- Increasing managerial frustration and sense of urgency – time, shareholder and corporate patience are running out.
- Many employees living in the past – strongly socialized to the 'good old days'.
- Many employees do not understand the external business environment and presenting organizational threats and opportunities.
- Management focus on organizational issues/culture change rather than business development and growth.

Key Success Factors – the system of management

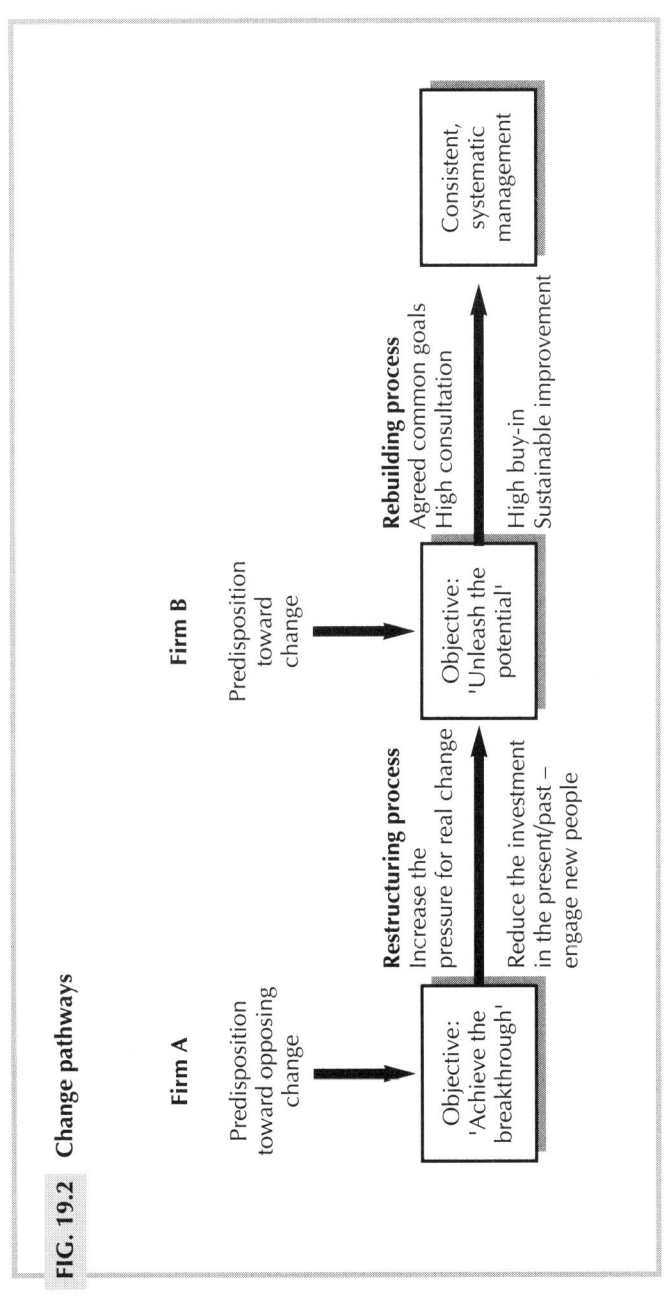

FIG. 19.2 Change pathways

- Management team dysfunctional behavior and high rate of executive team turnover, lots of 'shifting the deckchairs'.
- Passive management of underperformance and a lack of true accountability.
- High-control, risk-averse, 'self-propagating' culture.
- Insufficient experienced, change-capable managers and supervisors.
- Entrenched, adversarial employee/management relationships – minimal trust and strong socialization to past behavioral norms.
- Empowerment not accompanied with acceptance of responsibility.
- Perceived lack of common ground between employees and management.
- Track record of being unable to introduce and sustain real change.

In these environments, we have found that a 'significant activity/event' is generally required to break the deadlock, particularly where the time available for change is limited. Consequently, highly consultative, incremental, rebuilding processes typically have a low success rate. *Simply put, if it is a type A firm, it needs to break through before we can rebuild.* In fact we have observed a number of type A firms where the inappropriate, and sometimes, blind application of rebuilding approaches has actually exacerbated their performance problems and cultural deficiencies.

Contrastingly, firms that have successfully made the transition from type A to type B have employed combinations of a range of approaches that include those listed below.

- Plant and/or facility closure or rationalization or consolidation.
- Employee 'changeout' (CEO, executive, middle management, production employees).
- Management restructuring.
- Organizational restructuring.
- Workforce downsizing – typically 'one-off', not piecemeal/ incremental.
- External recruitment – significant infusion of new people: new faces, new attitudes, new needs and new expectations.
- A major event, e.g. a CEO presentation.
- Outsourcing.
- Active management of under-performance: termination of poor performers.
- Incentives and rewards for change.
- Changes to employee conditions of employment.
- Changes to work arrangements and practices.
- Stretching of employee comfort zones (hybrid roles and responsibilities, secondments/transfers, etc.).

Key Success Factors – the system of management

- Strategies to increase employee business awareness: education, benchmarking, etc.
- Strategies to build a critical mass of support and reduce resistance.
- Business restructuring: privatization, acquisitions, divestments, etc.
- Significant changes to business direction.
- Significant changes to established lines of business.
- Quality and customer service initiatives.
- Technological innovation.
- Growth and investment.
- Process redesign.
- Introduction of a world-class safety management culture.

Once a type A firm has undertaken a restructuring process, significant effort and time needs to be invested to change employee behavior, otherwise real change will stop once the process is completed. A restructured firm may opt for a change approach that unleashes the latent change potential of the organization created by the restructuring process[4] and progress into growth. Restructuring can clearly be a highly effective vehicle to overcome change resistance, change apathy and change skepticism as people at all levels come to recognize that the firm is absolutely committed to delivering on real change, change momentum has been developed, the change process takes the organizational spotlight and many fears of the unknown are addressed.

Firms with latent change potential that gain maximum benefit from a rebuilding process, i.e. type B firms, are characterized by:

- a stable, committed and energetic executive team who possess excellent leadership skills and who are prepared, and able, to lead the change process from the front;[5]
- a middle management group which embraces the chosen change directions and possesses the change management skills and savvy to 'make it happen';
- a critical mass of the workforce which supports the need for real change and wants to be dealt into the change process;
- business strategies, organizational development strategies and leadership styles that are appropriate for the particular competitive situation;
- a common bond and common goal: all employees are united in their quest to improve firm performance and profitability: all other requirements and demands are secondary to this goal.

The work environment at Firm B is developed to a such a point by interventions which enhance collaboration, participation and acceptance of responsibility. Personal development can be extremely effective vehicles to realize this latent potential. Type B firms typically achieve considerable success with processes and activities such as work and job redesign, joint problem-solving activities, teamwork development, interpersonal relationship development, developing workplace culture in accordance with agreed values, staff recruitment/development and appraisal innovations, job enrichment processes, performance management processes, efficiency and process improvement, etc. In these environments, these activities work and they stick.

How many companies have made the mistake of being in need of a serious restructure but instead attempt a rebuild, or vice-versa? Countless thousands have not recognized the essential 'difference in kind' of managerial approach and style needed for these two very different types of change and hence have failed.[6] Even worse, others have tried to do both types of change simultaneously which rarely produces the desired results. How can we expect people to commit fully to a business that treats them as 'dispensable commodities'? The confusion surrounding mixed agendas is further exacerbated by most people's limited understanding of the business rationale that necessitated major changes in direction and strategy to occur. Many firms are painstakingly undertaking rebuilding activity upon rebuilding activity but never making any real inroads into improvement (see Table 19.2). These organizations often do not have the right triggers for change, nor the time, nor the right 'type' of organizational mindset nor leadership style for rebuilding type processes to deliver. In these cases we simply cannot get alignment or distributed leadership, despite attempting to do all the 'right' things. Moreover, what improvements we do achieve will either be too slow, too marginal, unsustainable or a combination of all three.

Alternatively, we have also observed that managers in many other firms employ restructuring processes when there was no real need to do so. One or two relatively small changes in a couple of critical areas would have tipped the balance of the scales and created the critical level of support that they so desperately sought – there was simply no need for a bout of 'slash and burn'.

Table 19.2 Implementation pathways matrix

	Type A	Type B
Restructuring	**Achieve breakthrough**	Confused activity
Rebuilding	Lack of real progress	**Unleash potential**

Quotes from CEOs of leading firms that have effectively completed major change processes include the following.

> 'Our biggest mistake was failing to recognize that it's a lot easier to deal with the new problems created by a new management team and workforce than dealing with the old problems associated with 30 years of cultural baggage.'

> 'Restructure then rebuild. We tried to do both at once and failed. We also learned that you must understand how to change management style quickly … that means new faces, new roles and communication, communication and more communication.'

> 'Expect about one third of the executive team to leave and stabilize the team before you start any restructuring or rebuilding process.'

> 'Don't leave out your middle managers. You need to bring in some new blood and get them heavily involved in the process early.'

> 'If you're going to change-out your workforce make an event of it … do it once and do it properly as part of a well thought out change strategy.'

> 'In respect to culture – our biggest mistake was that we tried to make a dog into a pet.'

> 'There are only two types of change processes … those where you deal people in and those where you deal with people.'

KSF 4 – KNOW THE LIMITS OF RESTRUCTURING AND THE BUSINESS GROWTH BREAKPOINT: IS THE ORGANIZATION AT RISK OF BECOMING ANOREXIC?

Summary

Today, many organizations have either reached or are fast approaching the limits of performance improvement through strategies to reduce costs and improve efficiencies. Leading businesses develop a greater focus on the other side of the performance equation – namely revenue growth. These organizations view principles and practices that drive cost reduction as leverage opportunities for business growth.

Many firms fail to realize the limits of restructuring and the restructuring-rebuilding breakpoint. Therefore, their only change alternative is to move 'forward' through wave after wave of restructuring until ultimately there is very little left to restructure. Does this sound familiar? For some businesses, their relentless and possibly myopic focus on short-term cost reduction and efficiency improvement 'by any means' has resulted in an organization that has extinguished virtually all its sources of competitive advantage. These firms become hollow organizations which have passed the point of critical mass (see point 5, Figure 19.3). With no other source of performance improvement available, growth is fast becoming the dominant new paradigm which means that many firms must now confront the legacy of their past actions.

It is not easy to:

- acquire new customers when we have shed most of the old ones
- convince the board to invest more money in a business that has historically underperformed
- develop new products and services when we have outsourced most of our technical capability
- encourage involvement when we have been showering employees with pink slips
- become innovative when many of the more talented employees have already walked
- become externally market-focussed when internal operating problems are around every corner
- become fast changing and adaptable when we have been standardizing and systematizing the operations in a drive to reduce costs.

Alternatively, an organization can choose to view those attributes that were key in its rationalization activities as key drivers of growth by leveraging them in other ventures and areas of development opportunity. For example, we have often observed that integration has been a dominant principle in cost-reduction programs and resulted in changes to the relationships between suppliers, vendors, contractors and customers in ways that enhance alignment and reduce costs. These same practices, leveraged effectively, can be of immense value in developing new business ventures through strategic alliances, mergers and acquisitions, joint ventures and various forms of customer partnerships.

FIG. 19.3 Performance

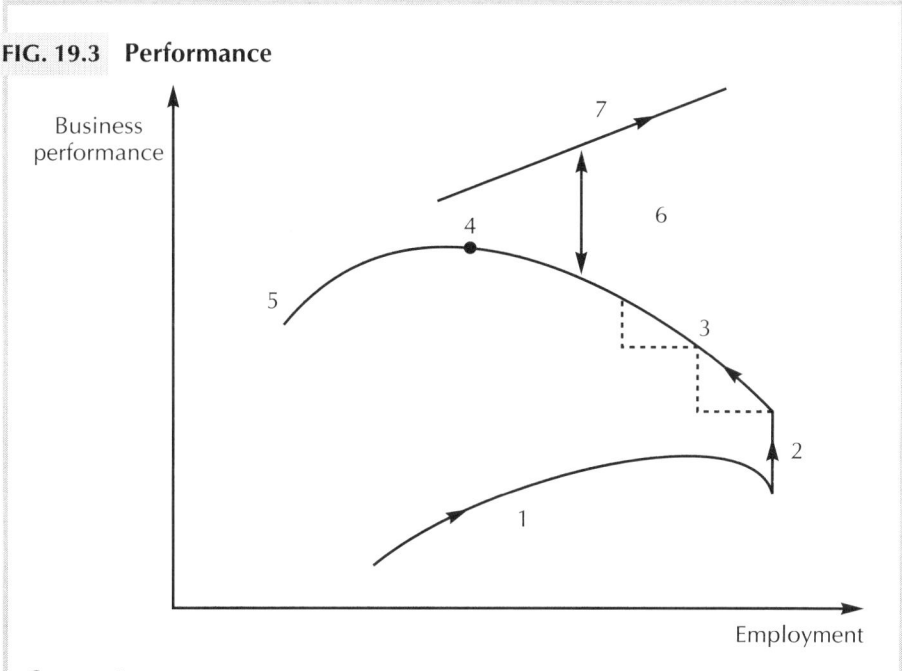

Company types:
1. The 1970s company – had employment growth with diminishing financial returns.
2. The 1980s company – adopted incremental business improvement strategies (e.g. quality management).
3. The 1990s rationalizing company – is fat and in need of restructuring and revitalization.
4. The 1990s wilderness company – is lean but continues to focus on restructuring and rationalization.
5. The 1990s dying company – is anorexic: has been stripped of its core capabilities and resources.
6. The 1990s oscillating company – periodically oscillates between growth and restructuring.
7. The 2000s growth company – has found new purpose, new meaning and new life.

KSF 5 – DEVELOP AN EXCEPTIONAL SENSE OF REALITY

Summary

Many organizations make poor decisions because they have a poor sense of reality. An exceptional sense of reality is essential for the effective application of the 14 principles of management. 'A good roadmap is of limited use in poor light.'

Why do some organizations undertake 'knee jerk' actions and reactions that are not really appropriate for their particular situation? We have argued earlier that it has a lot to do with some managers' preoccupation with the 'quick fix' and lack of systemic approach but is that all? We also contend that it has a lot to do with an inability, individual and collective, to see things as they really are i.e., their *sense of reality*. We have found a strong sense of reality to be a major differentiator of behavior between the best and the rest. Irrespective of how comprehensive the cognitive map used to review organizational effectiveness, the outcome will be poor without a good sense of reality.

Managers in many average performing firms in which we have worked, grossly overstate their organizational strengths and grossly understate their organizational weaknesses and vice versa. Still others never take the time to assess objectively their own organizational performance. These firms are not into diagnosis, they are into prescriptions. Often their insularity, and in some instances, downright arrogance, results in them believing they are much better than they really are or that they have a much longer time available to change than they have actually got. In particular, their perceptions of their own leadership capabilities and workforce behavior (attitudes toward change, preparedness to change, ability to change, etc.), either in a positive or negative sense, are often totally unrealistic.

Let's consider 'sense of reality' in a little more detail by reconsidering our example of the type A firm, which is predisposed to the application of a rebuilding approach. In these situations, we typically find falling profits spawning lots of change activity, fad surfing, empowerment without acceptance of responsibility, talented and experienced managers with a scattergun style, many employees sitting on the fence and union officials who are espousing all the right words but whose actions are basically reflecting past practices. Simply put, things are not working but the organization continues to 'muddle along' without ever really facing some basic home truths about its behavior.

Standard practice in management consulting may be to tell the company's executives that they should work with the existing management team, middle management group and general workforce in a highly participative way to reduce resistance and gain commitment. In sum, give managers clear change accountabilities, deal people into a process that designs their future and give them a stake in company success through rewards and eventually, real improvement will occur. However the truth may be that even if there is the time, this generally doesn't work – there may not be enough pressure for real change.

We have frequently observed that these are situations clouded in a veil of change rhetoric with firms committing to the rebuilding approach without sufficient initial clarity of understanding of the common ground and differences between the groups involved. Their failure to do this 'up-front' is symptomatic of a poor sense of reality. We argue that it is these approaches, variously characterized as 'vision of faith', 'let's keep talking about it', 'if we build it they will come' – the management consultant's dream – that are, in many respects, at the heart of the demise of modern management excellence. In this respect, standard management consulting has become part of the problem, not part of the solution, with too many organizations having ridden this horse for too long – and the odds of success are lengthening not shortening!

In our experience, if a sound foundation for rebuilding has not been established at the outset, the change process generally stalls, and in some instances collapses, at some later point in the process. It is only common sense – the pain is not avoided, but only deferred and inflated and everyone is eventually worse off. This includes the business, the workforce and the management. Executives who achieve success face reality up front and discuss and clarify goals, givens, concerns, expectations and positions. If issues cannot be resolved, *difficult* questions such as should we change out managers and employees, to what extent, when and how, need to be considered.[7] We need to face reality about the appropriateness and value of the rebuilding approach. We also need to ensure that we use both carrots and sticks to influence behavior. Not only do leading firms link performance achievements to individual and team rewards and incentives, but they also have processes and systems in place to identify performance shortfalls. As discussed in Chapter 1, they *actively manage underperformance*.

Leading firms demonstrate a strong sense of reality in many areas. They can realistically and objectively state their strengths/weaknesses in:

- *financial terms* (e.g. 'prices have nose-dived in our industry by 30 percent over the last 6 months')
- *change terms* (e.g. 'we stuck with change process X for way too long believing that it was eventually going to deliver … we should have seen the warning signs a lot earlier')
- *leadership terms* (e.g. we aren't good at living our values … we talk about empowerment and trust, but when things aren't going well we can't stop ourselves from diving in')
- *cultural terms* (e.g. 'our biggest problem is that people in Unit Y think that our past success assures our future – that just isn't the case')
- *employee terms* (e.g. 'I know that most of our employees in Unit Z believe in what we're trying to do and really want to be part of it … the team leaders have worked miracles')
- *market/competitor terms* (e.g. 'competitor X is no longer a real worry to us … we've taken over 20 percent of their market share in the last 18 months')
- *customer terms* (e.g. 'our customers are telling us that our inability to comply with delivery schedules is costing us and them business')
- *product terms* (e.g. 'we're doing well because the failure rates for product Y are three times less than those of our major competitor')
- *operational terms* (e.g. 'our parent company say that unless our cost structure is in the lowest industry quartile we'll be uncompetitive in the long term')
- *technological terms* (e.g. 'the technology in ABC unit is our biggest

strength – it not only makes us more efficient but the manufacturer is constantly developing new value-added features that we can readily retrofit').

This desire to seek the truth and see things for what they really are underpins these firms' no-nonsense/no-gimmicks approach to change and assures that they adopt an approach that is appropriate for their real needs.

The development of an effective sense of reality not only requires an extremely strong commitment to develop the 'out-front' principle but also the 'up-front' principle. Facing competitive truths is often a painful process and requires a high level of honesty and candor between individuals at all organizational levels. Employees have to be comfortable to tell the boss bad news and the boss has to know how the workforce interprets his or her response to bad news. We have frequently been involved in performance reviews involving representatives of the executive, middle management and the workforce and have found significant differences in performance perceptions across these groups. In our experience, many firms' poor sense of reality predisposes them toward discrediting differences rather than accepting that they exist and trying to work toward understanding and learning from them. Some executives spend way more time challenging the relevance of the measure and the rigor of the analysis whilst standing at the edge of the cliff. This extraordinary behavior is not uncommon in people and companies with a poor sense of reality.

KSF 6 – THE ABILITY TO AVOID 'FAD-SURFING'

Summary

Unless the organization understands and learns from its own change history and the successes and failures of others it will, in all probability, fail to recognize the fallacies of fad-surfing/cookbook management. Consequently, neither the critical mass of support for change nor the discipline and focus will evolve.

Almost by definition, leading firms resist fads and the temptation of the 'quick fix'. They see new management tools as simply that, tools to assist in the development of key organizational and behavioral attributes. They do not see them as the main event and certainly not as a panacea or savior. For example, we have seen a number of leading firms incorporate some re-engineering principles in their single integrated improvement initiative to assist in developing the principles of integration and distributed leadership. The critical differentiating factor here is that these firms can objectively and critically assess and analyze new ideas and 'pick the eyes out of them', implementing only those bits of them that add direct value to their current change activities. *They continuously evolve rather than continuously fragment their change plan.*

These firms also have effective gatekeeping processes to ensure that any changes made to their improvement initiatives are carefully controlled. This is very different to the ad hoc approach described in Chapter 1, Figure 1.2.

KSF 7 – KEEP IT RELEVANT AND KEEP IT SIMPLE

Summary

Good planning helps but the value of planning is increasingly in understanding the 'why' as much as the 'what'. Organizations succeed in this regard through investing in effective planning processes that are simple and that build understanding and commitment. This translates to doing less change than more – prioritizing principles for development and pursuing their development through a relatively small number of clearly targeted interventions

How many change roadmaps has each organization seen? Next time one comes forward, we should consider three questions. If our 'gut response' to any of these questions is 'no' then the plan is probably unlikely to succeed. Similarly, if we develop a plan to improve organizational effectiveness using the 14 principles that has similar properties, then it too is unlikely to succeed.

First, is it possible to tell what business we are actually in or what our organization actually does? If not, then the actions may well lack connectedness to critical business and operational issues, that is, fail the centrality test. Simply put, the plan lacks relevance and therefore will, in all probability, lack 'organizational grunt'. As a consequence it fails to engage people – get their attention over everything else that is going on back in the workplace.

Second, can the plan be resourced? Is the organization ready, able and prepared to commit to the level of participation and activity advocated? The answer to this question is often 'maybe' or 'it depends'. In our experience if we do not get a definite 'yes' before we start then we will certainly get a definite 'no' some time after we have started.

Third, how complicated is the plan? Can we clearly identify the critical, or foundation, change activities from the rest of the action? As discussed, most organizations fail from attempting too much, rather than too little, change. Indeed, successful change is systemic in nature but it is not diffused in intent. It is always possible to identify the few dominant 'stalking horses' for change from all the other actions that support these core initiatives. If we cannot do this, then there is a substantial risk that change effort will become too diffused as the focus shifts to individual blocks of action and excessive time is spent trying to understand the complex sets of interrelationships between activities. Leading firms do not seek to make all the connections between principles, practices, processes, competitiveness and performance in every detail. They often explicitly identify and make some of the major connections, but avoid becoming trapped in the complex maze of cause and effect.

Leading firms have the intuition, knowledge and confidence to avoid excessive detail. Conversely, 'analysis paralysis' can reign supreme in mediocre companies. By major connections, we mean things like knowing how one principle can be leveraged to help develop another or how a particular principle translates into practices or features that make a real difference to the business. For example, consider the electrical power distribution business and the principle of integration. Leading firms in this business know that the critical areas where this principle can make a difference include the mechanisms, technologies and processes to co-ordinate effectively the customer service center and field operations (i.e. quickly respond to outages and disturbances) and system control center and network scheduling (i.e. optimize network revenue generation). While the so called 'KISS' principle (Keep It Simple Stupid) has merit, things cannot be simplified to the extent that one should fire before taking careful aim. However, it is also sensible not to spend your whole life waiting for the perfect shot!

KSF 8 – GETTING INTO SPECIFICS: MANAGING THE DETAIL, NOT THE CONCEPT

Summary

Intellectually engaging in discussions about the principles and principles/business outcomes connections is a relatively easy task. Gaining agreement about the specific needs and requirements and translating them into an enduring set of behaviors and practices that take hold requires effective management of the detail.

How often have we all participated in workshops where, for many different reasons, agreement could not be reached around the detail? With the pressure of time what typically happens? The particular issue is taken up a few levels and progressively generalized until some form of agreement can be reached with some accompanying loose words around 'working through the detail' later. But the reality is that although our words may give us some comfort that we have agreement in intent, action and implementation stall because of a lack of agreement on specifics. For example it is hard to argue against the principle of alignment – it accords with common sense. But ask ten different managers what alignment means (and what their role is in its creation) and we're likely to get ten different answers, for example: people knowing what we stand for today and into the future, a core ideology that is reflected in everything we do, everyone living and breathing our values, doing business in ways that fit with what our customers really want, building ourselves into our customer's future etc. Then ask the same group of managers to describe what they believe each definition to actually look like, in behavioral and practice terms and we would get an even greater range of responses. It is through the discussion of the detail that the true understanding and value of the concept emerges.

We also need to challenge the conventional management paradigm around 'managing the fringes of everything and concentrate on managing the specifics of something'. We are not advocating that managers and change leaders are immersed in detail nor that they subsume the responsibilities of others, but we are saying that managerial time is a scarce commodity and its use needs to be clearly focussed in the right areas. The effectiveness of managerial action requires attention to detail in some key areas, some of which are often professionally, personally and politically 'high risk'.

> **Managerial time is a scarce commodity and its use needs to be clearly focussed in the right areas.**

The level of detail required depends on the strategic and change perspectives considered. For example, Walmart competes on the basis of ensuring that the customer believes the store and brand image to truly reflect service orientation, quality and value for money – replicating the Walmart DNA which was an extension of Sam Walton himself. In this environment, attention to detail from the displays at the front door, the ability to read the subtleties of the customer's body language and know when they really need help, through to the cleanliness of the toilets are extremely important. Line managers invest considerable personal time and effort signalling and reinforcing the value of 'the little things' to employees. Similarly when Compaq CEO, Eckhard Pfeffer, was bought in to combat the onslaught from Dell and Gateway in the early 1990s, he instituted a range of actions to transform the company from 'design and price later' to 'design to price'. The set of measures, accountabilities, financial disciplines and operating protocols introduced to achieve this cultural change had to be carefully managed and supported. This necessitated a high level of managerial attention to detail and the confronting of some specific behaviors. These included loosely defined product scopes, 'bottomless-pit' project budgets, placing a low priority on financial reporting, etc.

Contrast this situation to that of Andy Grove, the Intel CEO, in the mid 1990s. Grove saw the Internet as a huge opportunity and went to great lengths to marshal a brains trust of resources and then give it an 'open brief.' Grove went to considerable lengths to demonstrate to the team and to others the magnitude of the opportunity and the sense of urgency and the need to 'trust, empower and hold people accountable and at the same time, get out of their way'. Attention to detail in this case meant that 'the team could get on and do what they had been asked to do' and that the essential operating disciplines that existed in the rest of the organization were not compromised by this project.

KSF 9 – LEADERSHIP OF THE CHANGE PROCESS

Summary

The process of organizational change is usually complex and demanding, and strong leadership is a must. But this does not imply just strong executive management. In the most successful firms of the past decade and surely the next decade, this strength of leadership comes from the whole company.

In Chapter 3 we touched on a few leadership perspectives which we will further elaborate here. During the last 20 years or so, much has been written about the role and value of leadership in respect of organizational change and business success. What we consistently observe in leading organizations is that leadership is indeed a critical, if not *the* critical differentiating factor. In respect of change, it's not so much what an organization does that determines whether it is successful, but how it does it. By change leadership, we mean the core group of people, sometimes termed the *guiding coalition* (Kotter, 1995), from different parts of the organization who possess the fire, passion, authority, energy and influence to make real change happen and who can work closely together as a well-oiled team.

Leadership comes at all levels in the organization. In truly great companies, the operating staff are prepared to step up and lead from the front, challenge existing approaches and suggest and implement new ways (see Chapter 5). Supervisors take a step back and help to create the right environment for people to participate and give them the confidence and support to do so. Managers are prepared to tell it like it is, can communicate effectively, are truly committed to take the business forward and have absolute clarity about what they want. All these 'leaders' share a number of common attributes including 'the presence' factor, the ability to quickly obtain the respect and trust of those around them, being change-oriented, having the ability to influence, a preparedness to step out of the present and take 'a calculated risk'.

Effective change leadership is truly synergistic. The needs and demands of the process rise above factional interests and the actions of each and every individual combine to create a bedrock of stability and consistency in an environment of change. These people stand out – not by their status, role or skillset but by their personality, style and disposition. They have passionately embraced change and have a true affinity with people.

There are many different forms of leadership talent and if what we've got does not support what we need, then it is of very questionable value. For example, if we are in the product development business, e.g. Sony, we need leaders who are prepared to take a risk, are visionary, inspirational, conceptual, and who are able to engage people in the quest of creating their own future. Contrastingly, if we're in the process business like McDonald's, we need leaders who continually challenge the way things are done, are highly focussed, detail-minded, good finishers, methodical, like working with structure and who are able to engage people in the ideals of good customer service and continuous improvement. Contrast these behaviors with those of leaders operating in the strategic environment dominated by a marketing orientation. If it is a Benetton, we need a different type of leadership style: leaders who are a catalyst for action, have enormous stamina, are goal-oriented and decisive, comfortable with planning and scheduling, effective fire fighters, logic-based and pragmatic. Finally, if we are in the relationship business, like State Farm Insurance, we need leaders who are values and feelings-based, warm, empathetic, intuitive, perceptive, consensus seeking and collaborative.

Leadership style is contingent on strategic perspective.

KSF 10 – STAKEHOLDER ENGAGEMENT

Summary

The needs and aspirations of key internal and external groups who have power and influence over business performance need to be built into the review process.

Although stakeholder management is a much used phrase, it is seldom carried out well in practice. More often than not, it is observed in reactive form – explaining accidents and injuries to regulatory authorities, responding to customer complaints, explaining manufacturing plant down-time to the head office, explaining new service or product flops to investors, etc. We often liken stakeholder management to investment management: just as regular deposits of money help to secure our personal future, so too can regular deposits in stakeholder relationships help to secure our business's future by creating an environment, understanding and connectedness that ensures that everyone that has a possible stake in the business and is working toward the success of that business. However, if the necessary investments have not been made, then the support and infrastructure will not be there to support the business's short and long-term future and it risks either going it alone and/or losing a potentially powerful body of support. Proactive stakeholder management, through strategic planning exercises, corporate citizenship, collaborative stakeholder problem-solving forums, performance reviews, involvement in shaping legislative frameworks, etc., makes good business sense and it works.

There is another perspective of stakeholder management that merits consideration and attention. Just as we have argued that many organizations often fail to confront unacceptable employee performance, so too have we observed that many organizations fail to confront unacceptable stakeholder behavior: stakeholders who consistently fail to deliver on commitments they have made, stakeholders who breach confidences, stakeholders who take a tack different to that agreed, etc. Alternatively, the host organization may fail to deliver on agreed stakeholder commitments that it has made and fail to confront its own performance shortcomings.

SUMMARY

Key Success Factors should not be confused with the elements of a principles-based system of management, that is Figure 1.3 and the associated 14 principles we have articulated. Key Success Factors are crucial to the progression from Figure 1.2 to Figure 1.3 and provide a supplementary set of insights that should be considered in any change undertaken.

Notes
1. Some would argue that even this timeframe is too long due to combinations of business environment, business performance, organizational culture, staff capability, information and process.
2. When considering an organization's future change abilities, our experiences are consistent with those who applied Newton's Laws of Motion to Cultural change. Law 1: an organization's behavior will not change unless acted on by an outside force; Law 2: the amount of behavioral change produced will be directly proportional to the amount of effort put into it; and Law 3: the level of organizational resistance encountered will be equal and opposite to the amount of effort put into changing it. More turbulence requires more change which requires more organizational capacity for change.
3. By saying that a firm is predisposed toward change we are not rationalizing away the set of psychological issues and processes that accompany any change activity but we are saying that a critical mass refer to this commitment as 'latent alignment'.
4. Clearly a firm does not necessarily have to undertake restructuring to possess latent change potential. As shown in Figure 19.2, many firms are type B and already possess this potential. For type B firms the challenge is to unleash it in ways that are sustainable and that create maximum business value.
5. We have consistently observed that executives that are effective change leaders place considerably less emphasis on the written and spoken word and considerably more emphasis on their actions. To them, leadership of the change process is not synonymous with more values statements, missions, visions, videos, newsletters, etc., despite the fact that a very large percentage of companies currently consider them to be their number-one communication priority (Larkin, 1996). Effective leaders recognize that employees deduce what they really value by observing their behavior.
   Leading firms hold all members of the executive management team accountable for delivering on certain aspects of their change processes. They ensure that rhetoric is backed up by action. This not only helps to ensure that the change plan remains relevant and alive but also

Key Success Factors – the system of management

ensures that managers are not let off the hook. In too many firms we have seen senior managers distance themselves from change activities for a wide variety of reasons.

6. In many successful organizations we have observed that the transition between restructuring and rebuilding processes is accompanied with the appointment of a new CEO/Business Unit Manager.
7. Any change-out option is further complicated by the downsizing/infusion of new talent juggling act – firms often need to contend with the conflicting requirements of introducing new hires in an environment of downsizing and cost cutting. They also need to convince the body corporate and shareholders of the need for some short-term pain for long-term gain. A further complexity is the need to apply a different style of management for the change-out process: an issue frequently considered, seldom properly addressed.

CONCLUSION AND EPILOGUE

●●●●●●●●●●●●●●●●●

A company cannot increase its productivity. People can.
Robert Half

Why is it that for so many of us we have achieved a mediocre or poor rate of return on our organizational investments, when we know that leading companies are able consistently to do better? The typical situation is that effectiveness, efficiency, competitiveness, financial performance and cultural gains are small compared to the time, energy, resources and money that we commit to improvement on these. The typical result is frustration, fear, despair and disappointment, sometimes panic and always conflict. This situation is frequently accompanied with wave after wave of cost cutting and downsizing that can ultimately lead to an organizational mid-life crisis. But the world's best companies have shown us that it doesn't have to be that way.

Many leading organizations demonstrate that sustainable success can be 'built in'. This is not to say that crises and discontinuities can always be anticipated and avoided, for they clearly cannot in the new millennium that will be increasingly characterized by a series of 'external shocks' and discontinuities to economies and markets. However, the level of stakeholder confidence in the organization and the level of organizational integrity that exists in leading companies enables a more considered and collective response to be developed and implemented. Real change works and it sticks in these great companies that have the fundamental systems and principles in place. They are relatively robust to the changes and discontinuities that await all of us.

Leading organizations assure their continued prosperity through their own actions. They operate with something more fundamental in place that drives the behaviors of each and every employee and manager and that creates a platform of competitiveness that gives them considerable 'control' of their own destiny.

We have covered a lot of ground and considered many different issues in this book. Our approach is based on close observation of how and why some companies seem able to succeed and seem able to change successfully while so many others falter. We did not just 'sit in our offices' and dream up the systems and principles described in Parts 1 and 2 of this volume, quite the opposite.

Simply put, we set out to describe what we deduced as the fundamental drivers of what we observed in the world's best companies. There are at least three absolutely critical issues that we would ask the reader to consider in the context of their own organization. Leading organizations work hard at achieving the following:

- They manage using a fundamental set of axiomatic principles that guide all aspects of their behavior, at all levels and in all business dealings. They do not subscribe to fads or short-term quick fixes. They exude a confidence that they are working on the 'right' things and that the actions that they are taking will work, take hold, and result in real and sustainable improvement.
- They utilize these principles in a systematic framework that enables them to clearly articulate and connect principles, plans, actions, consequences and rewards. The high level of 'connectedness' that exists between these elements is no accident.
- They understand how organizational and cultural aspects of work relate to business strategy and business performance. They do not make investments in their organizations, cultures or people because they 'feel good', but rather, because they know they produce solid business results. There is a clear line of site between the 'soft' and 'hard' aspects of management.

Developing the principles-based management approach, a predisposition toward staying away from the fads, a structured management system, connecting principles, system and strategy across the organization are today's 'big ticket' leadership issues. They differentiate real leadership talent from plain vanilla management in the sense of care-taking or just administering businesses. It is on these issues that organizations require the nourishment of strong leadership – not the typical plethora of operational and interpersonal issues from which many executives that we know struggle to escape.

We are not so presumptuous to suggest that the 14 principles of management that we describe in this book define the 'future of management' as we know it. However we do strongly believe that they do take a step forward in creating a sound platform to progress our understanding of the field of management out of its current depths and reinstate some much needed professionalism and purpose back into this discipline.

These organizational perspectives are clearly not the domain or direct responsibility of any particular individual. Consequently, an organization, its leaders and its employees can expect to extract maximum value from the frameworks and models that we have described in this book if they use them as a set of perspectives against which past actions, experiences, future plans,

Conclusion and epilogue

failures and successes can be discussed, debated and analyzed. The answers don't lie in the models and technologies per se, but in the organization's ability to use this material to clarify more succinctly and understand its specific business and organizational situation and then create the critical mass of support and confidence to move forward. It is the triumvirate of models, people and process that constitutes the critical differentiating factor.

We have stressed throughout this book that there are no universal or magical recipes for success, although there are too many cookbooks advocating exactly 'how to do it' in the popular management press. The principles themselves are common to many excellent companies at a high level, but they can and do mean different things in different companies, because of the different context of each company. For example, Hewlett Packard and ABB both are very strong on alignment (Principle 1), but alignment is not specifically the same thing in these two companies.

So where might you start? We have provided a structured implementation framework that commences with the building of awareness, understanding and buy in. However, we know first-hand just how hard this is to do, particularly if you aren't the CEO. How do you go about getting the organization's attention? How do you get executives interested and prepared to discuss the central themes and issues that we have raised in this book, particularly when they may have been instrumental in developing or sanctioning some other course of action? How do you get people interested in longer term survival when they are 'up to their armpits in alligators'? As John Kotter of Harvard University suggests, you have to start by creating a strong sense of urgency – you need 'attention getters'. Attention getters need to be both logically and emotionally appealing to people, particularly those from whom you need an initial commitment in order to progress the central themes of this book.

We have found that confronting combinations of financial, market, competitor, product, customer, cultural, leadership and change realities often helps. On the other hand we do not subscribe to the general theory that we often hear about leaders having to 'manufacture a crisis' if they are not naturally having one. The good news is that astute executives and managers can be smarter than needing to be 'on fire' before they take action. Can we find ways, other than creating a crisis, to motivate people to engage in building the systems and principles needed to take us forward and then implementing integrated improvement strategies? The answer comes once again from leading companies such as GE, ABB and Medco, and is a resounding 'Yes'!

In addition, all people need to see and connect with the business and organization from a broad range of perspectives, and be held accountable for their actions. Throughout the book we have emphasized the power and value of good performance management practices: defining and agreeing standards, be they business, customer, operational, behavioral or ethical; recognizing and rewarding success and confronting failures.

A great starting point is a realistic assessment of how an organization measures up against the elements and connections of Figure 1.3, and the strength of the principles. Can a leadership team debate and agree its strengths and weaknesses against these measures? Yes. Given this, then a useful starting point is immediately established for breaking out of the cycle of fads, firefighting and short-termism. From these assessments, a mapping of business strategy to the strengths and weaknesses will show the way, in terms of what the change agenda should be, which we expressed as the integrated improvement initiative in Figure 1.3. Examples of this process are shown in Part 3 of this book. This should lead to no more than five or six management projects/initiatives, and they ought to be checked for fit and focus, or as described in Figure 1.3, integration. These initiatives can be focussed on strengthening the principles or the elements of Figure 1.3, such as the performance management system or the external benchmark inputs. These types of changes are different in nature from service improvement or cost-cutting projects or quality programs, in that they act to fundamentally and permanently improve the organization.

As a final point, we observe that leading companies are inclusive in their style and clear to all stakeholders in what they aspire to and how they operate. Just recently we asked one of our clients, the leadership team of a 5000-person division of a multinational company: 'How many brains do you use in this company in taking the company forward?'

The answer was a hundred, which we were told was an increase from the ten that would have been the answer a couple of years previously. Even a hundred people cannot achieve everything, no matter how hard they try. They can catalyze service standards, change, agility and innovativeness, but they can't fully implement any of these. So for many of our best organizations, it's about getting to the point achieved by Toyota, where intelligence is applied by virtually everyone – that is 'distributed intelligence' – in a systematic, disciplined manner. The world's best companies have led the way on this fundamental, and having achieved this, find that quality, service and efficiency are both possible and able to be improved on a continuing basis. Without this, it's the 'old model' of frustrated managers exhorting uninterested, recalcitrant workers to do more and better, with little real improvement being sustained beyond the temporary and fleeting surges that are achieved by fads.

Our hope is that this book has been clear enough to help leaders understand the choices that they do indeed have, that our 'tip of the iceberg' companies have grabbed and captured value from. Should you choose the 'world class' path, and we hope that many more organizations will, then we hope to have contributed to your knowledge of what is possible, how to start and what to use to guide actions.

BIBLIOGRAPHY

Adler, P.S. (1986) 'New technologies, new skills', *California Management Review*, Fall.

Adler P.S. (1993) 'Time-and-motion regained', *Harvard Business Review*, January–February.

Adler, P.S. and Cole, R.(1993) 'Designed for learning: a tale of two auto plants', *Sloan Management Review*, Spring.

Australian Manufacturing Council (1996) *Leading the Way*. Australian Manufacturing Council.

Barney, J. (1986) 'Organizational culture: can it be a sustained source of competitive advantage?', *Academy of Management Review*, 11.

Collins, J. C. and Porras, J. I. (1994) *Built to Last: Successful Habits of Visionary Companies*. Harper Business.

Fombrun, C. (1994) *Leading corporate change*. McGraw-Hill.

Greenwood, R. and Hinings, C.R. (1988) Organisation design types, tracks and the dynamics of strategic change', *Organisation Studies*, 9 (3).

Hamel, G. and Prahalad, C. (1989) 'Strategic intent', *Harvard Business Review*, 67 (3).

Hamermesh, G. (1996) *'Fad-free Management', The Six Principles that Drive Successful Companies and their Leaders*. Knowledge Exchange.

Hayes, R.H. and Pisano, G.P. (1994) Beyond world-class: the new manufacturing strategy', *Harvard Business Review*, January–February.

Heskett, J.L., Jones, T.O., Loveman, G.W., Sasser, W.E. and Schelinger, L.A. (1994) 'Putting The service profit chain to work', *Harvard Business Review*, March–April.

Jaikumar, R. and Bohn, R. (1988) 'The development of intelligent systems for intelligent use: a conceptual framework', in *Research on Technological Innovation Management and Policy*.

Kaplan, R.S. and Norton, D.P. (1996) *The Balanced Scorecard – Translating Strategy Into Action*. Harvard Business School Press.

Kotter, J. P. (1995) 'Leading change: why transformational efforts fail', *Harvard Business Review*, March–April.

Kotter, J.P. and Heskett, J. L. (1992) *Corporate Culture and Performance*. Free Press.

Larkin, P. (1996) 'Reaching and changing frontline employees', *Harvard Business Review*, May–June.

Lawler, E. III (1992) The *Ultimate Advantage: Creating The High Involvement Organization*. Jossey-Bass.

Mintzberg, H. (1979) 'An emerging strategy of direct research', *Administrative Science Quarterly*.

Mintzberg, H. (1994) *The Rise and Fall of Strategic Planning*. Prentice Hall.

Mintzberg, H. (1996) 'Musings on management', *Harvard Business Review*, March–April.
MIT Commission On Industrial Productivity (1989) *Made In America. Regaining the Competitive Edge*. Harper Perennial.
Peters, T. (1987) Thriving on Chaos: A Handbook for a Management Revolution. Knopf.
Peters, T. and Waterman, R. (1982) *In Search of Excellence*. Harper and Row.
Porter, M.E. (1985) Competitive Advantage. Free Press.
Porter, M.E. (1990) *The Competitive Advantage of Nations*. Free Press.
Prahalad, C. (1983) 'Developing strategic capability: an agenda for top management', *Human Resource Management*.
Prahalad, C. and Betis, R. (1984) 'The dominant logic: a new linkage between diversity and performance', *Sloan Management Review*.
Prahalad, C. K. and Hamel G. (1990) 'The core competence of the organisation', *Harvard Business Review*, May–June.
Quinn, J.B. (1984) ' Managing strategic change', *Sloan Management Review*.
Schein, E. (1985) *Organisational Culture and Leadership*. Jossey-Bass.
Schonberger, R. J. (1994) 'Human resource management lessons from a decade of total quality management and re-engineering', *California Management Review*, Summer.
Shapiro, E.C. (1995) *Fad Surfing in the Boardroom*. HarperCollins.
Skinner, W. (1978) *Manufacturing in Corporate Strategy*. John Wiley.
Skinner, W. (1985) *Manufacturing: The Formidable Competitive Weapon*. John Wiley.
Stalk, G. (1988) 'Time – the next source of competitive advantage', *Harvard Business Review*, July–August.
Stalk, G. Jr and Hout, T.M. (1990) *Competing Against Time: how time based competition is reshaping global markets*. New York.
Tichy, N. and Devanna, M. A. (1990) *The Transformational Leader*. John Wiley.
Treacy, M. and Wiesma, F. (1995) *The Discipline Of Market Leaders*. Addison-Wesley.
Ulrich, D. and Lake, D. (1991) *Organizational Capability*. John Wiley.
Walton, R. (1985) 'From control to commitment in the workplace', *Harvard Business Review*, January–February.
Waterman, R., Peters, T. and Phillips, J. (1980) 'A view of the organisation', *Business Horizons*, June (McKinsey 7S model).
Zuboff, S. (1988) *In the Age of the Smart Machine: the Future of Work and Power*. Basic Books.

INDEX

ABB *see* Asea Brown Boveri (ABB)
alignment 30
   areas of activity for increasing 44–6
   benefits 43
   case studies 36–7, 39, 40
   definition 35–41
   dimensions 38
   elements 35, 39
   evaluation 41–2
   improvement methods 43–6
   Kellogg, at 36–7
   management philosophy at ABB 39
   principles at Uncle Ben's 40–1
   summary 46
   values, of
      at Medco 22, 24, 40
      case studies 39, 40
Amazon (www) 97
American Express 73
AP 162
Apple Computers 115
Asea Brown Boveri (ABB) 84, 109–10, 115, 143, 244
   customer-value creation strategy at, case study 163–4
   distributed leadership at, case study 51
   resourcing the medium term, case study 90–1
   Technical Consulting 199
   time-focussing at, case study 102
   values, case study 39
AT&T 92
Australian Quality Award framework 12
Avis 4, 13, 14, 43, 60
AXA Insurance Group, market focus example 206–7

Balanced Scorecard Approach, quality award system 12
Baldrige quality award system in USA 12
Benetton 199
best companies, patterns followed, generally 1
BF Goodrich 14
Black & Decker 176
BMW 167
Boeing 4
British Airways 4, 60, 73–4, 78
business
   growth breakpoint, knowledge of 229–31
   management *see* management, management principles, management systems
business strategy
   changing nature, understanding 219–21
   integrated management 222–3

Canon 175
capabilities 30
   criteria to be satisfied 176
   definition 175–7
   evaluation 177–9
   examples 176–7
   focus on creating, from organizational improvement 177
   generally 175
   improvement 180
   principle, benefits of 179–80
   summary 181
Casio 175
Caterpillar 175
change
   embracing *see* embracing change

Index

process, leadership of 238–9
Chase Manhattan Bank 4
Chrysler 61, 62, 104
Citibank 9
Citicorp 73, 194
closed loop
  customer 15
  employee 15
  integrated 14–17
  investor 15, 16
  key management 16
  open loop and, considered 11–14
Coated Paper Corporation, relationship focus example 205–6
Coca Cola 168
company 'new'
  characteristics of 19–25
  example of 21–4
Compaq 237
Corolla 167
Crosby, Philip 145
customer loops 15
customer value 30
  competitive advantage, methods of establishment 166
  creation and focus, benefits of 170–1
  creation, case studies 161–2, 163–4, 168
  definition 161, 164–6
  evaluation of principle 169–70
  focus
    benefits of 170–1
    value of 166–9
  focussed companies, characteristics common to 173–4
  generally 161–3
  improvement and sustainment of 171–2
  internal processes, unseen by external consumer 165
  Medco, at 23
  service ethic 165–6
  summary 172

Dell Computers 98, 237
  mass customization at, case study 200
Deming 136
Denso 98, 168
discipline 30
  benefits of 144
  case study of system at Medco 138
  criticisms of 141–3
  definition 137–43
  distributed leadership and 24
  evaluation of principle 144
  formal authority, by, and self-discipline, comparison 135
  generally 133–5
  Henry Ford/Taylor approach 136, 143
  improvement and sustainment 145
  lack of standards, effect 137–8
  one best way, whether 136–7
  product and process standards 138–42
  reducing empowerment criticism 143
  service standards 138–9
  stifling creativity criticism 141–3
  summary 145–6
  systems, at Medco 138
distributed leadership 30
  ABB, at 51
  accountability 52
  benefits 55
  case studies 49, 51
  centralized and, contrasted 50
  definition 47–51
  Du Pont's Girraween Operation 50–1
  employees' process improvement 54–5
  employees' responsibility 49–51, 51–2
  empowerment and 47–8
  evaluation 51–5
  Ikea, at 49
  improvement 55–6
  key characteristics 48
  Medco, at 24
  strategic preferences and typical practices 211
  strategy, concentration on 53–4
  summary 57
  team behavior and 48
  widespread responsibility 51–2
Du Pont 4, 176
  charts 184
  Girraween Operation 50–1
Dun and Bradstreet 59, 73, 165

Edison Mission 14
embracing change 30
  behavior and attitudes, effect 14–116
  benefits 118–20

250

Index

change management, action principle of 113
  definition 113–17
  disposition towards 224–9
  evaluation 117–18
  generally 112–13
  implementation effectiveness 121–2
  improvement on the principle 120–2
  key questions 120
  organizational focus and 117
  process of, by leading organizations 116–17
  relationship of major change to performance 119
  summary 122
employee
  alignment and *see* alignment
  career planning 21
  characteristics where distributed leadership, 48 *see also under* distributed leadership
  embracing change 21
  loops 15
  Medco, at 22–3, 24
  process improvement 54–5
empowerment, distributed leadership and 47–8
Ericsson 4
  product focus example 203–4

fads
  fad-based companies 1
  importance of avoiding 234–5, 243
Federal Express 115
Fidelity 92
Fletcher Challenge 130
  learning focus, case study 125–7
focus
  customer value 161–174 *see also* customer value
  learning *see* learning focus
  market *see* market focus
  process *see* process focus
  product *see* product focus
  relationship *see* relationship focus
  strategic 197–211
    development of, key elements 198
    key principles 200–2
    preferences *see* strategic preferences

time *see* time-focussed, being
Ford 61, 104
  mass customization at Dell for, case study 200
Ford, Henry 136
Fuji 167

Gadsden 59
gap analysis 214
Gates, Bill 115
Gateway 237
GE Capital Finance 92, 142
General Electric 4, 60, 165, 222, 244
  discipline of fundamental process at 142, 144
  embracing change 114, 115
  learning focus at 125, 127, 130, 131
  out front, being 70, 78
General Motors 14, 61, 104, 114
  Fremont (California) plant 145
  Holden plant 89, 134
  joint venture with Toyota *see* NUMMI
  learning focus 123–4, 128, 130, 131
Goodyear Tire Company 167
Grove, Andy 237

Hewlett Packard 78, 97, 109, 115
  customer value at 165, 166, 171
  discipline of 137, 141, 143
  Hoshin Planning 91
  integration 59, 60, 66
  learning focus 125, 132
Hoechst 4
Holden's Engine Company 134
Homeside 166
Honda 4, 175
Hong Kong & Shanghai Bank 9

IBM 14
ICI 66–7, 139–40
  Botany plant 80, 86
IKEA 78, 97, 163, 165
  customer value creation at, case study 168
  distributed leadership at, case study 49
  out front and up front, case study 70
implementation
  adoption of management principles, approach to 196

251

Index

building awareness and executive buy-in 197
factual basis 195
fictional basis 195–6
focus, strategic 197–211
　development of, key elements 198
　key principles 200–2
　preferences *see* strategic preferences
gap analysis 214
growth strategies, effects 207
leadership demands, effect of growth strategies 207
models for 193–4
organizational systems
　end goals 195
　future directions 194–5
performance assessment 212–13
process
　generally 193–6
　process steps 196–215
project planning 214
review 214
Shell, rejuvenation strategy 194–5
strategic preferences *see* strategic preferences
summary 214–15
information
　transparency 80
　see also up front, being
integration 30
　benefits 64
　definition 60–2
　evaluation 63
　improvement, methods of 64–7
　methods 60–2
　performance assessment and 213
　principle of 59
　rewards and recognition systems 66–7
　scope 58–60
　summary 67
　typical practices and strategic preferences 210
Intel 4, 237
Internet banking 97
investor loops 15, 16

Jaguar 167
Jobs, Steven 115

'Kaizen' 141
Kanban systems 105–6
Kellogg 4, 59–60, 189
　alignment, case study 36–7
key success factors
　business growth breakpoint 229–31
　change process, leadership of 238–9
　disposition towards change 224–9
　'fad-surfing', avoidance 234–5
　identification 216–18
　integrated management 222–3
　magnitude of gap, knowledge of 224–9
　reality, exceptional sense 231–4
　relevance 235–6
　restructuring, knowledge of limits 229–31
　simplicity 235–6
　specifics, concentration on 236–8
　stakeholder engagement 239–40
　summary 240
　understanding change 219–21
Kodak 4, 14, 53, 144, 167
　Australia 132
　time-focussing at 104
　　case study 103

leadership
　distributed, as management principle *see* distributed leadership
　world-class, progress towards 19–25
learning focus 30
　benefits 130–1
　case study 125–7
　collective learning for company 123–4
　definition 125–9
　evaluation of learning principle 129
　generally 123–4
　improvement of 131
　learning centers 128–9
　learning-focussed organization, transformation to 124
　open learning concepts 124
　summary 132
　turnover and 127
Lexus 167
Lloyds Bank 9
loops
　customer 15
　employee 15

integrated closed loop 14–17
investor 15, 16
key management 16
open and closed, considered 11–14
LUTI system 130, 131

McDonald's 199, 239
  customer value 167, 171
  discipline of 134, 136, 139, 140, 141
  out front, being 70, 78
  time-focussing at 104, 108
McKinsey 7S framework 193
management
  1970s and 1980s, in 7–8
  ad hoc 9–10
  fundamental principles 5
  how and what is managed 6–9
  integrated 222–3
  key success factors *see* key success factors
  market turbulence 114
  possible standards of achievement 10–17
  present situation 9–10
  principles, by *see* management principles
  relationships, relevance 5–6
  success
    conclusions as to 242–5
    critical issues 243
    process for achievement generally 244–5
    sustainable, of leading organisations 242–5
  systems *see* management systems
  techniques, current practices generally 3–6
  world-class, progress towards 19–25
management principles
  adoption of *see* implementation
  alignment *see* alignment
  being disciplined *see* discipline
  being out front *see* out front, being
  being time-focussed *see* time–focussed, being
  being up front *see* up front, being
  capabilites *see* capabilities
  change management driven by 32
  customer value *see* customer value
  distributed leadership *see* distributed leadership
  embracing change *see* embracing change
  generally 27, 29
  guidance by, justification 31
  how firms rate 33–4
  how management by principles works 31–2
  how much management principles matter 33–4
  implementation of *see* implementation
  integration *see* integration
  key principles 29–32
  learning focus *see* learning focus
  measurement and reporting *see* measurement and reporting
  micro to macro *see* micro to macro
  resourcing the medium term *see* resourcing the medium term
management systems
  Australian Quality Award framework 12
  Balanced Scorecard Approach 12
  Baldrige system in USA 12
  loops
    closed and open, considered 11–14
    customer 15
    employee 15
    integrated closed loop 14–17
    investor 15, 16
    key management 16
market focus
  categorization matrix 207–8
  characteristics 199, 206
  distributed leadership practices 211
  example 206–7
  integration practices 210
market turbulence 114
Marriott 36, 176
Mars Corporation 186
  Uncle Ben's *see* Uncle Ben's
Matsushita 17
MBA 109
MBNA 4, 9
measurement and reporting 30
  benefits 158
  effective measurement systems 148
  evaluation 155–7
  improvement of, actions for 158–9

Index

information centers, role of 153
internal comparisons of performance, use of 154–5
management tactics 151–2
measures and data, ownership of 149–50
need to be up front 150–1
publication of output measures 149
service industries 152–3
special measures 157–8
strategy, need for 151, 152
summary 159–60
typical measures 147
Medco 4, 13, 14, 60, 97, 244
  alignment of values at 22, 24, 43
    case study 40
  as an industry leader, case study 81–2
  customer-value creation at, case study 161–2
  discipline of 134
    systems, case study 138
  example of new company, as 21–4
  measurement and reporting at 147
  rewards and recognition at 186
medium term, resourcing *see* resourcing the medium term
Mercedes 167
Merck–Medco *see* Medco
Merryl Lynch 166
micro to macro 30
  appeal to the heart 185–6
  benefits 188
  connections
    micro and macro, between 184
    operational and market effectiveness, between 185
  definitions 184
  evaluation 187–8
  generally 182–4
  improvement 188–9
  logic, undeniable 184–5
  performance assessment and 212
  rewards and recognition 186–7
  summary 190
Microsoft 14, 70, 73, 75, 115
Mitsubishi 17
Motorola 4, 144

National Bank 4, 9, 87, 162

Norwest Bank 4
NUMMI 4, 125, 145

open loop
  closed loop and, considered 11–14
  see also loops
operating discipline
  performance assessment and 213
  see also discipline
out front, being 30
  achievement of, reasons 73–4
  benefits 75–6
  case studies 70, 72–3
  evaluation 74–5
  factors 71
  generally 68–70
  industry leaders 69
  meaning 68–9, 78
  nature of 70–4
  practice dimensions 71–2
  status, improvement of 76–8
  summary 78

Pareto principle 117
performance assessment
  business/organizational 212–13
  integration 213
  micro-to-macro connection, lack 212
  operating discipline 213
  product quality problems 212
  systems discipline 213
Pfeffer, Eckhard 237
process focus 207
  categorization matrix 207–8
  characteristics 199, 200, 202
  distributed leadership practices 211
  example 202
  integration practices 210
Proctor and Gamble 4
product focus
  categorization matrix 207–8
  characteristics 199, 203
  distributed leadership practices 211
  example 204–5
  integration practices 210
product quality problems 212
project planning 214

reality, importance of sense of 231–4

relationship focus
  categorization matrix 207–8
  characteristics 199, 204–5
  distributed leadership practices 211
  integration practices 210
  mass customization at Dell, case study 200
reporting *see* measurement and reporting
resourcing the medium term 30
  ability for, transformation to 89
  attraction and retention of best people 97–9
  benefits 96–9
  case study 90–1
  definition 92–5
  distribution channel leadership 97
  evaluation 96
  generally 88–92
  improvement 99
  Medco, at 23
  next generation product leadership 96–7
  summary 99–100
  temporal focus and performance 94
restructuring, knowledge of limits of 229–31
Rolls Royce 167

Saturn 14
Schwab 92, 166
Shell 4, 141
  rejuvenation strategy 194–5
Siemens 4
Singapore Airlines 141
Smith, Fred 115
Sony 17, 78, 97, 115, 141
  innovation at 168, 199, 239
  learning focus at 125, 130
South Pacific Tyres, time-focussing at, case study 103
South West Airlines 4, 175
  process focus example 202
speed *see* time-focussed, being
stakeholder engagement 239–40
State Farm Insurance 4
  case study 72–3
strategic preferences
  categorizations 207–8
  distributed leadership practices 211

  growth strategies, effect 207
  integration practices 210
  market focus
    categorization matrix 207–8
    characteristics 199, 206
    distributed leadership practices 211
    example 206–7
    integration practices 210
  perspectives, consideration as 200
  process focus 207
    categorization matrix 207–8
    characteristics 199, 200, 202
    distributed leadership practices 211
    example 202
    integration practices 210
  product focus
    categorization matrix 207–8
    characteristics 199, 203
    distributed leadership practices 211
    example 205–6
    integration practices 210
  relationship focus
    categorization matrix 207–8
    characteristics 199, 204–5
    distributed leadership practices 211
    integration practices 210
    mass customization at Dell, case study 200
  types of 199–200
success, key factors *see* key success factors
systems
  discipline and performance assessment and 213 *see also* discipline
  management *see* management systems
  organizational development 222–3

TAC Insurance 77
Taco Bell 4
Tandy 176–7
'Taylorism' 136, 143
team behavior, distributed leadership and 48
3M 35, 78, 97, 125
time-focussed, being 30
  benefits of principle 108–9
  case studies 102, 103
  customer enquiries and orders, responsiveness 104
  evaluation 107

255

Index

generally 101–3
how and what to manage 102
improvement 109–11
Kanban systems 105–6
product development cycle time 104–5
reliability and time punctuality 105
sense of urgency 106, 107
summary 111
time based, definition 103–7
Toyota 98, 115, 167
   discipline of 134, 137
   joint venture with GM *see* NUMMI
   learning focus 125, 130
   out front, being 73, 78
turbulence in markets, factors causing 114

Uncle Ben's 59
Uncle Ben's pet food operation
   alignment 40–1
   being out front 69
   discipline 134–5
up front, being 30
   benefits 85–6
   case studies 70, 81–2
   definition 79, 82–5

evaluation 85
external relationships 84–5
generally 79–82
improvement of up-front status 86–7
meaning 79–80
measurement and reporting, in 150–1
Medco as industry leader 81–2
methods 80–2
mutual respect aspect 82–4
summary 87
superior performance and 86
transparency 80
'up-front' and 'backward' company, worker responses compared 83–4

Walmart 4, 175, 237
Walton, Sam 237
Welch, Jack 115, 222
Wells Fargo 9

Xerox 4, 14, 104, 137, 194
   learning focus at 125, 130

Young, John 115, 132